OFFA'S DYKE PATH

Lost in the Woods

Paul Amess

Kingston House Publishing

I would like to apologise to everyone I have ever offended. To everyone else, don't worry, I will get to you shortly.

CONTENTS

Title Page	
Dedication	
Introduction	1
Accidents Will Happen	21
The Flying Banana	43
When Animals Attack	89
Where Werewolves Were	136
Mad Dogs and Englishmen	160
Bells and Balls	195
Halfway	214
Vikings to Victorians	231
Homicidal Tendencies	261
The End is Nigh	290
The Final Push	319
Books In This Series	343

INTRODUCTION

I once read that Offa's Dyke Path was the stuff that dreams are made of. In fact, that statement was one of the reasons I originally decided to walk it in the first place, and so, on a sunny late spring day, I finally found myself setting out from Chepstow to do precisely that with three of my friends. On top of that, I simply need a break. My girlfriend keeps accusing me of cheating. She's starting to sound like my wife.

Over the next ten days or so, we would slowly make our way northwards towards Prestatyn, where the route finishes, following this most historical path and encountering some strange and mystical places and people, and doing our absolute best not to die or get lost in the woods, which, for me at least, was probably easier said than done.

But before I go on, there was something else that made me want to walk the walk, so to speak, and that was a movie I saw many moons ago. Arthur's Dyke tells the story of a strange group of disconnected friends reunited many years after first walking *the dyke*, as it is colloquially known. Whether, by doing this walk, they were attempting to recapture their youths or exorcising some long-held demons is up to the viewer to decide, as both explanations are entirely plausible.

Anyway, along their way, they were joined by an overweight, unfulfilled and unappreciated housewife who was in the midst of a mid-life crisis, and predictably, chaos ensues. A charming film in itself, it also showcased the immense natural beauty of Wales, having been filmed mainly on location in glorious Monmouthshire, which is at the southern end of the route. If I had been undecided about doing this walk before I saw that film, then by the end of it, I was firmly committed. And I mean committed in a sense that has absolutely nothing to do with a lunatic asylum, though some would say you probably belong in one if you enjoy such things as blistered feet and camping in the rain, which is much better known, of course, as walking in Wales.

I soon discovered one teeny, tiny problem, however. I had hoped to be able to follow in the footsteps, in the most literal sense, of the stars of the film. However, the movie had used more than a liberal amount of artistic licence when it came to locations, which meant this would not be possible, but more of that later.

As for the path itself, someone told me that it

had been there since 1971, which is not strictly true, as people have been walking up and down this route for longer than anyone can remember. And although it is named after Offa, the King of Mercia, who is thought to have built the dyke, there is a growing school of thought that claims the story is not quite as simple as that.

In fact, stretches of the dyke have now been dated all the way back to the 5th century, with some even going so far as saying that the *Lost Wall of Severus,* a mysterious fortification thought to have been built by the Roman Emperor Septimus Severus, might actually be Offa's Dyke. However, it is important to mention that none of this is known for sure, and Roman historians also interchangeably conflate the Severan Wall with the Antonine Wall in modern-day Scotland, as well as with the much more famous Hadrian's Wall. Indeed, the 8th-century monk, poet and all-round genius *The Venerable Bede* also linked the Severan Wall with Hadrian's Wall, describing a *rampart made of sods cut out of the ground fronted with a trench*, which muddies the waters even further, almost literally.

As for Offa's Dyke then, there is surprisingly little in the historical record detailing either its construction or its subsequent history. This is not because of some grand conspiracy but simply because historical sources during the era in which it was supposedly built are incredibly few and far between. And although its construction may well have started as far back as the 5th century, the first mention of the dyke came over a hundred years later, though it wasn't actually referred to as Offa's Dyke until over half a millennium later, sometime in the twelfth century.

Archaeological records are not much help either, as the areas the dyke passes through are all pretty much devoid of coins, ceramics, and any other such items that the bearded boffins with spades generally use to date their finds. And if you think I'm being sexist by referring to archaeologists as bearded boffins, I'm actually referring to the ladies. Archaeologists, you see, are a certain type of person, if you know what I mean. Very nice and polite and all that, but let's just say gritty.

Anyway, those very boffins have also searched in, on and around the dyke for any signs of wood, which they could pass on to their equally brainy colleagues who can do absolute magic with tree rings and date the dyke that way. But guess what? They haven't found a single scrap, so dendrochronology is of no use either, which is a shame because it took me ages to figure out how to spell it, something for which I think King Offa would have been very proud of me.

But who was Offa anyway? Well, he certainly was a king, ruling much of England during the 8th century, with his kingdom stretching from Sussex in the south all the way to the far north of the land. He had a bit of a reputation, too, primarily because in 796 AD, he had a bit of a falling out with a rival king, Ethelbert of East Anglia, and ultimately had him beheaded, but more of that in a bit.

Historians previously looked at Offa's legacy as one that was working to unify the land into an actual country, but this view is no longer the consensus, and in fact, many now consider Offa to have been a power-mad ego-maniac who left not a legacy, but merely a reputation, which quite frankly reminds me of some of our more modern so-called leaders.

And as for the evidence that it was Offa who even built the dyke, there is only one actual source to cite, and that is in a history of Alfred the Great rather unimaginatively called *The Life of King Alfred* written by a monk called Asser. In his book, Asser writes that *a certain vigorous king called Offa . . . who terrified the neighbouring kings . . . had a great dyke built between Wales and Mercia from sea to sea.* However, it should be noted that Asser only put pen to paper, or more accurately, quill to parchment, in around 893 AD, almost a hundred years after Offa's death in 796 AD.

What is odd, though, is that Asser completely failed to mention anything regarding Offa's Dyke in his earlier and much better-known work, *The Anglo-Saxon Chronicle.* Furthermore, all later historical accounts regarding Offa seem to be derived solely from Asser's somewhat late and solitary account.

Other great chroniclers of the time, such as John of Worcester, William of Malmesbury, Henry of Huntingdon, and Bob of Bradford, all fail to mention the dyke at all, although I must confess that I made that last one up, just to check if you were still awake.

And while accounts of the dyke did become more common after the Norman conquest of 1066, there seems to be only one other pre-conquest account, which is in a survey of Tidenham, near Chepstow, thought to date from about 1050 AD or thereabouts, but even then, it is only mentioned in passing and is referred to simply as *the dyke*.

For the next concrete mention of the dyke, we must fast forward almost a hundred years after William the Conqueror stumbled onto the scene, specifically to 1165 AD. This mention is credited to Reginald of Durham, who was writing about the life of Saint Oswald, King of Northumbria, and, in particular, about the site of the king's death at the Battle of Maserfield. Notably, the spot is only referenced in relation to *"King Offa's dyke, which divides England from North Wales"*. Reginald goes on to provide an explanation for the dyke, too, describing it as a *"securer bastion against his (Offa's) enemies, the Welsh"*.

After this date, references to the dyke become somewhat prolific, partly because more records have managed to survive from that era but also due to the many wars between the English and the Welsh during this time. Documents from 1184, 1200 and 1233 all reference the dyke and give us various snippets of information, including its location as well as a statement that King Offa *"girdled the Welsh into a small corner of their Wales by means of the dyke which still bears his name"*.

In 1159, John of Salisbury wrote of his admiration of Earl Harold of Wessex and his policy stating that any Welshman found east of the dyke was to lose his right hand, which seems a bit harsh. Another English chronicler, Walter Map, mentioned something similar, though in his case, whichever Welsh miscreant dared to venture into England was to lose a foot, though he never mentioned which one. To be honest, it wouldn't really matter, as the loss of either would be inconvenient, to say the least.

It is probably fair to say, however, that every single one of these accounts might be said to be somewhat biased, as they are all essentially English. The first Welsh mention of the dyke comes from the late 13th century when Gerald of Wales wrote that *"Offa had a dyke made as a defence between him and the Welsh so that it might be easier for him to resist the attack of his enemies. And that is called Offa's Dyke from that day to this"*.

What is sure, though, is that the dyke has never formed the actual border between England

and Wales, a myth that somehow originated in the twelfth century and which persists to this day, similar to the myth that Hadrian's Wall forms the border between Scotland and England, which it never has.

All of this is interesting, but for me, the most fascinating discovery was that Offa was not Welsh. I had always presumed him to have come from Wales and had also assumed that he built his dyke to protect his homeland. The actual truth, however, seems to be the complete opposite, but there you go. Offa was English, you see, at least sort of, as England did not technically exist at the time he was alive, but anyway, he was from Mercia, an area which is now known as the Midlands, which makes him about as English as you could probably get. And Offa had his capital in Tamworth, which is where he was crowned and where he chose to spend every single Christmas, and I don't blame him one bit, as it is a lovely little town with lots of nice pubs and a great little pie shop.

I once went there on a stag weekend that got a bit out of control, but on a positive note, I can confirm that the police cells are nice and warm and very comfortable. Unfortunately, the lovely people who run the Castle Hotel no longer accept bookings from large groups of males who may or may not have claimed that the reason for their visit was to attend a conference on the merits of recycled packaging in the 21st century and not in any way to go on a massive bender, and I'm quoting my good friend Rob now, who also got absolutely obliterated that night though somehow managed to avoid getting arrested. It can be quite hard to describe Rob, but to give you a rough idea, everyone has a friend who they shouldn't be allowed to sit next to at a serious function. For me, that friend is Rob.

Anyway, moving on, he turns out to be not a very nice chap at all, and I mean Offa, not Rob, though he certainly has his moments, too. It was while he was in Tamworth, and I still mean Offa, not Rob, that he was said to have had Ethelbert, the King of East Anglia, popped off in the middle of the night, which is surprising, as Ethelbert was actually Offa's son-in-law. Allegedly, old Ethelbert became just a little bit greedy and started minting coins with his own image upon them, which was strictly against the rules of the day. Offa was presumably not impressed when he popped down to the medieval equivalent of the supermarket one morning and saw somebody else's head on his change, and on May 20th, 794 AD, he had his trusty manservant Grimbert, which is an excellent name by the way, carefully remove Ethelbert's head, and that was the end of that.

Or at least it would have been had the finely named Grimbert not been just a little bit careless when disposing of Ethelbert's rotting corpse. As Grimbert was taking the evidence away in the middle of the night, Ethelbert's head somehow fell off the back of a cart and landed in a ditch, where it was later found by a somewhat bemused peasant.

Not surprisingly, when Mrs Ethelbert found out, who, you may remember, was King Offa's daughter, she was not very happy at all about the fact that her dear old daddy had been chopping bits of her husband off and leaving them lying all over the land. She made her considerable displeasure abundantly clear to her father, the king, and whatever she said to him must have worked. Offa then spent several years trying to make it up to her, though I'm not sure what exactly you could do that would compensate for murdering and dismembering one of your closest relatives and then trying to get away with it by hiding the body here, there and everywhere. Anyway, Offa even went on a Pilgrimage to Rome in an effort to make amends, but despite his best efforts, things were never quite the same.

Anyway, for various reasons, the route of Offa's Dyke path is extremely interesting and crosses the border between England and Wales over 20 times, passing through a total of eight counties. Whether you go north or south is entirely up to you, and when I had a quick glance through some guidebooks, I discovered you can actually buy one which follows your preferred direction. We're starting in the south, though, and heading north, as this is the right way to do it, and all those who say otherwise are stupid and should thus be dipped in tar, feathered, and thrown overboard to the sharks.

As already mentioned, what made me finally want to do this walk was the 2001 movie called Arthur's Dyke which we briefly discussed earlier, featuring British actors Pauline Quirke and Brian Conley, along with several other equally distinguished stars of the time.

The premise of the movie is a group of friends meeting up for a reunion a couple of decades after having previously walked the route while at university, with Quirke thrown in as Janet, the wild card stranger who joins the already eclectic mix.

Things soon go awry, with Dennis Waterman appearing in the guise of an atopic private investigator, who seems to be allergic to almost everything judging by the amount of time he spends emptying the contents of his nose into a handkerchief. Another relatively well-known actor, Brian Conley, plays Quirke's jealous husband, who is intent on tracking down his absent wife, convinced she has gone off on some kind of ambulistic orgy.

The film sells the trail well, and if you haven't already seen it, any effort to watch it will be well-rewarded, showcasing the beautiful Welsh countryside in all its glory, along with more than the occasional pub and more laughs than you can count.

As for the actual path, it starts in lovely Chepstow, as I may have already mentioned, and also, as I have already mentioned, it finishes in sunny Prestatyn, on the far northern shores of Wales, at least ten days, 177 miles and countless blisters away on foot.

The chances of making it depend on many factors, but mainly on how stubborn you are. Being of a very stubborn sort indeed, I intend to absolutely and completely refuse to give up under any circumstances whatsoever. My three companions feel precisely the same, and we have collectively decided that there is only one thing that could stop us, and that would be death himself, the grim reaper.

And if I do happen to die along the way, then please accept my most sincere apologies, as the words will probably stop mid-way through this book. I will obviously try to avoid that, as I expect it would rather annoy you and you might even demand your money back, which would rather annoy my accountant.

Anyway, Chepstow is an attractive little town. It is, in fact, the first place you come to when you flash your passport and suddenly find yourself in deepest, darkest Wales, and furthermore, it is actually the easternmost town in the country. Go any further east than Chepstow, and you will immediately find yourself rather wet-footed and in the middle of the River Wye, and go further still, and you will find it is people with English accents who would be asking what on earth you were doing and why you didn't use the bloody bridge.

The town was also rather important hundreds of years ago, attested by the fact that it has a rather fancy castle. In fact, Chepstow Castle is commonly referred to as being the oldest castle in the United Kingdom. That is really saying something when you think about it and certainly shouldn't be taken with a pinch of salt as we have some genuinely ancient stuff dotted around this land of ours, and I'm not referring to myself at all, although everyone keeps reminding me that I really am getting on a bit.

Anyway, this old relic, and I mean the castle, not me, has been rattling around for over a thousand years, having been built by a guy called William FitzOsbern just after the Norman conquest in 1066. FitzOsbern was actually the cousin of William the Conqueror, often considered the mastermind behind what is commonly referred to as the last invasion of England, but we shouldn't forget that Wales was in the Norman's sights as well. Furthermore, it was actually FitzOsbern who was one of the most vocal proponents of the invasion, and without him, it might never have happened at all.

Following the successful operation, which saw the English King Harold apparently killed by a rather painful arrow to the eye, at least in popular folklore anyway, FitzOsbern was generously rewarded for his allegiance to William the Conqueror, who was much more interestingly known as William the Bastard, by the way, as he was, in fact, the illegitimate son of Duke Robert the 1st of Normandy. I can't possibly think why they don't teach us this stuff in school, but there you go.

Anyway, FitzOsbern was given significant land holdings around the country, probably because he had been able to influence the military campaign in William's favour due to intelligence he received from his younger brother, the rather curiously named Osbern FitzOsbern. Osbern was actually the chaplain to Edward the Confessor, one of the last Anglo-Saxon kings of England, based at an influential church in Sussex where King Harold also went to pray. Thus, Osbern FitzOsbern was ideally placed to snoop on the royal conversations and learn all sorts of sneaky secrets that he could pass on to his older, sneakier brother.

Back to Chepstow Castle, though, and after the conquest, the place soon began to fall into disrepair, basically because it wasn't really needed anymore, until, that is, a Welshman called Owain Glyndwr started to cause a bit of trouble around the year 1400.

Owain had actually been quite close to the English, having studied law in London, after which he served in various English armies. At some point, however, he clearly remembered his Welsh roots, and on September 16th, 1400, he was proclaimed Prince of Wales by a band of brave but apparently reckless Welsh noblemen with high aspirations and surprising amounts of optimism.

Subsequently, they all went on a bit of a rampage, burning lots of quaint English towns, including some not too far from Offa's Dyke Path, particularly Welshpool and Oswestry.

The English, not surprisingly, were less than happy at this turn of events and branded Owain both a rebel and a traitor. None of this mattered, though, as Owain had already met his first objective, which was challenging the very foundations of English rule in Wales. While the English were certainly less than happy with Owain Glyndwr, Shakespeare was much kinder to him in his works, referring to him as a great magician, which stems from a belief that he was somehow able to control the weather.

Others followed Owain's lead, including one of his own cousins, who quite cheekily tricked his way into Conwy Castle and successfully held it for two months. But Owain didn't just rely on his fellow Welshmen, as he courted international support, too. As the old saying goes, the enemy of my enemy is my friend, and Owain persuaded the fiendish French to join the party, which resulted in a substantial force of heavily accented, quite rude, but very romantic

European types landing at Milford Haven in 1405 and marching as far as Worcester. So please don't believe the hype they teach you at school when they tell you that your glorious little island hasn't been invaded for almost a thousand years because that's pure propaganda, I'm afraid. In fact, this invasion was actually just one of many that have occurred over the last millennium or so.

Ultimately, however, things didn't go all that great for either the Welsh in general or Owain in particular. His last days saw him hiding out from an English army intent on hunting him down like some kind of wild animal, and reliable accounts state that he finally died, aged 61, on September 20th, 1415. And although his final resting place is not known, and may never be, a recently revealed family secret suggests he may have been buried at Monnington-on-Wye, halfway between Hay-on-Wye, which is in Wales, and Hereford, which is in England. Unfortunately, for Owain, at least, this means he may be buried in England, which would probably make him turn in his grave.

Anyway, going back to FitzOsbern and Chepstow, the place is much quieter nowadays, though the castle did briefly become relatively famous, at least to us nerdy types anyway, after starring in the 50th-anniversary episode of Doctor Who, which is probably why it looked so familiar to me. Others of a more advanced age may remember the castle from the 1980s Terry Gilliam classic *Jabberwocky,* and the very oldest among us may even recognise it from the 1913 silent movie version of *Ivanhoe*, though obviously, I'm far too young for such foolishness, but my good friend Rob probably remembers it well.

And although Cheptsow is the starting point of our grand tour of Offa's Dyke, it used to be the finishing point of another tour, the Wye Valley Tour, when the actual Grand Tour of a trip across Europe became somewhat impractical due to the risks of being killed by one of Napoleon's armies who were rather partial to stabbing the British in general and the English in particular, probably due to years of continuous warfare.

Thus, instead of the delights of Paris, Rome and Milan, our ancestors instead decamped to the glorious delights of Ross-on-Wye and spent a day or two drifting gently downstream on the beautiful River Wye all the way to Chepstow. The tour became particularly popular after a man called William Gilpin published a travel book about the route, which bore a ridiculously long title typical of that era but which we will simply call *Observations*.

Other writers followed, including Thomas Fosbroke, who compared the area to a Grecian Temple because of its innate natural beauty, thereby elevating the tour among the upper classes to that of *the highest level of classical beauty*.

And, of course, as already mentioned, Napoleon helped to elevate the popularity of the tour as well, but this had less to do with its beauty and more to do with British travellers becoming increasingly wary of travelling to a continent ravaged by war and populated by unfriendly Europeans where they risked taking a bullet in the back or a bayonet in the belly, a bit like a fortnight in Benidorm today really.

It was Gilpin alone, however, who was largely responsible for introducing us to the idea of *properly picturesque* scenery, which resulted in hordes of predominantly English tourists descending upon this particular little corner of Wales to experience such delights as the Devil's Pulpit and trampling across not only the land but the customs of those who lived upon it as well as each other, so numerous were the tourists. And picturesque, by the way, meant something like *that particular kind of beauty which is agreeable in a picture*.

At the height of the picturesque craze, for that is what it was, up to ten boats a day would set off from Ross-on-Wye, stuffed with fat, old, filthy rich people who had both too much time and too much money on their hands. They would while away the hours on board gazing out at the passing landscapes, often painting their own unique versions of it or even reading the works of Gilpin and Fosbroke as they sailed by, which seems a bit pointless when you think about it as they would miss the scenery entirely if they had their head stuck in a dusty old book.

Regardless, most tours followed more or less the same itinerary, lazily meandering along the course of the Wye and enjoying its lofty banks, with the first stop usually being Goodrich Castle. Next would come the looming ironworks at New Weir, where many would marvel at the various man-made amendments to the natural environment, particularly around the waterfall, and would consider them as enhancing in nature, and this, perhaps bizarrely, included the sound effects such as booming hammers coming from within the works which were so loud that they would often out-compete the waterfall itself.

The boats would then take them past and beneath Symonds Yat, an almost 500-foot-high cliff, which apparently impressed upon our ancestors a certain sense of the sublime, such was its greatness. However, this impression was probably at least partly due to Gilpin and Fosbroke simply calling it sublime.

Travellers would then spend the night in Monmouth at one of its many splendid inns, carrying on the following day past a series of tiny hamlets and more beauty than you could shake a stick at before arriving at the tour's greatest spectacle, Tintern Abbey. There, our learned friends would marvel at the bare columns and overgrown vegetation of this once mighty structure, more often than not reciting William Wordsworth's poem *Lines*.

It should be pointed out that the full title of his poem is actually, and I kid you not, *Lines composed a few miles above Tintern Abbey.* I'm sure you will agree that this does not exactly roll off the tongue, which explains why I initially used the somewhat abridged title. And furthermore, regarding the title of said poem, while I hate to describe anything done by Wordsworth with the following words, it is, quite frankly, a bit crap.

While the tourists absolutely loved the abbey, Gilpin himself was not all that impressed, describing it in such terms as *the parts are beautiful, but the whole is ill-shaped*, so I can only conclude that, much like Wordsworth, Gilpin was probably a bit above his station, or perhaps even a bit dim, or maybe both, because the abbey really is, much like most of this walk, truly beautiful.

ACCIDENTS WILL HAPPEN

Chepstow to Not Very Far Really

We had arrived at Chepstow in the early evening, following perhaps the longest bus journey known to humanity, after setting off from our homes in the far north of England just after the crack of dawn. I remember sitting on the bus thinking that Columbus probably got to the New World quicker than this. The journey, quite bizarrely, had included a transfer in London, meaning we spent almost a full day travelling, which is perhaps why things went south so quickly after we started walking.

We had prepared ourselves for this walk, though, as should anyone considering a long-distance walk. I recently had a thorough checkup at my doctor's surgery, for instance. He said, *"Don't eat anything fatty"*. I replied, *"What, like bacon and eggs?"* and he said, *"No fatty, don't eat anything"*. I had a hearing test, too, as I had a suspected ear infection, and the guy doing it asked me if I could describe the symptoms. I told him that Homer was a fat guy and Marge had blue hair. I failed the test.

We, by the way, included me, obviously, along with my good friends Rob and James, as well as a new face, to me at least, which was Mark, and we were all very happy when we finally stumbled off the bus in Chepstow.

Mark, incidentally, nearly never made it. Just over half an hour or so after setting off, he received an alarming phone call. As soon as he answered it, his face drained of all colour. We immediately knew something was drastically wrong, though at this stage, we had no idea what it was, and our minds wandered through all sorts of possibilities.

No one dared interrupt, and as we listened in, trying to glean any details we could, we figured there had been some kind of accident. Mark was on that phone for around fifteen minutes, though it felt like an hour, but either way, we knew it was serious. Ironically, the bus driver, who admittedly did not know the circumstances, put out an announcement basically telling Mark to get off his phone as he was disturbing the other passengers, of which I counted eight, and that included the four of us.

When he finally hung up, I asked him if he was okay, knowing full well that he wasn't, but it's difficult to know what to say in these circumstances. He took a minute to compose himself and then told us what had happened.

His wife had been involved in a car accident, he said, and another car had hit her head on. Whilst she was shaken, she was luckily okay, more or less, though the car was probably going to be a write-off.

We all stood and looked at each other, feeling both speechless and helpless, as he carried on.

She had been approaching a junction, and whether or not the other car had jumped the lights was not known, though it seemed likely. Paramedics had given her the once over and were satisfied that she was, luckily and surprisingly, uninjured, but the look on Mark's face told us he was obviously still very concerned.

I immediately told Mark that, obviously, we would not blame him for going home if he felt the need, especially given that he could probably have been home within the hour, such was our slow progress.

Mark then spent the next forty minutes variously on the phone with his insurance company, the breakdown recovery people, and then, surprisingly, a garage.

It turned out that it wasn't their car his wife had been driving, but it was a courtesy car provided when their own vehicle had been rear-ended the previous week. This was going to be complicated, I thought.

Ultimately, after speaking to his wife again and getting assurances that all was okay, he decided to continue with the walk after all, and although I did not really know him, I suspect he came pretty close to going home.

I had a call as well, though luckily, it was not as serious as Mark's. My wife rang and asked me if I'd seen the dog bowl. I said I didn't know he could. I can be a dick like that, and as a consequence, it is probably good that I am away for a few days, as she is currently in a bit of a mood with me. She asked me if there was anything about her that annoyed me and then got all offended during the PowerPoint presentation. She also berated me for what I did to the dishwasher before I left. In every relationship, you see, there is one person who stacks the dishwasher like a Scandinavian architect, while the other stacks it like a raccoon on crystal meth. I am that other.

Anyway, back to Mark, as what was going to be his first long-distance walk had started on shaky ground anyway, even before the car accident. He had invited us all around to his house the week before as he wasn't a hundred percent sure about what to pack in his rucksack, and as a lure, he promised us pizzas. He must already know us well, I remember thinking.

We took a critical look at what he had put in there, and actually, most of it was probably essential. There were, however, one or two items we advised him to leave behind, mainly because someone else already had one, and that included things such as first aid kits and pans and the like.

He had also invested in an expensive lightweight inflatable mattress, which we definitely deemed to be essential, but as it was still in its packaging, Rob advised him to blow it up to make sure it didn't deflate. Better to find out now than on the first night of our trip, Rob suggested.

Once inflated, Mark placed it against the wall in what must have been his gaming corner, which contained a chess set, a dartboard, and various board games and the like. The plan was to leave it an hour or so to see if it deflated while we carried on looking at the rest of his gear.

This involved wandering off to the garden to put his tent up, basically to make sure all the poles and pegs were present. There were, alarmingly, no poles, but Mark told us that this tent relied on using your own hiking sticks as poles, which was a good idea as it saved weight, unless you left your poles somewhere, of course. And while the tent was up, he sprayed it with waterproofing treatment, after which we went back inside.

The pizzas arrived soon after that, and it was as we were eating them that something unfortunate happened. Out of the corner of my eye, I saw something fall from the wall, after which I heard a pop followed by a long hiss. One of the darts had, quite inexplicably, decided to detach itself from the board, had fallen straight down and landed on, of all things, Mark's somewhat pricey new blow-up bed.

The long hiss continued, and while I wanted to laugh, as did Rob and James, Mark's face was a picture. Again, I didn't really know him all that well then, and he probably wouldn't have appreciated my sense of humour, but luckily, my silliness only lasted a few seconds.

Suggestions were made for repairing it, but I had a better idea and told him to just send it back and pretend it was faulty when he bought it. I have no scruples, apparently.

Oh, and on top of that, I inadvertently smashed Mark's favourite cup whilst we had been in the garden. This possibly wasn't the best start to our friendship, and I should probably point out that he hasn't invited us back since.

Back to the bus journey though, which had actually proven to be an incredibly cheap way of travelling to the start of our walk, and on the way to London, I had delighted in talking to Frankie, an American student from Utah who was enjoying a gap year before returning to the States to start her illustrious career as a copywriter. When I asked her what a copywriter does, however, she thought for a minute and then simply said *copywrites things*, which didn't shed much light on the issue, to be honest.

After extolling the virtues of Wales to her,

which she had carelessly failed to include in her tour of our wonderful little island, we bade our goodbyes within the bowels of London's surprisingly busy Victoria coach station. We then made the second leg of the journey in complete, utter and absolute silence, apart from, of course, the family of rambunctious children who were seated directly behind us and who graciously kicked the backs of our chairs every thirty seconds or so for the next two hundred miles, presumably just to make sure we were all still alive.

We stepped off the bus in Chepstow just in time to enjoy the last of the daylight, and after a quick look at my map, we were off, heading straight for the starting point of Offa's Dyke Path. Not only would this stretch our legs, which were desperately in need of a good stretching after many hours on that horrible bus, but it would also knock a couple of miles off tomorrow's schedule and hopefully allow us a more leisurely day.

Rob said he had to ring his wife before we set off, though, just to let her know we had arrived, which set alarm bells off in my head. I know what he is like on the phone, and he can be hours, so I shared a little tip. Start every phone call with, "*My battery is almost dead*". That way, you can end the call when you're bored.

We wandered through the town centre in the general direction usually known as east, or so we thought, and we probably should have used a map, but one thing about us stubborn old men is that we always think we know exactly where we are going, even when we don't really have a clue.

This is why, after passing by what looked like a fancy medieval arch, we ended up near Chepstow Castle, which was nice but was not where we wanted to be, so after a quick look anyway, I admitted defeat, dug out the map, and headed towards where we actually wanted to be, which was the southern terminus of the path near Sedbury Cliffs, quite some distance away and in the entirely opposite direction to the one we had been going in.

Walking back through the town, we considered getting some food, but we had already eaten a bagful of snacks on the journey down here, which, admittedly, had not been very healthy. It doesn't matter how old you are, you see. Buying snacks for a road trip should always look like a 9-year-old had won the lottery.

Anyway, I wanted to lose a bit of weight on this walk if I could. I was a tad overweight, and something I had heard a few weeks earlier had jarred me and forced me to finally confront my lifestyle. Life is like a box of chocolates. It doesn't last long if you're fat. And while I say I am fat, which I am, I wish I were as fat as I was the first time I thought I was fat, if you know what I mean.

I had considered dieting, and I even tried it

once. It didn't work, not because I wasn't any good at it, but because I was too good. I don't mean to brag, but I finished my 14-day diet in a little under 3 hours.

Anyway, we passed on the food, as it is actually a waste of money. Think about it. Every penny you have spent on it has been flushed down the toilet, so instead of eating, we pushed straight on.

The first obstacle was the River Wye, luckily spanned by a beast of a bridge that carried cars and trains as well as pedestrians. A quick hop along a path just after crossing it led us onto a housing estate, and from there, we were finally able to make our way to the cliffs in mere minutes.

Although there isn't a lot to see at Sedbury Cliffs, there is a plaque that marks the start or the end of the walk, take your pick, so after a quick photo opportunity, we were finally on our way for real, heading north on a walk that would lead us through forests and mountains, valleys and farms, and would take us through all four seasons, often on the same day. In other words, we were about to get absolutely battered by old Mother Nature herself.

When we had first planned this trip, we had considered coming down on the train, but because none of us was particularly keen on re-mortgaging our homes and spending the rest of our lives up to our necks in debt, we had chosen the cheaper alternative of the bus instead. In one way, this was a shame because it meant we would not see Chepstow train station, which was a bit of a film star, or so I had initially thought.

About a year before this walk, I had come down here for a week on a sort of reconnaissance mission and had spent a few days gently driving along the route of Offa's Dyke Path, stopping at all of the key places. I even brought my wife and youngest son, and we made fond memories together where I vividly remember telling them about the history of all the exciting places we visited. They must have really enjoyed it, as it tired them out so much that they spent the entire week yawning and falling asleep, although, in retrospect, I did wonder if they had been just a little bit bored. Come to think of it, neither of them has spoken to me since.

Anyway, one of the places we visited was Chepstow train station, and the first thing I noticed about it was that it did not look much like Chepstow train station, which is odd because all the signs said Chepstow. However, I was foolishly basing my belief in reality solely on the movie Arthur's Dyke, particularly the bit where Janet, one of the stars, gets off the train to begin her ultimate walk along Offa's Dyke at, as you may have guessed, Chepstow railway station.

It turns out, then, that they actually used Abergavenny train station as a stand-in and simply borrowed Chepstow's signs for a couple of days, which must have confused the hell out of whichever poor commuters had been passing through whilst they were filming. While I'm not sure why the producers chose to do this, I'm sure they had a good reason, but regardless, Chepstow train station is very nice in itself, and I think they certainly missed a trick by not using it.

Muttering under my breath something about artistic licence as I recalled this happy memory, we wandered on northwards and soon passed the Wye Bridge again, which made me feel like we were finally on Offa's Dyke Path for real.

This was still an urban environment, though, and in fact, this part of Chepstow resembled a well-to-do leafy suburb. Accordingly, a couple of dog walkers gave me a cheery good evening but only after a somewhat suspicious glance, and one of them asked if I was on the dyke, which I thought was an odd way of putting it, but I replied in the positive nonetheless.

All national trails are waymarked with a little acorn symbol, and we soon came across our first one just a few hundred yards further on, pointing left into what looked like a park of some kind, and we obediently followed it. It wasn't a park, however, but was simply an even leafier little street with some very lovely and rather expensive-looking houses.

We almost took a wrong turn here straight into someone's garden, but I realised the error at the last moment, which meant that we ended up on a tiny lane that then became a narrow footpath. Unfortunately, this was our first mistake, and the next half a mile involved a pointless detour down, around and back up a hill. I thought it best not to mention it to the lads, however, who were already chuntering loudly among themselves about mileages and directions and whatnot. And I say our mistake, though technically I was the one who had the map, but I do like to share, and anyway, I'm admitting nothing.

A short while later, I found what I was looking for, which was that beautiful little acorn symbol, indicating we were back on the path. A gate then led us into an actual field, and this meant two things. We were now entering the wilderness, and we really were on Offa's Dyke Path, as the town bit hadn't really counted, at least not in my mind.

A gentle hill led slowly upwards, first past another dog walker and then past a ruined tower. The tower, imaginatively called Tutshill Tower after the village in which it stands, is a bit of a historical mystery. Some say it was defensive in nature, and its construction was perhaps linked to nearby Chepstow Castle, while others say it is a ruined windmill. Another opinion is that it was merely a folly, so we will probably never know for sure, though the windmill theory is most likely.

One certainty is that Tutshill is linked to none

other than Harry Potter, as Joanne Rowling lived and went to school here as a child. Better known, of course, as J.K. Rowling, she attended Tutshill Primary School and then went on to study at the secondary school in nearby Sedbury, which apparently set her up pretty well to go on and become one of the wealthiest women on the planet, so it can't have been all bad.

She may have remembered her roots when it came to her writing, as it has been suggested that Severus Snape was based on one or more of her teachers here, and in her seventh book, *Harry Potter and the Deathly Hallows*, a small part of it is set within the nearby Forest of Dean, which Tutshill sits on the very south-western end of.

And the Forest of Dean, by the way, which Offa's Dyke Path technically skirts for the next few miles, is something of a haven for wild boar. When I was first told this, I thought of cute little piggies and the like, but the person who told me soon dismissed such folly. Wild boar can be huge, and they can be dangerous, I was warned, and I should exercise immense caution when hopping and skipping through the trees, apparently, especially as I was basically a nice chubby snack on legs with lots of lovely meat for the fiendish porkers to feed on should I somehow find myself incapacitated in the woods.

They live in family groups and are very wary of other forestry visitors, particularly of the human variety. They can be surprisingly big and, considering their size, can move incredibly quickly. And while they have pretty poor eyesight, they have an excellent sense of smell, which is probably bad news for stinky backpackers, so make sure you have a good wash before coming out here. Luckily, with this being day one of our walk, we were all about as fresh as we were ever going to be. For anyone doing this walk north to south, however, with Chepstow as your finishing point, well, it was nice knowing you.

Boar are much more likely to see you before you see them, too, due to the sounds that you make as you clumsily tramp along on Offa's Dyke Path, with your camping pans clanging and rattling against each other, and your loud huffing and puffing alerting anything and everything within 500 yards that you are totally out of shape, and therefore fair game for anything that fancies a quick but satisfyingly large meal of fat, meat and bone, but mainly fat in my case.

If they do hear you, they will definitely come and investigate, and while some people mistake this curiosity for aggressive behaviour, they are generally just being nosey, at least initially. Get too close, however, and all hell can break loose.

In the first instance, one of the sows will generally place herself between the family group and whichever miserable walker has been stupid enough to stumble across them. They might even perform a mock charge if they really feel threatened, such as if you attempt to get even closer so that you can get a nice photo for whatever social media rocks your boat or perhaps because you're just an imbecile.

Don't worry, however, as there is an easy way to tell if that charge really is a mock one or is perhaps the real thing, and this is as follows. If you suddenly find yourself lying face down with a broken hip, a fractured skull and a dislocated shoulder, then it probably wasn't a mock charge. And I'm being serious too, perhaps deadly serious, as all those injuries have been attributed to wild boar at one time or another. And a complete lack of natural predators means their numbers are only increasing, making interesting encounters ever more likely.

Male boars, by the way, don't live in these family groups but instead live alone, shirking all parental responsibility and generally living a day-to-day existence. I'm sure my wife would make some correlation there with men, but anyway, the males can be a bit awkward and will often refuse to move away. Generally, however, their bark is worse than their bite, and they are not as tough as they might make themselves out to be. In summary, it really is the females with the piglets that you should be wary of.

We carried on along the path, chased briefly by a herd of curious cows just past Tutshill Tower, and the path took us next towards an old manor house, where we bumped into a rather lovely couple. We stopped to talk to them for a while, and the next minute, we were being given a tour of their beautiful walled garden, within which they grew endless varieties of flowers, vegetables, herbs and who knows what else. I spied an excellent place to camp in the corner, but unfortunately, we had only done a couple of miles, and we had aimed for a few more. Inevitably, we waved goodbye to our new friends Robert and Sarah and moved on, though in retrospect, because of what happened shortly after, we probably should have stayed.

We followed the path which next took us along the edge of a wood where a craggy cliff soon signalled imminent death should anyone be unfortunate enough to flop over it, and this was Wintour's Leap. According to legend, many moons ago, a man called Sir John Wintour survived a 200-foot horseback jump from the top of this cliff whilst being chased by Parliamentarian forces during the Civil War, but as usual, the story is not quite as simple as that, and the fog of history has certainly muddied the waters somewhat.

Wintour, then, was firmly on the side of the king during the war. He wasn't a soldier by trade but had been born into money and had inherited some iron mines from his father. Unfortunately, he wasn't very popular locally, as he tended to meddle in the affairs of the peasants, particularly regarding their right to use common land for things such as grazing, and the old devil even fenced off large areas and claimed it as his own.

Subsequently, when the war began, Wintour didn't just have the Parliamentarians to worry about, but the locals too, who knew an opportunity when they saw one and proceeded to smash down many of the fences he had built.

As a consequence, Wintour had no choice but to fortify his house, particularly when he went off to fight against the Parliamentarians on behalf of the king.

Just as Wintour wasn't a popular landowner, he wasn't a popular commander either, and in fact, many accounts describe him as being a poor soldier who often lost his battles but somehow managed to escape, and there were even hints of cowardice. A noted historian of the time, Sir John Corbet, even described him as a man who *delighted more in petty and cunning contrivance than open gallantry,* which brings us back to Wintour's Leap.

Upon closer inspection, the incident that led to the legend of Sir John's leap from the top of this cliff actually turns out to be two incidents which have been consolidated by the sands of time.

The first one was in 1644 when Wintour joined with the awesomely named Prince Rupert to attempt to re-occupy a place called Beachley, which was a crossing point of the River Severn just next to the outflow of the River Wye, which is at almost the exact point where the Offa's Dyke Path begins and where we had been just a couple of hours before.

The action failed dismally, and Wintour was chased north by Parliamentarian forces, led by the more than capable Sir Edward Massey, all the way back to Sedbury, where he managed to scramble down a cliff and escape in a boat. At no time, however, did his efforts involve gallantly jumping from the top of a cliff on horseback, which is a part of the story he probably added later that night after a couple of pints of grog in whatever ye olde English pub he inevitably ended up in.

The following year, Wintour suddenly found himself once again outsmarted and outgunned by the Parliamentarians, once again led by General Massey, this time in the vicinity of Lancault, a mile or two north of his last incident but right beneath what we now call Wintour's Leap, but once again, there was not a single flying horse in sight.

Furthermore, Massey now looked to be in a position to take possession of Wintour's house, so rather than let this happen, Wintour burned it down himself, and that was the end of that. Talk about cutting off your nose to spite your face.

Still, the tales of Wintour's escapes were greatly embellished over time, gradually becoming a single incident that was about as far from an accurate account of what actually happened as it could ever be. However, because it was such a good story, it was retold many times until it became more or less fact.

For now, though, a maze of paths, gates, fields and styles led us seemingly this way and that before dumping us on a short section of road, after which we almost missed a small fingerpost directing us once more into a muddy field and, by the looks of it, a forest.

We had been following each other in single file purely because the path was very narrow, and being the slowest, I was at the back. Therefore, I only heard what happened next and never saw it, but when I finally caught up with the others, Rob was lying sprawled across the floor with the other two leaning over him, who looked incredibly concerned indeed, but only if incredibly concerned means they looked like they were both about to burst out laughing.

The clumsy oaf had slipped on a rock, after which his ankle had given way, though, on the plus side, he looked to be in quite a bit of pain. Unfortunately, Rob was our first aider, so short of digging a hole and burying him there and then, there was little we could do, other than leave him for the wild boar, of course. He would probably feed them for a week. Doing so, however, would mean that we would have to deal with an incredibly angry Mrs Rob when we got home, so instead, a decision was quickly made to retreat a hundred yards or so to a field we had just passed through, where we could reassess the situation in the rapidly fading daylight.

It was here that we saw a village perhaps a quarter of a mile back, and the wonders of technology told James that there was a pub there. I'm not good with computers and the like, so it's good to have a youngster with us. Up until a couple of weeks ago, I thought Instagram simply meant having your granny on speed dial.

Anyway, when we are out on these walks, we do like to support the local economy as much as we can, so after checking if Rob could make it that far, we decamped to The Rising Sun in Woodcroft, and it's a good job we did.

James was probably the most presentable and well-spoken of the four of us, so we volunteered him to go and ask the landlord if perhaps, pretty please, we could pitch our tents in his beer garden for the night, thank you very much. We explained the situation that our clumsily crippled friend found himself in, and while Jules, which happened to be the name of our new best friend, looked on sympathetically, he said that, unfortunately, we couldn't camp there because the other villagers might not like a bunch of smelly hikers messing the place up, which was fair enough. He didn't actually use those words, of course, but we knew exactly what he meant.

He did, however, tell us that we could camp in his garden, which was very nice of him. It overlooked Wintour's Leap, he said, and there was even an electrical socket and a water supply if we needed such luxuries, which we certainly did. A jacuzzi and a mini-bar would be nice, too, I thought.

That was all for later, though, and for now, we took turns buying rounds of drinks and supporting the local economy I mentioned earlier. We sat chatting in the beer garden for quite a while, which was pleasantly warm, and after a couple of drinks, Rob said that his ankle didn't hurt as much, at which point we thought it best to go and find our campsite.

Unfortunately, after a couple of beers and a long day, the human body becomes a bit stupid. As such, it took us around twenty minutes and a few wrong turns, one of which involved climbing over somebody's garden fence, before we finally stumbled across our campsite for the night. By now, it was pretty much dark, though we somehow managed to get our tents up by torchlight, which is when I realised that the batteries in my torch were dead. Luckily, I had brought some spares, but why is it that things like eggs come in flimsy cardboard boxes, yet batteries come in a package that only a chainsaw can open? It took me longer to open it than it took to put four tents up.

Anyway, just moments later, we found ourselves sitting and enjoying a mild, late spring or early summer night, take your pick, under an almost cloudless sky, though there was no sign of that jacuzzi or mini-bar.

Rob had found a small bottle of something spicy in his rucksack, too, which he passed around and shared, and as we sat and enjoyed the spectacle of a star-filled sky gradually revealing its immense natural beauty, we chatted about this and that for half an hour, but then decided that the sensible thing to do would be to go to bed, which made me very happy. It was not so much the sleep that made me happy, but when I crawled into my sleeping bag, I found one of my favourite socks, which I had presumed to be lost forever.

Some people are solving major world problems, and I'm happy because I found a missing sock in my sleeping bag.

THE FLYING BANANA

Woodcroft to Hendre Farm

When we woke up the following day, our campsite looked spectacular. Set on a high cliff overlooking the River Wye, we could not have picked a more beautiful spot, which is why it was a shame that our tents looked as if they had been put up in the dark by a bunch of drunken idiots. On reflection, of course, they had.

Three of those tents were quite near each other, but Rob's was further away, and this was by design. Rob was, and I'm afraid there is no way to put this diplomatically, England's loudest snorer. Despite our preventative measures, however, James, Mark and I had still endured an almost sleepless night, and we collectively scoffed at Rob's suggestion that he had not slept much because of the pain in his ankle. Judging by the animal-like noises emanating from his tent for the last eight hours or so, Rob had had lots of sleep indeed, as well as some exciting dreams, apparently.

Rob's wife regularly gets angry with him for his snoring habits, and he said he struggles when it comes to appeasing her as he doesn't really understand women, so I decided to give him some pointers. I started with the fact that you can learn a lot about a woman by her hands. For instance, if they're placed around your neck, she's probably slightly upset. Also, telling a woman to calm down works about as well as baptising a cat. And finally, and I love this one, if you line up all your exes in chronological order, you can see a flow chart of your mental illness over the years.

Oh, and I almost forgot. Don't annoy them, ever, especially the older ones. The older they get, you see, the less *"life in prison"* is a deterrent.

Women are changing, though, and are coming up with increasingly sneaky ways to bamboozle us, particularly on the internet. I have never really been into the whole Facebook thing, and when I say Facebook, I actually refer to all of that digital crap, but mainly Facebook. In fact, being popular on Facebook is like sitting at the cool table in the cafeteria of a mental hospital.

Anyway, one of those changes involves how women love to apply filters to their photographs. Please stop doing this. How can we find you if you go missing and look like Angelina Jolie on

Instagram and a potato in real life?

I try to avoid technology, too. My wife has one of those Alexa things in the house that listens in on all your conversations, and I said that I didn't feel comfortable with her listening to me all the time. Luckily, there's a male version, too, she told me. It doesn't listen to a thing anyone says.

We brewed a quick coffee and got ourselves ready. I put on some deodorant, which was really just a token gesture when you think about it, as keeping clean on the trail is not really an option. I had actually bought it specially for this trip, and as I put it on, I read the instructions. The label said *remove cap and push up bottom*. I can barely walk, but when I fart, the air around me smells lovely.

After we had packed our gear away in almost military style, we were back on the trail in no time at all, taking it easy at first, mainly just to see how Rob's ankle did, which was surprisingly well. We had a bit of a squeaky-bum moment, however, as we passed the spot where he had fallen the night before, and we may or may not have made considerable fun of him and asked him if he wanted anyone to hold his hand, but that's what friends are for.

We soon passed a vast manor house with impeccably kept gardens, but it had an almost Disney-like look to it, meaning it was far too clean and fresh. I later found out that it was more or less new, as far as stately homes go anyway, having been built in 2005. Tidenham Manor, as it is known, has, in fact, recently been sold for a rather large stack of cash. I made a mental note to buy it myself if I ever win big on the horses.

Just behind the house, by the way, is the north end of something called the Tidenham Tunnel. If you come here in the summer months, you will find it open, as it is only closed during the off-season in order to protect its resident bat population. It is basically a very long but disused railway tunnel, which has now been repurposed for walkers and cyclists.

In fact, at 1,120 yards, the tunnel is incredibly long indeed. When it was built in 1875, it took 20 months to complete, and the rate of progress was a mere 2 yards per day, which was considered good going back then.

Linking Chepstow and Monmouth, the line was sadly never what you could call a commercial success. The hordes of tourists, who had been expected to come and visit the beautiful Wye Valley, never materialized, and while passenger services ceased in the 1960s, the line did somehow manage to survive for freight until the early 1990s, when the very last train to use the line left Tintern Quarry for good.

Perhaps the best thing about the line had been the introduction of the Flying Banana. While this wasn't actually a banana and also never flew in the strictest sense of the word, the Flying Banana was a streamlined passenger railcar that had to be seen to be believed. If you could conjure up in your handsome little head what a futuristic-looking train might have been expected to look like way back in the early postwar years, then you are probably picturing a flying banana, though in this case, some lunatic actually built it. The Banana was also the first diesel-powered railcar to be built, and it actually started running in the 1940s, so it was way ahead of its time. And if you want to see one, go to the National Railway Museum in York, which is where I saw it.

After less than half a mile of road walking, a discreet sign pointed into the woods to our left, and after hopping over both the road and the gate, we immediately found ourselves in a dense forest. Just a few feet away from the road, the only sound to be heard was the birds singing in the trees, and it was magical. The path here was good underfoot, and the canopy of trees was apparently protecting us from a bit of a shower, which I could hear but not feel. I would not have minded anyway, as I quite like walking in the wet. My wife doesn't like to walk in the rain, though, because it sets her face back to factory settings.

There was a good section of Offa's Dyke within these woods, and that was the Tidenham section. Now in the care of English Heritage, although care in this case simply looks overgrown if I am brutally honest, the dyke is at least relatively safe and should be here for many generations to come, which was unfortunate, as I suddenly felt the need to find a toilet, if you know what I mean. Not wanting to desecrate a national monument, I decided to try and hold on, but on that note, I recently bought a toilet brush. Long story short, they're overrated, and I'm going back to toilet paper.

I gave up any and all hope of knowing where I was as I made my way through the trees, but I didn't need to know, as the path was obvious, and anyway, I was just enjoying being in the moment. I think the only time I knew where I was whilst in those woods was when I caught up with the others at the Devil's Pulpit, where we stopped to take a short break.

The Devil's Pulpit is basically a tiny outcropping of rocks offering an exceptional view down to Tintern Abbey, which sits on the other side of the River Wye. The name derives from a myth about the devil herself, who, according to legend, used to sit on these very rocks and hurl insults at the monks in the valley below. This seems a bit petty when you think about it, especially considering that the devil probably had the power to inflict plagues across whole continents, which, quite frankly, sounds a lot more fun than just screaming randomly at some overly religious types, but maybe that's just me.

And if you're feeling particularly courageous

and perhaps just a tad reckless, you could even scramble onto the rocks for a selfie, but I wouldn't recommend it. There is an increasing death toll among certain groups, and dare I say it, the younger of those among us, who are increasingly dying in evermore bizarre circumstances whilst trying to take adventurous pictures of themselves, often merely to impress their many thousands of followers on the social media channel of their choosing. This is perhaps partly because of a psychological phenomenon called optimism bias, which is when people think nothing bad will ever happen to them.

Perhaps somewhat surprisingly, many of these incidents occur whilst driving, and in the United States alone, 33,000 people were injured in 2014 while taking a selfie at the wheel, which reminds me just how much I love Americans, bless them, even if only for their entertainment value. I feel sorry for Canadians, though, who, as a society in general, must probably feel like they live in the apartment above a meth lab.

The problem is just as bad in India, however, which accounted for over half of all selfie deaths in 2016, and the authorities have even gone to the lengths of establishing official *"no selfie zones",* with fines for those who break the rules, or at least those who break the rules and survive.

Russia is also up there at the top of the list, which, perhaps not surprisingly, is dominated by men, and young ones at that. There is a reason for this, as the male brain does not become fully formed until the mid to late twenties, and consequently, young men, in particular, are notorious risk-takers or, alternatively, are simply stupid.

Like so many things nowadays, the Americans started this craze, which doesn't surprise me at all. In particular, three individuals kicked it all off in 2011 when they posed for a selfie in front of a train. Nobody actually knows exactly what happened, and in fact, everyone presumed they had been tragically killed whilst trying to cross the line. However, that all changed when investigators discovered the selfie on one of the deceased persons' phones. Bizarrely, however, that group had consisted solely of girls, which is unusual in the extreme.

After that, things just get crazy, and people have died in all sorts of manners. One incident involved a young man shooting himself while trying to take a photo with a gun pointing at his head, while another involved two Russians posing with a hand grenade, but for some unknown reason, they had pulled the pin out.

Others have chosen to have their final snap taken with one cute and fluffy animal or another, resulting in death by bull, bison or bear, and in one case, an extremely pissed-off elephant.

Other little gems include lots of electrocutions, usually involving overhead railway lines, as well as countless falls from bridges, cliffs, balconies, waterfalls or dams, along with anything else you can possibly think of, with one bright spark even somehow managing to fall into a volcano.

Hopefully, however, no such adventures awaited us as Rob, Mark, James, and I leaned over the side of the Devil's Pulpit for a truly awesome shot. Well, stuff like that never happens to us, does it?

I sometimes go off on a tangent like that, but I was drawn back into the now when brilliant sunshine broke through the clouds and illuminated Tintern Abbey almost like a theatre spotlight.

The abbey far below us was actually the first Cistercian Abbey in Wales, which was built by an order of monks in 1131 AD. It was intended to be as remote as possible from any cities and their associated vices, as were most abbeys, churches and monasteries, and I can honestly say they did a great job with this one. However, the ruins of the abbey we see today are far removed from the original, which was initially built without towers or bells, as per the simplicity of the Cistercian order.

In fact, what can be seen today are the remains of a significant rebuild around 1300 AD, though unfortunately, Henry VIII came along not much later with his dissolution of the monasteries in 1536 and smashed the place to smithereens. As a result, the lead was ripped from the roof, and what was left of the ruins was gifted to the Earl of Chepstow, which meant the end of 400 years of worship at Tintern Abbey.

Luckily, the place still fared better than most, and one of the earliest surviving images we have of the abbey is an engraving by famous brothers Samuel and Nathaniel Buck. Dating from 1732, the image is clearly recognisable when compared to the modern ruins, which can only be a good thing, as it suggests the deterioration of the place has slowed if not actually stopped.

However, in the late 1700s, Tintern Abbey was unfortunately purchased by a man named the Duke of Beaufort, who immediately went on a restoration spree. While this may sound good, it was, in fact, very bad indeed because restoration back then was nothing like what we would think of today.

For instance, one of the first things the duke did was to hammer lots of little bronze letters into the floor all over the grounds, following which, for whatever reason, he planted lots of creeping, crawling and climbing plants that almost immediately began to threaten the structural integrity of the building in general, though in particular, the fragile arches and the slender hallways.

More depictions of the place exist, luckily for us, and which thankfully suggest that whatever harm he did, the Duke of Beaufort didn't quite manage to destroy the place entirely.

For instance, famous artist Thomas Gainsborough popped by in 1782 and drew a picture showing the abbey apparently covered in camouflage that would delight any soldier, though, to be honest, his drawing was more of a sketch, suggesting he couldn't really be bothered.

William Turner was next, who was really called Joseph Mallord William Turner, by the way. I don't know much about him, but it is said that he had many mistresses and illegitimate children, and apparently, he was noted for being incredibly rude to people when travelling around the country. He even urinated out of the window of a moving train once, so I bet he was good at a party.

Anyway, he came along shortly after Gainsborough, in 1794, to be exact, and he did a much better job with his painting. He drew the abbey, or at least the ruins, predominantly covered in foliage, presumably thanks to the misguided efforts of the grand old Duke of Beaufort.

Perhaps not surprisingly, the first photo of the abbey is also exceedingly old, coming along as it did as far back as 1858, which surprised me as I didn't think photos were even a thing back then. Roger Fenton's snaps show us, once again, an abbey covered in ivy but also with piles of ruined stones stacked neatly for the tourists, but those stones were moved on many years ago, which, incidentally, is precisely what we did next, moving on through the woods.

Eventually, we left the trees behind after descending a fine wooden staircase, emerging onto a hillside just east of Brockweir that offered tremendous views of the Wye Valley to the west, and I could just make out Brockweir Bridge far below us. It was on this hill that the path split, offering a choice of high or low route for anyone following the course of the dyke, though we had already decided to take the more picturesque lower route, which is definitely the more popular option for chubby old men with bad knees and dodgy ankles.

If you do choose to follow the high route, it will take you up a steep hill known as Saint Briavel's Common. The low route, on the other hand, will guide you gently along the banks of the River Wye, so it was here that we left the hills behind for a while. Before we moved on, though, I wanted to have a quick look around Brockweir, for there was something I wanted to see, and you may or may not be surprised to discover that the thing in question was a pub.

It wasn't beer I was after, though. The pub in question was the Brockweir Inn, made moderately famous, at least locally, for playing a cameo role in Arthur's Dyke. It was here where our diverse group of hikers wandered in after an exhausting day of walking, only to discover a band of rowdy soldiers having just a little bit too good of a time.

Chaos and banter ensued, and the cheeky squaddies ended up in something of a fight with an outmatched group of ageing backpackers, ultimately resulting in said backpackers being evicted from the pub by a somewhat irate landlord.

Alas, given the early hour, the pub was never going to be open, not that it even looked like a pub in real life, so Brockweir was, for me, just a single solitary moment on a very long path.

Just around the corner, though, next to the bridge, a bunch of people had set up a food stand. I thought they were selling it, but it was free, so I helped myself to a big slice of watermelon and an energy bar as Rob spoke to one of the organisers. Apparently, there was some kind of ultra marathon on, and every now and then, a runner would roll up, devour something sweet and sickly, and then jog on.

Rob explained to Steve, the guy who was managing the refreshment stand, what we were doing, which was basically walking 177 miles or thereabouts and carrying everything on our backs. This made Steve's jaw drop, but when he told us that his runners were doing the Wye Valley Ultramarathon, our jaws dropped, too. The mad people who had actually volunteered for it were running 35 miles in less than 5 hours, and when I interrupted and asked why, Steve looked more than a little puzzled but then asked us why we were doing our thing. I didn't want to say it was because we were stupid, but I got his point.

There is science behind a 35-mile run, Steve went on. Apparently, covering such a distance gives the maximum benefit when it comes to endurance training, as the human body simply can't adapt to anything longer. In fact, running further offers no advantages and merely increases the chance of injury, so there you go.

The next hour of this walk, which we spent ambling upstream along the riverbank of the Wye, was one of absolute peace and serenity, apart from the two Eurofighter Typhoons that tried their hardest to smash everybody's windows as they flew upriver, emerging from behind me at approximately five times the speed of sound, and almost sending me into spasms of shock in the process. And while I'm sure they weren't actually going that fast, probably due to the laws of physics being a bit boring around here, it certainly seemed as if they were.

Once I had recovered, and once the animals had all come back out of hiding and resuscitated all of their mates who had variously suffered from heart attacks and strokes, I shared the path with rabbits, crows, sheep, jackdaws and even a rather large and noisy frog, though I mean the amphibian sort, not one of our cousins from across the channel. Rob, James and Mark were somewhere far ahead of me, and every now and then, as a reminder of the crazy race that was currently taking place, a mad and exhausted jogger would pass us from behind.

This made me think about running for a minute, but then I realised one thing. I have never seen anyone jogging and smiling, so that's all I need to know about that. In fact, if you do ever see me jogging, please kill whatever the fuck is chasing me. In fairness, though, there are positive things that can be said about jogging. Starting your day with an early morning run, for instance, is actually quite a good way of ensuring that it cannot possibly get any worse.

The first of the year's flowers were now very definitely blooming, and I got a sense that spring had very much sprung, judging by the colourful clumps that dotted the riverbank.

I did, however, have to work hard to avoid the piles of poo, an occupational hazard for a walker, of course, but as I said, all in all, this was a lovely, calming section of the walk and one that I very much enjoyed. More than anything, I saw it as a three-mile chance to rest my knees before heading back up the hills just after Bigsweir Bridge.

It was all open country as well, apart from a half-mile section near the end, but this was just as pleasant and peaceful, though in an entirely different way.

It was a bit of a shock, then, when I emerged from the last of the trees only to encounter what must have been a school trip as dozens of young children waddled along, two by two, chaperoned by at least half a dozen teachers, who quite frankly didn't look all that much older than the kids.

I stood aside as they passed, and while I noticed that they were all immaculately dressed in splendid uniforms, suggesting a school of some repute, possibly Hogwarts by the looks of things, they were also all incredibly polite. By the time they had passed me by, the word *hello* no longer sounded like a word at all, but just sounded like an odd noise, as all words tend to do when repeated incessantly for what seemed like a thousand times but was probably only around fifty.

Bigsweir Bridge was next, but it was merely just a bridge unless you also considered a set of traffic lights and an old toll house to be anything of significance, which I did not.

It was, however, beautiful in and of itself, with its graceful ironwork spanning the River Wye linking Monmouthshire, Wales, with Gloucestershire, England.

It was right here, at Bigsweir Bridge, that Janet first met up with the gang that was Arthur, Andy and Jeffrey in the movie Arthur's Dyke, which is one of the clues to the inconsistencies of the film. Basically, if she had started out at Chepstow, as the film suggests, which was really Abergavenny, of course, then there is no way she could have met them here and then spent the night in the barn back at Brocksweir after getting thrown out of the pub for fighting. Sometimes, it's just best not to know the magic of the movies, I mused.

After crossing the bridge and taking the obligatory moment for a photo or two, we passed a sign welcoming us into Gloucestershire, undoubtedly one of the most difficult English counties to spell and probably one of the most commonly misspelt due to its truncated pronunciation. Regardless of how it is spelt, you see, it is simply pronounced as *Glos-ter-shire.*

English place names have nothing on their Welsh counterparts of course. In England, we have the delightful examples of Towcester, pronounced *toaster*, and Bicester, pronounced *bister,* and even Cholmondeley, which for whatever reason is pronounced *Chum-lee*, along with my own little favourite, Belvoir Castle. When spoken, it sounds exactly like *beaver,* so you have to wonder why people bother wasting all of those letters in the first place. I can only think that these places were named with Scrabble in mind for all those extra points.

When it comes to Wales, though, their place names are on a different level altogether. One of the reasons, apparently, is the Welsh language's absolute disregard for vowels, which can make some place names look like total gibberish to uneducated, ill-informed buffoons such as us English in general and myself in particular.

For starters, we have Bwlchgwyn, a delightful

little village near Wrexham and incidentally not all that far away from Offa's Dyke Path. If you have ever been to Bwlchgwyn, then you might have noticed that it has a lovely little church and a rather pretty pub, and in fact, they are almost right next door to each other. However, and as previously mentioned, you might also have noticed that it has absolutely no vowels, none whatsoever, which makes it unpronounceable to me and millions of others who are unaware of the fact that in Welsh, the letters w and y seem to double up as those missing vowels.

Another one, Cwmystwyth, is a smart little village not too far from Aberystwyth, which itself is not exactly all that easy to pronounce. Cwmystwyth actually sounds something like *cum-uss-twith,* and from this, I can glean that the "w" generally sounds like "u", while "y" replaces the letter "i". This is only a general rule, however, at least as far as I can see, as the equally unpronounceable Ynysybwl seems to sound something like un-niss-uh-bull. Compared to that, then, Gloucestershire is a walk in the park.

The walk in this park was a steep one, though, as the path next followed the road, slowly ascending an uncomfortably steep hill. Next to the sign that welcomed us to Gloucestershire was another one that welcomed us to the Forest of Dean, which immediately put me on alert for those hordes of rampaging wild boar, but all that came around the corner was a rusty old Ford

Fiesta.

A sign halfway up pointed us off into some woods, Cadora Woods, so we duly obliged and began what was to be a several-mile woodland walk. The paths here were generally good, and I spied occasional glimpses of what I supposed was the dyke. The track had its ups and downs, but it wasn't anything excessive, though it was a bit steeper when we seemed to move from one wood to the other just before a steep descent down into Redbrook.

The village was a welcome breath of fresh air, and of course, there was a toilet. The sun had come out too, so after popping into the village stores for a sugar-rich can of full-on Coke and a rather expensive sandwich that would hopefully give me an energy boost, we all took our backpacks off and sat on a picnic table, watching the world go by. After a minute, our shoes came off as well, and then our socks, but thankfully, there wasn't anybody around to witness the wilting of the nearby flowers.

It was nice to get air to my feet, and as I sat and rested, I realised how little distance we had covered so far. Not that we were in a rush, though. On our past walks, we had always had a schedule to keep and somewhere to be. Although we aimed to be in Monmouth by the end of today, or possibly even further, we had no actual timetable as such.

And yes, it might be dark when we got there,

which is not ideal for tramping through strange and unfamiliar fields and woods or for putting tents up, but the point was we had all the time in the world, so this was a walk we could afford to savour, which is precisely what we intended to do.

The temptation to go to the pub surfaced, but only very briefly, before we decided that we would instead wait and save that particular pleasure for the end of the day. We had already passed one pub just before the shop, which was the Bell Inn, and there was another option available just over the river, the Boat Inn. However, that one would involve crossing an international border, sort of, which was still formed by the River Wye at this point between England and Wales.

Anyone wishing to do so can cross here on the old railway bridge, called the Penhallt Viaduct. While it looks old, rusty and rickety, it has been lovingly restored, and a pedestrian walkway has been added to the old structure, so it is perfectly safe. Please let me know if you make it across, though, because I'm not risking it.

With our rest over and with a slight chill beginning to come over me because we had stopped, it was time to move on, so after putting my socks and shoes back on, as well as my backpack, I once again found myself heading north in the footsteps of my most distinguished companions.

A little bit of roadside walking was a shock here due to the noisy traffic that kept zooming past. I guessed I had already grown accustomed to the peace and tranquillity of the woods, so I was grateful when the path left the seemingly busy road after just a few hundred yards.

Unfortunately, but as always, the path began to take us uphill along a quiet side street, but after just a few hundred yards more, we found ourselves back on a main road, though one not as busy as it had been down in the village.

The road did get rather narrow as we went higher, and I kept having to duck into the hedge every time a car came along, so I was pleased indeed when I saw that little acorn directing me off and to the left, even though it did point up yet another hill. I presumed the others had taken the same route, as the climb had really held me back, but I hoped to catch them later on, maybe in Prestatyn.

And while I didn't know it at the time, this road also forms the border between England and Wales, so as I had made my way up it, I imagined I probably crossed that border at least a dozen times in just a few minutes of walking.

When I turned off, I thought the path was going to take me straight into some more woods, but after a brief tickle by just a handful of trees, I emerged onto a farm track and found myself at the foot of a broad and open valley, where I saw the others waiting for me up ahead.

A farm almost immediately on my right seemed to be populated by lots of young farmers who looked nothing like farmers, and I noticed accents from as far south as London and as far north as Scotland. They were walking in the opposite direction to me, and as they passed, I said hello to one of them and discovered that this farm gave young city kids a chance to come and do some incredibly farmy things, which presumably included getting covered in cow shit by the looks of most of them. Apparently, this sort of thing has become incredibly popular since broadcaster Jeremy Clarkson made his documentary about life on the farm. Anyway, they all looked really happy, and I was a teeny bit jealous, especially when I found out they were going down to the pub.

I trudged on, feeling somewhat dismayed at our earlier decision not to stop at the Boat or the Bell back in Redbrook, and made my way slowly but steadily up the valley. Although I kept expecting to enter the forest, this never happened, and the path followed the tree line, meaning I had fantastic views to the east for much of the time.

It was along here that I met someone who was also walking Offa's Dyke Path. As I got talking to Doug, who had stopped for a rest and to nurse an early blister, I discovered he had started at almost the same time as us this morning but had set off from Sedbury Cliffs. I was puzzled for a minute as to how he had passed us by, but he said that he had taken the high route between Brockweir and Bigsweir, which immediately solved that little puzzle.

Doug was a bit older than me, and as we got chatting, I discovered that he was from Glasgow and was a retired policeman. I racked my brain for a minute just in case there was something in there that might suggest I needed to run, but I came to the conclusion that I was not on Glasgow's list of its ten most wanted and, therefore, had nothing to fear.

He was doing Offa's Dyke, he said, because he had never done it, which was as good a reason as any, I guess. As we talked, I happened to mention the movie Arthur's Dyke, which Doug said he had never heard of, though he seemed suddenly keen to watch it once I had brought it up. I almost mentioned a certain website where you could get any movie for free until I remembered his police links, so I kept my mouth firmly shut about that.

We talked about other walks we had both done and discovered we also had the West Highland Way and the Coast to Coast in common. Bizarrely, we had done these at more or less the same time, in 2020 and 2016, respectively, and just a couple of months apart.

It looked like Doug was comfortable where he was, and although I wasn't in a rush, I sensed he would rather walk alone, so after our little chat, I wished him well and moved on.

It would be unlikely for us to bump into each other again, we had concluded, as while we were possibly stopping in Monmouth tonight, Doug was heading to the Hog's Head Pub near Abergavenny, which is not a pub I had heard of. He gave me a good tip and told me they have glamping pods available for backpackers, and the food is good, too, so I promised him I would look the place up later. It might even be our stopping point for tomorrow, I pondered. I did ask him for some directions before moving on, however, as I had lost track of my exact whereabouts. I do wish, though, that when I ask for directions, people wouldn't use words like west.

Moving on once more along the edge of the trees, it wasn't long before we came across the Kymin, which was a surprise for two reasons. First, I had thought it to be further away, and second, it was absolutely full of people.

In case you're wondering, the Kymin is technically the name of a hill, upon which stand a couple of interesting monuments, namely the roundhouse and the naval temple, which are what I actually meant when I referred to the Kymin. Both were built in the years leading up to 1800 by people with far too much money, and they built them so they could come up here to socialise out of the weather, though by that, they meant drinking. While it was nice today, the weather up here can be a bit soggy, you see, and that is putting it mildly, so those well-heeled party types built the roundhouse so that they had somewhere to stay dry while they partied.

Nowadays, the roundhouse looks like a cross between a lighthouse and a castle, and apparently, you can see ten different counties from its windows, as well as two countries, of course.

Of the two structures, the Naval Temple is definitely the more interesting of the two. It was built to commemorate the British Victory at the Battle of the Nile in 1798, led by Lord Horatio Nelson. This might seem like a distant and unimportant battle, but it was crucial to the history of the country much later on when other threats surfaced, mainly one led by a mad Austrian with a funny moustache, who most people think was German.

At the Battle of the Nile then, Nelson and his fleet delivered a resounding victory over the French, trapping Napoleon Bonaparte. Being English myself, I cannot claim to be a fan of Napoleon, but he did have one redeeming character. He was notorious for not opening his mail for up to three weeks, basically because most of his letters were sent to notify him of various problems, which is why he came up with this cunning approach. By not opening his letters for such a long time, you see, Napoleon discovered that most of those problems tended to resolve themselves one way or another and, therefore, no longer required his attention, leaving him free to concentrate on other issues, such as getting a good thrashing from the British.

Anyway, the result of the battle served to isolate Napoleon's armies in Egypt, which resulted in their eventual defeat and paved the way for the British to retake Malta, which had been held by the French since they had seized it just a few months before. In turn, this finally secured British control of the Mediterranean Sea, which was vital if they wanted to hang on to things like India, which they most certainly did.

Thus, when a mad, bad Adolf Hitler also decided to try and conquer the world, he came well and truly unstuck, which was at least partly down to the fact that the British controlled the Mediterranean, which you could argue came about in the first place because Napoleon refused to open a letter warning him of an impending British attack. And while the temple definitely commemorates Nelson, it also pays tribute to fifteen other admirals, a couple of whom are certainly worthy of mention for various reasons.

One was Edward Boscamen, who distinguished himself in a very little-known war called *The War of Jenkin's Ear*. The Brits have a bit of a mad reputation when it comes to history, and this war only helps to fuel that, as it is precisely what it sounds like. When British sailor Robert Jenkins allegedly had his ear amputated by Spanish coastguards who searched his ship for contraband, Britain did the only thing it could do under the circumstances and declared war on an entire country. The war, which would last a staggering nine years, resulted in the deaths of tens of thousands of people and left hundreds of ships at the bottom of the sea. All because of an ear. You couldn't make it up.

The other was Admiral George Rodney, who spent most of his surprisingly successful naval career chasing down plunder and treasure rather than actually fighting. Apparently, as per the rules of war at that time, commanders could claim prize money, which correlated to the size of every successful engagement. Unfortunately, this only served as an incentive for greedy, crazy people like Admiral Rodney. He even used his warships as escorts for the treasure ships carrying all of his booty home rather than directing them to actually fight the enemy.

Things came to a head when the Americans decided they wanted a bit of independence from the madness of King George and his high taxes, as it was actually Admiral Rodney who was in command of the British Fleet at Yorktown, one of the most decisive battles of the American War of Independence.

Again, Rodney was somewhat side-tracked as he galivanted around the Caribbean, plundering whatever ships he could find for yet more prize money, demonstrating that he was only ever really interested in his own interests and that of his family, with actual warfare coming a distant third. He even wrote regular letters to his family, promising to buy new houses and gifts for his children with his newfound riches, and he made his own son the captain of a ship when he was just fifteen years old. Such was Rodney's reputation for trouble, the Earl of Sandwich, who, in 1762, famously asked for meat to be served between two slices of bread, inadvertently creating a clever new snack just like the one I had back at Redbrook, even communicated to his superiors at the Admiralty his concerns that Rodney might provoke a war with Spain purely for personal gain.

Anyway, to cut a long story short, because Admiral Rodney was otherwise engaged, the British lost Yorktown, a result which foretold the end of British rule in the colonies and the birth of a new nation, the United States of America. On a positive note, he retired on a vast navy pension, lived in a huge country pile, and lived happily ever after, and to hell with the empire.

Nowadays, the temple is generally used as a place to rest by chubby hikers such as ourselves, but back in the day, even Nelson himself visited it to see what all the fuss was about. And apparently, he was pretty impressed, particularly by the statue of Britannia that adorned the top, which actually blew away at some point but has now thankfully been replaced.

We left the crowds behind and moved on towards Monmouth, which was clearly visible from the Kymin, and while there may well have been a direct path down the steep hill and through the trees, we walked along the road instead, which offered a more leisurely descent and probably had better views, particularly of the surrounding woodlands.

The area that we now know as Monmouthshire was mainly covered by forests in ancient times, and up until the time of the Romans' arrival in 75 AD, it remained relatively sparsely populated.

When the Romans finally left in the late 4th century, the area increasingly found itself under English control, courtesy of the Anglo-Saxons, and King Henry VIII formalised this control in 1536 with the creation of the county of Monmouthshire, an entity which remains more or less the same today. However, over the following centuries, it was often considered to be a part of England, though today, of course, it is most definitely and completely entirely Welsh.

Much more recently, it was the Savoy Theatre in Monmouth that itself became a part of history when it saw the world premiere of Arthur's Dyke, and which is where we headed first, though we did pass the Queen's Head pub on the way into the town, worth mentioning because it was there that someone once tried to assassinate the Lord Protector Oliver Cromwell after he had deposed the king. It is said that the assassin was chased into the bar and shot dead, and Cromwell lived to fight another day.

I finally found the tiny cinema just near the end of a charming pedestrianised shopping area. It is apparently the oldest in Wales and has been in business since 1930, a year that was right at the end of the silent-movie era and just in time for movies with sound, otherwise known as talkies, which had appeared a couple of years earlier and had originated in America. Interestingly, when the first British-made movie with sound appeared, which was called Blackmail, it was promoted with the tagline *"See and hear it! Our mother tongue spoken as it should be!"*

If Arthur's Dyke had been on, I would have gone in to watch it, but as it was, we carried on, heading for the King's Head, which was a pub and not an actual king's head, because that would be weird.

Luckily, the place was empty, which meant the smell of sweaty feet didn't put anyone off their food. Once our footwear was removed and taken out the back to be burned, which allowed a cheesy odour to perforate the entire neighbourhood, we spent a good hour refreshing ourselves with pizzas, pasta, pies and pints.

The barman cum waiter was very friendly, but he looked like he was under the influence of something which could only be described as the good stuff, although I don't do drugs myself. At my age, I get the same effect from just standing up too fast. Anyway, many countries are legalising things like cocaine while, at the same time, making straws illegal. That must be frustrating.

The King's Head had lots of those informative little history posters that pubs tend to have, and one told me all about Geoffrey of Monmouth, but it didn't quite tell the whole story.

While Geoffrey of Monmouth struck me as being a rather interesting character, there are probably two things about him that we should be aware of. The first is that he was not actually called Geoffrey, and the second is that he probably wasn't from Monmouth, either. In fact, any factual description of him would be relatively brief, as we know next to nothing about him with absolute certainty.

He was probably born somewhere hereabouts, though, sometime around 1100 AD, although no one really knows for sure. In fact, we should get used to the fact that much of what we know about him is, at best, a guess and, at worst, total fiction, which is a rule we should probably apply to much of his work, too.

Geoffrey was, you see, something of a writer, and a rather prolific one at that. His best work, however, was *The History of the Kings of Britain*, although we should once again caution ourselves before we delve into this interesting little nugget of historical creativity.

For instance, although he has been described as *arguably the most influential secular writer of medieval Britain,* others have denounced him as a *dishonest, fibbing, unscrupulous, massive manuscript maker-upper,* though the truth, as usual, probably lies somewhere in between.

His *History of the Kings of Britain* was thought to have been written somewhere around the year 1136, and the book describes in surprisingly specific detail the pre-Roman history of the Britons. Drawing from a wide variety of historical sources, some written and some oral, the work is greatly influenced by the likes of the Venerable Bede, who we met earlier when discussing the Severan Wall and who is widely considered to be the *Father of English History.*

However, although it is written in Latin and can be something of a challenging read, the *History of the Kings of Britain* reminded me of a tabloid gossip column, as it relates tales of plotting, incest, marriage and subterfuge between the various rising and falling dynasties that dominated the two-thousand or so years before the arrival of the Romans who finally civilized us with things such as central heating, toilets and, of all things, bikinis.

If Geoffrey had left his works at that, basically a compendium of earlier sources, then all might have been well, but unfortunately, he was also somewhat creative in his storytelling and filled in the many gaps in the history of the English with, how can I put it, a load of old twaddle.

In his writing, Geoffrey does, however, give us the first complete account of none other than King Arthur himself and includes countless ancillary accounts of the likes of Merlin, Camelot, Guinevere and everything else that is all so familiar to us nowadays when it comes to one of the oldest of English legends. In fact, it was precisely Geoffrey's writings that made Arthur so famous in the first place, but unfortunately, much of it was simply made up by him as he put quill to parchment by inadequate candlelight so many moons ago, probably after supping too much mead.

There is one thing he tells us about Arthur that is true, though. Apparently, as well as his sword Excalibur, he also had a much-treasured spear called Rhongomyniad, which Geoffrey simply called, of all names, Ron, and which, in turn, tells us just how lazy old Geoffrey of Monmouth really was.

But Geoffrey's history did much more than popularize his Arthurian tales. It also provided us with a sort of national genealogy, though a somewhat sketchy one at that. For instance, it was Geoffrey who gave us much of the source material that was later utilized by the great bard himself. Had there been no Geoffrey, then it is likely that there would have been no Shakespeare, either. Geoffrey's King Leir, for instance, became Shakespeare's King Lear, and of course, in a world without Shakespeare, we would all have enjoyed school a whole lot more than we actually did.

Furthermore, it is entirely possible that Geoffrey was descended from the Bretons of northern France, who came over here with William the Conqueror in 1066, as Geoff talks highly of such people while somewhat trash-talking those who were by then known as the Welsh. Shame on him, perhaps, but then we really should remember that it is always the victors who write the history books.

And whatever his roots, Geoffrey did rather well for himself, probably because of his strong links with the landed gentry. He became a canon and then a priest and was also a magister, which is basically a specialist teacher of particular importance. After some time, he received yet another promotion and became a bishop, although in his case, presumably because of his expertise and nothing whatsoever to do with nepotism or the fact that he was exceptionally well connected, of course, his promotion to bishop came only ten days after he became a priest.

And as for his name, well, he was really called Galfridus.

All of this was very interesting, to me at least, but it really was time to move on. We had considered staying close by, having already covered a fair distance today, but our attempts at finding a nearby campsite proved futile. One insisted on a minimum two-night stay, while another said they didn't accept stinky English hikers. They didn't actually say that, but we knew what they meant.

While we were still in the pub, we also checked the weather forecast, as we had heard rumours of a coming storm. One certainly looked to be on the way, so it wasn't long before we had shoved the rest of our food down our necks, swilled our pints, put our backpacks back on, and made our way through most of Monmouth.

James had managed to get hold of a campsite a few miles further on, which unfortunately meant more walking, though we did have plenty of daylight left. On the plus side, whatever mileage we did today, we wouldn't have to do tomorrow, so off we went, and our route took us directly across the impressive Monnow Bridge.

Described as probably the finest example of a medieval bridge in the country and painted by such high-profile artists as the now familiar William Turner, probably England's most-loved romantic artist and the so-called *painter of light*, Monnow Bridge, so named because it crosses the River Monnow, really has to be seen to be believed. It is essentially the last of its kind in the country, as people wiser than you or I who worked in the planning departments of councils throughout the United Kingdom decided to demolish anything and everything that looked remotely similar in either the late 19th or early 20th centuries, though a couple of similar bridges do survive in Europe.

Basically, Monnow Bridge is a fortified bridge with a tower at one end, which once also boasted a fine portcullis designed to keep out undesirables, in this case, the Welsh. Don't have a go at me for such comments either, as I'm just relaying history. Anyway, the Welsh ultimately had the last laugh, as Monmouth and, therefore, the bridge, now firmly form part of their country, and it is a very beautiful one at that.

It is thought to have been completed in 1272 when it replaced an earlier wooden bridge built by those industrious Normans, and while its purpose may well have been defensive, it was also used to collect tolls from anyone trying to get into the town. Over the years, it has also been used as a jail, and in more modern times, a farmers' market has been held here at the end of every month.

Those clever people called dendrochronologists have helped date the original wooden bridge after finding timbers beneath the existing one, where tree ring analysis suggests that the wood came from trees chopped down in the mid-1100s, although that bridge is thought to have been destroyed by fire during the Battle of Monmouth in 1233.

Nowadays, the bridge is reserved purely for pedestrians, mainly chubby tourists, by the way, so I blended in pretty well today. I had a wander up and down it and made sure I went through each archway twice just for the hell of it, mainly because I was feeling a bit wild and crazy. I deliberately ignored two pensioners who had the most bemused looks on their faces and who were clearly feeling sorry for the poor bedraggled soul that they were so interested in observing, which was me.

I particularly sought out the grooves that would have guided the portcullis, and I also noticed some defensive drop boxes, which are exactly what they sound like. These would have enabled any defenders to drop things on potential attackers and are also known as murder holes, which is a much better name, in my opinion. Items dropped could have included rocks, boiling water, arrows and, my own personal favourite, sheep shit, which, in Wales at least, has always been in plentiful supply, of course. If you wanted to spice things up even more, you could also set fire to your dung bombs before you threw them at your enemies, which would spoil their day even more.

Incidentally, flaming sheep shit didn't stay at the top of my list of offensive projectiles for very long. I later found out that medieval peoples had even been known, on occasion, to have tumbled dead bodies onto their enemies, which in my humble opinion, is probably an even worse way to die than being covered in poop. Perhaps they even set fire to the bodies before they dropped them. I know I would have.

The gatehouse, by the way, is actually a later addition, and the two pedestrian portals came later still, as late as the 1800s. This was mainly to ease the flow of traffic and to ensure that our dear ancestors didn't keep getting run over by horses and carts, which, while still not ideal, was probably preferable to death by fiery poop.

Considering its age, the bridge fared pretty well for several centuries, though by the 1700s, it was beginning to fall into disrepair and required a bit of a facelift. Workmen were brought in, who soon patched things up, and for their troubles, according to the records, they received 100 gallons of ale. I just hope they paid them after they had finished the work and not before.

It has survived remarkably well since, although there has been the odd hiccup every now and then. In 1982, for instance, a double-decker bus almost remodelled the bridge completely when it crashed into the large central arch. This is precisely why it is now closed to traffic and why I found myself walking across it today.

After passing a small roundabout which bore a signpost pointing towards Newcastle, though presumably not the Newcastle I was familiar with, which was around 300 miles away to the north, I got the distinct impression that we had nearly left Monmouth. A further roundabout took us onto a small housing estate, after which we turned onto a narrow track, and after passing a few pleasant cottages, we finally found ourselves back out into the open countryside, or at least on the edge of it. Overhead, however, the skies had darkened considerably, and the clouds now looked to be threatening to drop their loads on us at any time, if you pardon the expression.

We were heading west, and low hills looked to be our first destination, which was confirmed when we left the road and joined a muddy footpath where I spent the next half a mile dodging puddles and trying to catch up with the others. For the half mile after that, I didn't even bother dodging them, as it was impossible, but luckily, my recently waxed and oiled boots seemed to be holding up surprisingly well against the sudden onslaught.

It was here that we passed Rockfield Farm, which was just to our north. I had hoped to be able to see it, which was questionable because of the hills, but today, the poor visibility made any chance of a glance wholly impossible.

Rockfield Farm is perhaps one of the most unlikely places I had expected to come across on this walk. I had first heard of it whilst watching a documentary on the BBC, and while it may actually be a farm, of sorts, with cows and pigs and great piles of shit and the like, that is not why it was of interest to me.

Music-loving brothers Kingsley and Charles Ward had been lucky enough to have grown up on the farm, then owned by their parents, at the height of the rock and roll era in the 1950s, and the pair were particularly enthralled by the likes of Elvis and his pelvic thrusting.

Wanting to get in on the action themselves, and I mean the music, not the thrusting, though you never know, Charles bought himself a guitar, and the brothers soon began calling themselves the Charles Kingsley Combo. After borrowing a tape deck from some bloke they met in a pub, the pair quickly managed to record a couple of songs. Being somewhat sure of themselves, they next decided to drive hundreds of miles to the offices of music producers EMI to demonstrate their tremendous talents. However, once there, they discovered they had inadvertently driven to a record-pressing factory instead, so they probably felt a bit stupid, at least for a while.

Soon redirected to the actual offices, however, they somehow managed to blag a meeting with one of the firm's top producers, and although he ultimately decided not to sign them, this was still a foot in the doorway for the ambitious Kingsley brothers.

A year later, the brothers once again found themselves in a recording studio, but as well as making music, they also took note of what was going on around them. When they returned home, they set up their own studio in an unused attic, and by 1961, they were well and truly in the music business themselves, recording several local bands one after the other.

Things hummed along quite nicely for a few years, and as word slowly spread of the world's first residential recording studio, Rockfield Farm soon morphed into Rockfield Studios, eventually drawing in some rather well-known bands.

In fact, one of the earlier hits recorded at the studio was *How Long* by *Ace*, which, funnily enough, eventually became the theme tune to Pauline Quirke's hit movie *Arthur's Dyke*. Perhaps this local link explained the choice of song.

More prominent bands soon came along, of all kinds, including the likes of everyone from *Black Sabbath* to *Joan Armatrading*, but the real milestone, at least as far as I am concerned, was when *Queen* recorded *Bohemian Rhapsody*, right here, in the heart of the beautiful Welsh countryside. Who knew?

After that, almost anyone and everyone visited Rockfield at one time or another, including Simple Minds, The Stranglers, and The Stone Roses, and that's just the ones beginning with "S".

The latter arrived in 1993, originally intending to stop for a month, although they ultimately spent over a year there, which not only saved the farm financially but also served to attract even bigger names to the studio.

And perhaps the biggest band to turn up at the farm must be Oasis, with the mischievous Gallagher brothers rolling up here in 1995. By the time they left, they had mastered perhaps their most famous song ever, *Wonderwall*, and in fact, the wonderwall in question is actually on the farm, where Liam famously sat atop it surrounded by microphones as he sang his song while tuned into the sounds of the farm all around him. Quite bizarrely, it is said they recorded the song in half a day, as the brothers wanted to get finished as quickly as possible so they could go to the pub and get pissed.

My wife and I actually had a bit of a falling out over that song. I'm a fan you see, whilst she isn't, and a couple of weeks ago, she asked me to stop singing Wonderwall. I said, "*Maybe......*"

Apparently, people still turn up today to sit on that wall, or at least try to, though they are usually chased off by a very displeased farmer with a rather bitey dog. Trust me, I know this, as I called in on our reconnaissance trip last year.

I trudged on through the mud, and at one point or another, I became conscious of the fact that my feet were about twice as heavy as they had been when I set off. Great clumps of mud were stuck to the bottoms of each shoe, and as well as making them heavier, it also made each step a slippery gamble, which I thought would make a good name for this walk if they ever wanted to change it.

The fields turned into woods, which soon became a full-blown forest called Kings Wood. I had hoped that the trees would give at least some shelter from the blazing sun that was now beating down on us, but it didn't. The going here was brutal, with short but sharp hills coming one after another. And all the while, the sound of thunder began to get louder and louder.

Very soon, an oppressive sky hung above the hills all around us in the manner that a shroud would hang over a coffin. It was pretty foreboding, and I reckoned that the chances of us getting wet in the next hour were somewhere north of one hundred percent, and I was right.

We had been walking separately, but I caught up with the others at the top of one of the small hills, where we all sheltered under a tree while a short shower doused everything around us. This probably wasn't the best idea, considering the constant sound of thunder was getting closer and closer, and we could see bolts of lightning all around as well, so we soon moved on.

The rain was steady for a while but then got slightly heavier, and we discovered that the thunder was all the encouragement we needed. By the time we emerged out of the woods and onto a road, however, we were definitely starting to get wet.

Luckily, the campsite at Hendre Farm appeared once we rounded a final bend, and we were soon knocking on the reception door and dropping our backpacks, after which we, too, dropped onto a couple of handy benches.

The farmer was friendly and took our cash in as efficient a manner as possible, and then told us we could camp more or less wherever we wanted as the site was mostly empty tonight, mainly because of the vicious weather forecast, which predicted torrential downpours and flash flooding. He seemed to take great delight in telling us that last bit, by the way. We all looked at each other, slowly digesting this news, and figured it would be best to get the tents up as soon as possible, but then fate intervened, and the heavens opened up like nothing I had ever seen before.

Rain was bouncing off the floor, and the gutters on the farmhouse were overflowing, but the porch sheltered us just enough to keep us dry, although pooling water on the floor did momentarily threaten James' rucksack. The farmer came back out and seemed to be smiling intently at us, almost but not quite actually laughing. He asked us if we knew about when God had made it rain for forty days and forty nights, and after exchanging puzzled looks with each other, I offered up a feeble yes. *Good summer for Wales that was*, he quipped, before disappearing into his nice, dry farmhouse.

We stared in disbelief at the downpour going on all around us, which went on for around ten minutes or so, after which it stopped as suddenly as it had started. This meant only one thing - it was time to move out and get the tents up. Luckily for us, the rain held off for most of the rest of the night, other than for a couple of short showers, but we were tucked away in our sleeping bags by then, so it didn't matter.

We also managed to get showers ourselves, though of the lovely, warm kind, which made one hell of a difference and lifted our spirits immensely. I did stub my little toe on the doorframe of the shower, though, which caused me to shout some interesting words to everyone within three miles. As it turns out, a little known fact about your little toe is that it is there simply to make sure all the furniture of the house is in place, although incidents such as this have led me to start believing that my sole purpose in life is to serve as a cautionary tale to others.

I happened to catch a glimpse of myself in a mirror, too, which was a bit of a shocking sight. I had only been walking for a couple of days, yet it looked like I had been on some kind of months-long expedition into the jungle with absolutely no supplies whatsoever.

Looking at my broken self, I could only conclude that growing older is just one body part after another saying, *"Ha ha. Do you think that's bad? Watch this".*

We were all utterly shattered, and I think everyone was dozing off by 9pm, which reminded me of my childhood when my bedtime was also 9pm. I vividly remember that I couldn't wait to be grown up so I could go to bed anytime I wanted. Turns out it's 9pm. In fact, my childhood punishments were going to bed early, not leaving the house and not going to a party. These are now my adult goals. In fact, my best party trick is not going.

Everyone was probably asleep by half past, though Rob's snoring woke us up a mere ten minutes later. I had thought we'd killed him and buried him in the woods, but apparently, that was just a dream.

WHEN ANIMALS ATTACK

Hendre Farm to LLanthony

I didn't really want to move when I woke up this morning, mainly because I am a person who wants to do a lot of things trapped in the body of a person who wants to sleep a lot. Nonetheless, I bravely, gallantly and single-handedly dragged myself out of bed and somehow managed to get ready, almost but not quite like a real adult.

And as we left the campsite behind, I noticed that the bluebells and daisies were definitely flowering all around. I had thought about the wisdom of doing this walk in springtime, and before we set off, I had figured that it would be an experience defined by the weather. Foreign types tend to laugh at us Brits and our apparent obsession with our climate, but we are fortunate enough to live in a part of the world that throws different weather, indeed different seasons, at us almost every day.

Thus, whenever we venture off into the wilds of our most interesting little island, it is not unusual to take sun tan cream and hats and gloves on the same trip, as well as waterproof jackets and swimwear, just in case. I can't imagine the various peoples of Florida or California having to face this dilemma, but then they probably have their own issues, such as bears and school shooters, so there you go.

Anyway, I had erred on the side of caution on this walk and had brought everything I could possibly envisage needing on a trip such as this. For instance, I didn't particularly relish the thought of camping at this time of year, particularly in light of yesterday's experience of the rain, which had almost driven me to start building an ark when I had passed a farm with a plentiful supply of lumber, yet I had brought a lightweight tent and sleeping bag nonetheless.

The sleeping bag had already earned its weight, so to speak, when I had used it last night. In fact, before I left home, I meticulously weighed everything in my bag and considered lightweight alternatives, as carrying a bag full of supplies for 177 miles can soon start to get you down. And the fact that I had managed to keep it all dry helped, too, as wet stuff is inevitably heavier than dry stuff. My tent, however, was far from dry, but I was never going to get it dry now, and it probably weighed twice what it should have.

As we stepped away from the farm beneath a brilliant blue sky and a slowly rising sun, I couldn't have imagined weather more different from last night, and I hoped and prayed that the improved conditions would last.

And while the paths and tracks were still somewhat saturated, they were far better than expected, and we could at least make our way along them without having to splash through countless muddy puddles.

I had hoped to make a slight diversion to nearby Raglan Castle, but this had been a foolish aspiration as the place was more than a couple of miles off the path, which was a shame. Raglan Castle, you see, is yet another famous movie location, though I use the word famous rather recklessly.

Way back in 1977, Terry Gilliam brought his production of *Time Bandits* to experience the delights of Raglan Castle, along with its stellar cast, which included Michael Palin, Sean Connery, John Cleese and Ian Holm, who is perhaps better known for playing Bilbo Baggins in *The Lord of the Rings*.

Anyway, it was at Raglan where Ian Holm's character, Napoleon, famously enjoyed watching what were then called midgets or dwarves beat the living daylights out of each other. Nowadays, it is deemed politically unacceptable to call them such things, and the term little people is preferred, which I think actually sounds more condescending and derogatory, but what do I know. I'm just an old bloke with a degree in international politics and a wealth of experience, but hey, let's call them little people. Anyway, they can still hit each other if they want to, but before you ask, no, we can't hit them.

Before it became a Hollywood star, Raglan Castle was an actual castle and had battles and kings and the like. It was built by Sir William Thomas around 1525, who also had a much better name, the Blue Knight of Gwent, which made me wonder if he swore a lot.

During the Civil War, the castle was held by the Royalists loyal to King Charles, which made the Parliamentarians so angry that they destroyed it, a bit like a toddler would when they couldn't have their favourite toy. The technical term for this is "*slighted*", but this word wholly fails to convey what actually happened here. In reality, you see, the castle was absolutely smashed to smithereens, and what remains today is classed as a mere romantic ruin, as there is not a lot left. This is partly because, after it was slighted, the rather dodgy locals stole most of the brickwork. Every cloud has a silver lining, as they say, and consequently, there are now some rather fine and fancy and surprisingly sturdy-looking houses scattered across the area, so it's a shame we would have to miss them.

If you do make a visit, I should warn you that

the castle is haunted by, of all things, a naughty librarian. In my experience, librarians aren't all that scary, but apparently, the one at Raglan is. He taunts visitors from the darkened doorways and twisting stairwells of the castle and is said to be protecting a hidden treasure trove of priceless books and manuscripts that were stashed away in a secret tunnel somewhere deep beneath the ruins. And while the library was the first thing that was destroyed during the war, it is said that the hidden books remain to this day, guarded by a ghost that, quite frankly, sounds like it belongs in an episode of Scooby Doo.

We made good progress though we did encounter the odd flooded field, and within an hour, we arrived at Saint Michael's Church, which is a sort of famous stopping point along this part of Offa's Dyke Path. The local villagers maintain supplies of tea and biscuits for hungry hikers, and in no time at all, we took advantage of all the facilities the church had to offer, including a nice, clean toilet. I didn't really need to go, but I went anyway. This is a sign of getting old, by the way, when you can't walk past a bathroom without thinking, *"Well, I might as well go while I'm passing"*.

These little bits of trail magic really help those passing through, so we made sure to drop a good donation into the collection box, which, due to a breakdown in communication between Rob and me, meant the church actually received two donations that morning. Obviously, it was Rob's fault. It always is.

We couldn't stay all day, though, and we were soon back on the move, but the next place we came to was a rather strange one. About a mile or so after the church, we had been expecting to pass through an orchard. Apparently, this part of the country has many orchards, most of which supply apples to the cider industry.

However, when we got to Penrhos Orchard just south of Llantilio Crossenny, we discovered all the trees had mysteriously vanished. It was a strange sight, but a little further on, we found a few uprooted trees that had simply been left lying around, and this provided clear evidence of what had recently gone on here. To say it was almost apocalyptic would be an understatement, and the whole experience was somewhat jarring, not least because I like to enjoy a nice glass of cider every now and then.

I later found out that, despite my best efforts at propping up the industry with my occasional purchases, cider sales have been consistently dropping in the UK for several years, and coupled with higher yields from orchards up and down the country, the one at Penrhos Farm became, and I quote, *surplus to requirements*. It had been the size of 140 football pitches, which is always a good metric when it comes to measuring things, but to be honest, I would have no idea how big 140 football pitches would actually be other than saying the obvious and that it would be a long walk around it. Personally, I actually prefer to use London buses or bananas when demonstrating size, but that's just me.

And while we're here, it's probably worth mentioning that the phrase "*an apple a day keeps the doctor away*" actually originated in Wales, though this was probably a marketing ploy because they had so many bloody apples that they couldn't shift. In fact, the original phrase was "*eat an apple on going to bed, and you'll keep the doctor from earning his bread*", though this wasn't quite as catchy, so, not surprisingly, it never caught on. Winston Churchill actually improved the phrase immensely, though, as he said, "*An apple a day keeps the doctor away...as long as you aim well*". However, the whole premise is bullshit anyway. Apples are dangerous. Just ask Eve, Snow White, Blackberry or any pig at a hog roast.

Anyway, we plodded on and soon came to the tiny village of Llantilio Crossenny, where I was hoping to find a shop that sold snacks. Unfortunately, I found absolutely nothing other than an interesting little church, though I couldn't really eat that. The church was dedicated to Saint Teilo, who was a new saint for me, but Saint Teilo is quite appropriately the patron saint of fruit, so it's more than a little ironic that they just chopped all those apple trees down.

Saint Teilo, in fact, is perhaps the second most famous saint in Wales, with Saint David somewhat obviously being the absolute top dog. Teilo actually grew up with David in the days before either of them became saints, and they may well have been cousins. They spent many years together and even went on a pilgrimage to Jerusalem.

Teilo really shot to fame when he spent some time in France, though. It is said that he saved the locals of Brittany from a winged dragon, which he subsequently caught, tamed, and kept as a pet, which makes perfect sense, but only if you've done a line of acid or maybe munched a shedload of magic mushrooms.

However, it is because of what happened after his death that Teilo became really famous. Back in the day, churches loved to have relics on display from former saints, and when I say relics, what I actually mean is body parts. True believers would travel hundreds of miles on pilgrimages to see such wonders, often spending vast sums of money in the process, which meant that displaying relics was big business.

Anyway, when Saint Teilo died, there was a dispute over his remains, which were claimed by three different churches. They all wanted to put him on display so they could sell plenty of tickets and make lots of lovely money, but the obvious problem was that there was only one set of remains.

Luckily, a quick miracle was at hand, and one night, Saint Teilo's body magically multiplied itself into three, meaning that each church now had a nice, fresh corpse to show to the pilgrims, which was convenient, to say the least.

The genuinely worrying thing, of course, is where on earth the other bodies really came from. It is said that the actual remains of Saint Teilo are in Llandaff Cathedral in Cardiff, the capital city of Wales, which means that the other two churches claiming to hold Saint Teilo, in Llandeilo and Penally, also both in Wales, must logically be holding two random dead dudes, which is just a little bit creepy if you ask me.

Needless to say, we didn't stop long at Llantilio Crosseny, which meant that our next stop was the White Castle, just a few miles along the route, though unfortunately and perhaps inevitably, it was at the top of a hill. However, just after the church, we saw a sign pointing towards the famous Hog's Head pub, so we did the only thing we could and took a quick diversion to support the local economy.

The pub really was just around the corner, and once we arrived, we dumped our backpacks on the tables outside and headed toward the doors. Imagine our disappointment then, when we found the doors to be locked, and as I squinted through the glass windows into the darkened interior, the only sign of life was a vicious but tiny dog, who was clearly trying to hit well above his station.

Even though the pub was shut, we decided to rest a little and take advantage of the tables and chairs, and I decided to unpack my tent to let it dry in the sun. The others followed suit, and as we were doing so, I heard a key turn in the door, after which a head appeared.

The vicious dog flew out, yapping this way and that, but it proved to be a paper tiger and was soon rolling on the floor and enjoying a good old-fashioned belly rub. The head belonged to a lady who came out and spoke to us, and she said she would go and find the owner to see if he would open up. He appeared just moments later, which meant the day had certainly taken a turn for the better.

Just five minutes later, we were all sitting enjoying a nice refreshing drink in the late morning sunshine, though we had made the place look like a Chinese laundry by hanging our tents here, there and everywhere. Dale, the owner, had come out for a chat, and he proved to be a very funny man, and he confirmed that Doug had passed through the previous night, whom we had met way back on the trail, just past Redbrook. I think he was surprised when he discovered we were also walking Offa's Dyke Path and that we intended to do the entire route, as when he heard this, he looked us all up and down and raised his eyebrows a little. In fairness, our rough appearance on what was only the second proper day of our walk probably didn't lend the best impression.

When I asked him if he wanted to come with us, he just laughed and said that he would if he could, but he was currently undergoing reconstructive surgery on his legs and feet following a serious accident a few months previously. He then produced some incredibly impressive but quite graphic photos of broken bones and skin grafts and the like, which made me grateful that we were not eating here despite my now incessant tummy rumblings. Apparently, he had fallen off a ladder.

We could have stayed there all day, and the urge to get a second drink was powerful, though this would inevitably have involved a third and a fourth and so on. So it was with some reluctance that we repacked our gear, which was now very much dry, thanked Dale for his hospitality, and ventured back to the path, only getting mildly lost and having to dodge through a row of conifers, which Mark announced he was very much allergic to.

It was only a short hop, skip and a jump to the White Castle, though it was mainly uphill, but by the time we got to the top, Mark had not suffered any kind of significant reaction other than a couple of rather impressive sneezes. I, however, found myself completely out of breath, but because there were some normal people in the car park, I tried to hide it. I am one of those who tries to breathe quietly while walking uphill, you see, so bystanders can't hear me fighting for my life.

The route of the path more or less encircled the castle, so it was no great diversion to go and have a proper look around, but I took my rucksack off and left it at the entrance so I could let my back rest while I did so, and if somebody stole it, then so be it. If the worst did happen and I was unable to continue the walk, I pondered, I would simply have to go home, put my feet up in front of the fire and eat waffles instead.

White Castle was originally built by the Normans shortly after the invasion of 1066 to protect trade routes between Wales and Hereford. The original was probably built by William FitzOsbern, the same FitzOsbern who built Chepstow Castle, and this castle's name derives from the fact that it was initially covered in a white rendering, but that is long gone, and all that remains is a crumbling ruin. Talking of crumbling ruins, Rob's ankle was hurting again, so he grabbed a seat while the rest of us explored the castle, which was surprisingly big.

What stands today is probably not the original castle, but one built later by Edward I, who woke up one morning and suddenly decided he wanted to conquer all of Wales.

This urge to conquer came about because a man called Llewelyn the Great had earlier annoyed the English King, Henry III, mainly when he drove the English out of Wales entirely in the early 1200s. Llewelyn didn't stop at the border either, and he took his armies as far as Shrewsbury, which was well into England. When Edward was crowned in 1272, he became determined to sort this out once and for all and to take back all of Wales, and in doing so, he built a formidable chain of castles, mainly just to remind the Welsh who the boss really was.

Even today, it's easy to understand why the White Castle has been described as *a masterpiece of military engineering*, although by the 1600s, it was instead being described as *ruinous and decayed,* at least in terms of its military usefulness.

Still, it remains impressive to this day, at least to a simpleton such as myself, and as I wandered around it, I was particularly impressed by the unusual arrowslits. While on most castles, these tend to be symmetrical and in the shape of a cross, at White Castle, the horizontal bits are offset. Apparently, this was a feature that supposedly enabled archers to fire over a wider arc. However, tests in the 1980s showed the slits to be incredibly vulnerable to incoming fire. I immediately found myself wondering how they discovered this exactly while at the same time feeling sorry for the poor apprentices or students who were presumably forced to partake in this exercise of friendly fire.

The castle also has some more recent but

equally fascinating history. During the Second World War, prominent Nazi and Hitler's Deputy Führer Rudolph Hess was brought here, where he was allowed to paint pretty pictures and feed the swans. Hess had originally stolen a plane on a supposedly unofficial trip to explore prospects of peace with the British, but when he landed, he was immediately locked up, and that was the end of that. Churchill was in no mood to negotiate, and if Hess had taken any notice of Churchill's somewhat indignant speeches, he probably would have known this.

We didn't hang about at the castle for too long. In all honesty, there wasn't much to see here, but it would have been a nice place to stop for a picnic, particularly on a sunny day such as today, so it's a shame we didn't have any food. And unfortunately, nobody stole my rucksack, which meant no waffles for me.

More muddy paths and fields led us on our merry way, including a nice little bridge that crossed a bubbling stream that I presumed to be the same one we had crossed a couple of times yesterday. I checked later and discovered it was called the River Trothy, and it was indeed the very same one.

Those same fields contained lots of Sunday dinners' worth of sheep, all recently washed and looking immaculate, something I suspect had more to do with the rainy weather than the farmer employing a woolly hairdresser.

Caggle Street was next, a tiny slither of a village that totally lived up to its name in that it was little more than a street, though there was an interesting little chapel with a finely kept graveyard where the inhabitants literally were pushing up daisies.

After Caggle Street, it was back into the hills, though I almost took a wrong turn and wandered up someone's driveway, although the footpath was just a few feet after that. Thousands more sheep filled these hillsides, and my mind drifted to things like mint sauce and barbecues, a sure sign that I was now getting very hungry.

A single-tracked road led me into the wonderfully named and very Welsh-sounding Llangattock Lingoed, where I headed straight to the church to rest my legs and wait for the others to catch me up because, for some inexplicable reason, I was at the front for once. The exterior of the church was unique, half-rendered, painted white, and perhaps a little rough-looking, but the interior was exquisite, with a vaulted ceiling much like Saint Michael's Church yesterday. There was also a 15th-century wall painting, which, not surprisingly, looked a little past its best, but aren't we all?

As well as Offa's Dyke Path passing through the village, another long-distance walk slices through the place, and that is the Cistercian Way. Not only that, but this path more or less shares the same route as Offa's Dyke from Monmouth all the way to Hay-on-Wye, where it veers off to the northwest, only to once again cross paths with the dyke a little later on near Welshpool.

The Cistercian Way, apparently, is much more than a long-distance walk. Linking up the great monasteries of the Cistercian order, it also takes in the little churches of the Welsh hills, as well as some unique geology, and thrown in for good measure are some castles, stone-aged burial mounds and even the industrial heritage of the 19th and 20th centuries. For a minute, I wondered if I had perhaps chosen to do the wrong walk until I realised that the last bit sounds a lot like industrial estates to me, in which case I will stick with the dyke, thank you very much.

The others caught me up soon enough, and after the briefest of discussions, we all headed straight for the village pub, the Hunter's Moon Inn, whose reputation for fine food apparently precedes it.

I had expected it to be packed, bearing in mind the sun had decided to make an appearance, and while there were undoubtedly a few people enjoying the beginnings of summer in the beer garden, we still managed to find a table right by the door.

A brief moment of hesitation and panic followed when we went inside to order some food because the young lady behind the bar said she would have to check if there was anything left. I found this odd, as it was hardly late, but thankfully, she came back more or less straight away and said that the chef could accommodate us. I was tempted to say that I didn't want to move in and I just wanted some food, but I thought it best to keep my stupid mouth shut and my silly jokes to myself.

Drinks were ordered, and we enjoyed chatting and rehydrating ourselves while we waited for our meals. While it was not the cheapest pub around, the quality of the food was pretty good, and it arrived surprisingly quickly. Separate little bowls contained potatoes, carrots, broccoli and the like, and various cuts of meat adorned our respective plates, while Mark, who is a vegetablearian, had opted for the nut roast.

We had all been ravenous when we arrived at the Hunter's Moon, so by the time we had finished stuffing our faces, there was barely a morsel of food left on any of our plates other than a big lump of nut roast on Mark's, which apparently, had not been very nice. The timing was lucky because, just then, the chef came out to see if we had all enjoyed our meals.

Even if I hadn't, I'm not sure I would have mentioned it, as he was a big guy with what could only be described as a weathered look and an impressively long knife. Luckily, I really had enjoyed my Sunday dinner, which was fortunate because I reckoned the chef was also a human lie detector, which was bad news for Mark and his dodgy nut roast.

We considered puddings, but we were all stuffed beyond belief, and anyway, the choice didn't look great. The menu offered *gluten-free, sugarless vegan brownies*, but it should have read *compost*.

We spent as long as we dared at the pub, but the inevitable time came to move on. However, after stuffing ourselves silly, getting going again was a bit of a challenge, but soon enough, we were back on the dyke, albeit moving incredibly slowly.

The path skirted around a hill for a bit, then dipped down into a valley and went up the other side, albeit a bit more precipitously than it had gone down, which is usually the case, of course. I was once again at the back, and James was at the front, being the youngest and fittest as he was. He did have the grace to wait for us all at the top of the biggest hill while we oldies slowly closed the gap, and when I caught up with him, he was busy doing one-handed push-ups to pass the time, treating his body as the temple that it was. My body is also a temple. Ancient and crumbling. Probably cursed or haunted.

We were approximately halfway to Pandy, from Llangattock anyway, where I bumped into a dog walker, and I mean that in the most literal sense. I stopped to let her pass on a narrow bit of path just as she did the same, but then we both went for it at the same time. To say I almost knocked her into next week would be an understatement, and while she muttered something under her breath, probably something along the lines of *idiot,* I apologised profusely.

There had been a big puddle blocking part of the path here, hence the bottleneck, and as we both went to pass, one of us was destined for a splashy end. Luckily, it wasn't me, which explains my profuse apology, as my newest friend ended up ankle-deep in the finest Welsh mud.

Luckily, she was wearing tough-looking boots, and although the dog didn't fare as well as his owner, for he definitely was a he, if you know what I mean, he didn't seem to mind the fact that he was wallowing knee-deep in sloppy brown stuff. And before you say that dogs don't have knees, they actually do, but only on the back legs.

Anyway, the now soggy lady asked me where I was heading, so I told her my route, and she spent a good few minutes talking about walking in general and Wales in particular. She was originally from London, she told me, but had moved out here when she retired and now spent her days tramping around with Barney. I had presumed Barney was the mud-covered dog until she told me he was at work today, and it turned out that Barney was her husband, and the dog was Rufus.

She whispered his name as she said it, as apparently, when he hears it, he goes barking mad, literally, which suggested we were now talking about the dog, but quite frankly, I was getting more than a little confused as she had not stopped talking for what seemed like an eternity, not even to breathe. And when she did finally stop, she didn't wait for any kind of reply from me but simply said goodbye, and with that, she was gone.

Pandy was just a couple of miles away, she had told me, and she also mentioned that there was a very fine pub there. I expected her to talk about the Old Pandy Inn, but instead, she told me about the Skirrid Mountain Inn, named after the mountain that stands behind it and which is Wales' oldest pub, she had added proudly.

This completely changed both my dining options and intentions, as there was no way I was going to miss out on a chance to visit the oldest pub in Wales, even if I had just stuffed my face. Thanking her for her kind understanding when pushed into a puddle by an imbecile and also for the fantastic little snippet about the Skirrid Inn, I waddled off along the muddy and slippery path, taking careful steps along the absolutely treacherous surface. Nevertheless, I fell anyway after just a dozen yards.

She definitely saw me fall, I mused, as I dragged myself back onto my feet, and I figured it was simply karma.

Pandy was closer than I had thought. I emerged from the path onto a surprisingly busy road that brought me quickly back to civilization and also allowed me to catch up with the guys. From here, we discovered that we now had the luxury of something we had not seen for a while, which was proper footpaths as opposed to sloppy rivers of mud.

The pub was a few hundred feet to the south, or so we thought, so we immediately set off and soon saw it in the distance. Unfortunately, this pub turned out not to be the Skirrid after all, but it was the Rising Sun, so we carried on. However, we now found ourselves on a smaller road that ran parallel to the main one, which was much more pleasant.

After wandering along a small lane that was hedged in on both sides, always a pet-hate for me due to the problems I usually encountered when trying to secrete myself into said hedge when one large vehicle or another inevitably comes by, and after passing countless immaculately kept houses and bungalows, we finally arrived at the Skirrid, which it has to be said, was some distance off our route.

The first thing I noticed was the rather snazzy sign hanging outside, which at first glance looked like an erupting volcano but which I more or less immediately realised actually showed a bolt of lightning hitting a mountain, presumably the Skirrid from which the pub derives its name.

Most pubs, if not all, have signs such as these, largely because of an English king, Richard II, who passed an act in 1393 mandating the hanging of them.

It is a common misconception, however, that these signs were hung simply because people back then were generally illiterate. While they may well have been unable to read such names as *The Bucket of Blood* or *The Drunken Duck*, they would definitely have been able to recognise pictures of such things unless perhaps they had already been in either of those pubs for several hours. My own personal favourite, by the way, is from my own neck of the woods and is *The Goat and Compasses*, which is allegedly a corruption of the phrase *God encompasses us all*, two completely different phrases that presumably sound a lot like each other when you are either wholly obliterated after downing twenty pints or simply have a Hull accent, as do I.

Anyway, that is only half the story, as the king wanted signs hung outside of pubs not to help his stupid alcoholic peasant citizens but to make it easier for an official ale taster to find them so he could inspect the quality of the ales on sale, which doesn't sound like a bad job at all and is one that my somewhat negligent school careers officer forgot to inform me was even a possibility.

And ale taster really was an actual occupation

back then. In fact, none other than William Shakespeare's dear old dad was an ale taster who spent his time swanning around his local pubs, checking the quality and strength of the beers on sale and making sure they were priced appropriately. Tasters even had the power to reduce the price of ales they deemed to be inferior, and if they genuinely had serious doubts about a pub, they could ultimately force its closure, at which point its sign would be removed as a signal to everyone around to keep the hell away.

Not so for the Skirrid, of course, so we went in, claimed a table and perused the menu. A swift pint soon lubricated each of our throats, and we enjoyed a friendly conversation with the landlord, who was very talkative and who didn't at all mind repeatedly visiting our table to continue our little chat in between all of the rude customers who kept wanting to order food and drink and the like. Anyway, we learned all sorts about this most interesting little pub.

He told us it was 900 years old, that it is haunted, and that there used to be trials and executions held here, but then added that he had put an end to all that malarkey a couple of years ago.

I shared what little I knew about pub names and also happened to mention Shakespeare's dad being an ale taster as a roundabout way of asking if he had any jobs going. His eyes lit up at this, and he then told us that this very pub had its own claim to fame regarding the great bard himself.

Apparently, Shakespeare gained his inspiration for the character Puck in *A Midsummer Night's Dream* from a visit to the Skirrid. Notorious for his many mischievous deeds, I recalled my schoolday education, which unfortunately included far too much Shakespeare, and I remembered Puck as a fun-loving and somewhat mischievous hobgoblin and wondered if Shakespeare had been influenced by a member of staff here. Furthermore, the pub had once been home to the last real Prince of Wales, apparently. Other than that, however, Eric, which, I decided, was probably the landlord's name, knew no more.

Alas, poor Eric, and that was that.

I always like to double-check these seemingly tall tales, and while some of them may have merit, others simply turn out to be modern marketing ploys designed to lure in unsuspecting tourists such as ourselves for a big spend.

For instance, the pub was actually dated to around the mid-1600s, so there is no way it could be 900 years old, though there may well have been an inn on the same site before the current incarnation. As for its other history, while there is a myth, there is no hard evidence, so it is merely folklore that suggests it was here that

Welsh folk hero Owain Glyndwr, who was the self-proclaimed Prince of Wales, used this pub as his base for an uprising against Henry IV, King of England, in the early 1400s.

The pub is also said to have been used as a court of law, with some executions having been carried out here too. Indeed, the present owners have themselves hung a rather photogenic noose above the staircase, presumably as a gentle reminder to encourage you to pay your bill before heading off. Some even claim that Judge George Jeffreys, a notorious English judge perhaps better known as *The Hanging Judge*, held court here, which is not beyond the realms of possibility, as his jurisdiction is said to have stretched from Chester in the north to nearby Monmouth, here in the south of Wales.

More recently, the pub featured on one or two of those so-called reality television programmes, specifically *Most Haunted* and *Extreme Ghost Stories*. I have watched one or two of these sad little programmes, and all they have ever demonstrated to me is that ghosts don't exist and that second-rate presenters will do absolutely anything to get ratings.

By now, we had been in the pub for about half an hour, so we figured we should probably get going, though we had a bit of a decision to make. That choice was either to continue onwards or to spend the night in Abergavenny, which was just a few miles away to the south.

Abergavenny, although not actually on the route of the walk per se, remains an important stop for many hikers following in King Offa's footsteps, plus it was the location of the train station used in the movie Arthur's Dyke. Just a short taxi or bus ride would take us to a plethora of hotels, pubs and restaurants where we could enjoy a well-earned soak in the bath, and if anyone fancied it, they could go to one of those health and beauty spas where little fishes will happily nibble on your feet, blissfully unaware of the state they might be in after the first part of this walk.

There is, however, one other reason to mention Abergavenny, and that is because it was both the birthplace and home of a young lady called Miriam Kate Williams. She was born there in 1874 to Irish parents, though Williams was proudly Welsh through and through.

At some point in her youth, she became interested in physical fitness in general and bodybuilding in particular, which is a clue to her later life, for while Williams was never all that well-known by her name as such, any Victorian worth his or her salt would have instantly known who you were on about if you mentioned her stage-name, which was Vulcana.

I had first come across Vulcana on one of my other little walks, *54 Degrees North*, through a somewhat admittedly tenuous link, so it was a pleasure to come across her again and to find out where she actually lived and grew up and went to toilet and whatnot.

Anyway, while she might have achieved at least moderate fame for her weightlifting and bodybuilding exploits, she also found herself firmly in the news in 1910, something that made her vastly more famous than her work ever did.

Williams had been close friends with another performer, you see, one who went by the name of Belle Elmore but whose real name was Cora Crippen. Cora was married to a doctor called Hawley, and as you may have already guessed, Hawley was, in fact, the notorious Victorian murderer otherwise known as Doctor Crippen.

The good doctor, or come to think of it, the not-so-good doctor, had fallen out of love with Cora and, rather inconveniently, had fallen in love with his typist, Ethel Le Neve. Subsequently, he came up with a hare-brained scheme to kill his wife, bury her beneath their basement, and live happily ever after with Ethel.

Unfortunately for him, he didn't take into account the fact that while he might not necessarily miss Cora, other people definitely would, and one of those other people was none other than Miriam Kate Williams, a.k.a. Vulcana.

She reported her friend's mysterious disappearance to the police, who duly searched the Crippen family home but found absolutely no trace of the missing Cora. Meanwhile, Doctor Crippen concocted a story about how his wife had left him and fled to America with another man and even suggested that she had died in California.

While this story, coming from a seemingly respectable doctor, actually satisfied the police, Crippen misjudged the situation entirely, and he incorrectly presumed the game to be up. Faster than you could say, *not guilty, your honour*, he had fled with Ethel to Brussels, where, after a brief stay, the pair boarded the SS Montrose and steamed off to Canada, literally sailing off into the sunset.

Alarmed by the sudden and mysterious disappearance of more or less everyone involved in this story, London's finest returned to the Crippen family home and, after a more thorough search, discovered grisly remains beneath the basement floor, which amounted to not much more than a human torso.

And although this was in the days before forensics and the like, the police still figured that something was up and worked hard to track Crippen's whereabouts. Newspapers ran this sensational story for several days, and word soon spread around the globe about the now-infamous murderer.

Not surprisingly, witnesses began to come forward, stating they had seen the outlaw couple, and this included the captain of the Montrose. Apparently, the flaw in Crippen's plan had been to travel first class, and had he not done so, it is unlikely he would have ever met the captain and would, therefore, have escaped. However, another significant component of his undoing was that Crippen had decided to disguise Ethel as, of all things, a young boy, perhaps to satisfy a little fetish of his.

Anyway, when Scotland Yard discovered the pair were on their way to Canada on a lumbering steamship, they came up with a cunning plan. They would dispatch their top copper, Chief Inspector Walter Dew, on a faster ship, who would race to Canada, where he would promptly arrest them both.

This unlikely plan worked, too. Dew was also in Canada before you could say *not guilty, your honour*, and on the day of Crippen and Le Neve's arrival, he disguised himself as a ship's pilot and boarded the Montrose. Once on board, the captain invited some of the first-class passengers to meet the pilot, as was the custom, although, of course, in this case, it was just a ruse to get Crippen in front of Inspector Dew of the yard.

Historical accounts reveal that Crippen was actually most relieved to have been caught, and he is said to have held out his hands to be cuffed, while others dispute this. A bit like the fog of war, it seems that time and history have a fog of their own.

Regardless, Crippen was tried and convicted in a court of law, and on the 23rd of November 1910, he was hanged to death at Pentonville

Prison in London by John Ellis, incidentally the same man who later executed Herbert Armstrong in 1922, who we will learn all about when we get to Hay-on-Wye. As for Le Neve, she was exonerated of all guilt and returned to Canada, while Vulcana went back to her life on stage.

Anyway, other than that, Vulcana lived an interesting life of her own. She met and fell in love with a strongman called William Hedley Roberts, but again, he was better known by his stage name, Atlas. And the fact that Roberts already had a wife and family did not seem to be a hindrance to their blossoming romance, and after meeting, it is said they never parted, ever.

Perhaps somewhat bizarrely, though, the pair concocted a strange story for the general public, which stated they were actually brother and sister, which you might have thought would have raised some questions later when she started popping children out. All in all, they had six little ankle-biters, though they never married, presumably because Roberts had never actually bothered to divorce his first wife, something almost unheard of at the time. And the reason this never became a scandal is because they somehow managed to keep it all a secret and out of the public eye.

Retiring in later life, Vulcana lived an otherwise simple and somewhat uneventful existence, though she did manage to get hit by a car in London in 1939. Bizarrely, in the immediate aftermath of the accident, she heard her own death pronounced, which must have been something of a shock. And while she did suffer some brain damage, she lived another seven years and passed away in 1946, just after Atlas, the love of her life.

As it was, with there being still several hours of daylight left, and because the weather was fine, we decided to carry on heading north.

We had been putting it off as we knew what was coming next, which was a steep climb. The next part of our route would take us straight up Hatterall Hill, you see, which would be followed by a ridge walk of several miles. Hay Bluff stood at the far end of the ridge, many miles away, after which we would drop down into Hay-on-Wye, but that would not be until tomorrow.

Hatterrall Hill would actually signal the start of the section across the Black Mountains, somewhere I had not been before, so I did not know what to expect. And while I knew that we wouldn't fully cross the mountains by the end of today, I had been told of a good camping site near Llanthony, which I hoped we could take advantage of, particularly as the weather was about the nicest it could possibly be and was ideal for camping.

By the time we got back to Pandy, however, where we had initially joined the road, clouds had moved over what had previously been a brilliant blue sky, and the temperature had dropped more than a few degrees, though this was good as it would help to keep us cool.

Had we not gone to the pub, Offa's Dyke Path would have merely crossed straight over the road here and into the field opposite, which is exactly what we did next, or is what we tried to do anyway.

We had stopped for a few moments to rest at the Lancaster Arms, which had once been a pub but was now a guesthouse. I had gone to knock on the door to ask if we could refill our various water bottles, and as I was returning to the others, I noticed a man walking his dog.

Greetings were exchanged, at which point James moved off, passing close by the dog, which immediately decided it rather liked James and became somewhat attached to him. What I mean by that, however, is that its teeth became somewhat attached to him. Out of nowhere, the dastardly mutt suddenly went crazy and lunged at James' legs, sinking its teeth fully and firmly into his left calf muscle, or so it seemed.

Obviously, James was not too happy with this turn of events and kicked his leg accordingly. I would like to say that the vicious beast flipped upside down and over the hedge, but it didn't, though James did manage to free his leg.

The strange thing is that the dog's owner just stood there, doing nothing. He didn't pull the dog away or apologise or anything else, though when I passed by a few seconds later, he did ask me if James was okay. The adrenaline was flowing, and I'm pretty sure my reply was something like no, he bloody wasn't.

Stepping back onto the soft grass surface actually came as something of a relief after the last couple of miles on the tarmac, and I followed the others along the edge of a field before crossing a river, a railway and a road, in precisely that order.

In the field next to the path, in between the railway and the road, I noticed a rather prominent mound upon which grew a few trees and presumed it to be a burial mound of some sort, though it is actually the motte of a Norman castle that once stood here.

Behind that was a mound of an altogether different nature, and that was the Skirrid, the mountain that had a very distinct shape which, once seen, can never be unseen. The shape is the result of a landslip that occurred sometime during the last ice age, and there are some nice walks to be had on the hill today. Apparently, Rudolph Hess was known to enjoy walking on the mountain every now and then while he was held at Maindiff Court just a few miles south near Abergavenny, but only when he had finished painting the White Castle, presumably, and feeding the swans.

A narrow track took us slowly uphill, and after a while, we left the road to cut a corner out of a field before joining the exact same road again a few hundred yards further on. James, who had been ahead of us, had stayed on the road, but he had been moving so fast that we still never managed to catch him up.

When we rejoined the road, the views had improved considerably, and we could see all the way back down into the valley we had come from. We must have climbed higher than I had thought, I pondered.

A pleasant country lane was my guide for the next half a mile, which provided an impressive canopy of branches in full bloom. We had all split up again but had agreed to meet at the top of the ridge, so for now, I was on my own.

Rounding a bend and passing a farm, I was greeted with a fantastic view extending far down a distant valley with an impressive hill beyond that, and I was really enjoying the spectacle until I realised that this was the direction I would soon be heading in, and those slopes were the exact ones I would shortly have to drag myself up.

Indeed, just a few moments later, one of those cunning little fingerposts directed me off the road, into the trees, and up that very same hill, signalling the fact that our climb up to the top of Hatterrall Ridge had finally begun, but not before I encountered three strange men with an axe.

I stopped in my tracks when I saw them, and thoughts flashed through my mind of being chopped into little pieces and deposited here and there throughout the woods.

I was somewhat lost for words until the one with the axe realised the optics of the situation and told me they were just looking for somewhere to wild camp. Judging by their looks, I'm not sure any of them had ever been camping before, and in fact, I'm not sure if any of them had even been into the countryside before, as they looked so out of place.

The fact that they had also tried to drive their battered old BMW up a steep footpath suggested they were very much out of their depth, and after a brief conversation about the legalities of wild camping, I said my goodbyes and left them behind. I must admit that I did look over my shoulder once or twice, just to make sure that there wasn't anyone running after me swinging a hatchet around, and I only felt safe after I had gone another half mile or so.

The trees soon petered out as I climbed higher, and breaking the tree line left me on the side of a ridge with views to the east that would not be suitable for anyone who suffered from vertigo. The sky had cleared again, and you could see for miles, so I stopped for a quick rest. While this did indeed allow me to savour the view, if I am being brutally honest, it was mainly so that I could get my breath back.

Whilst I sat, I particularly enjoyed watching some lunatics flinging themselves off the side of the hill. They never fell to their deaths, though, as they were paragliders, all hanging beneath a small parachute and sporting dinky little motors as backpacks that propelled them along. While I'm not sure I would want to have a go myself, it certainly looked like it was quicker than walking.

A little further on, the view was even more impressive, and I was even more out of breath. A small sign suggested there was something of interest here, too, though it was too worn to read.

My trusty map, however, told me this was Pentywyn Hill Fort, which was an Iron Age fort with little to see nowadays other than raised earthen banks, though who knows what could be underground, as the place has never been thoroughly investigated, which seems a shame. This might be something to do with the fact that the fort sits right on the border of England and Wales, which would presumably make getting permission for an archaeological dig challenging in itself and something of a bureaucratic nightmare.

Before doing this walk, I had read that anyone covering the entire route of Offa's Dyke would cross the English and Welsh border around twenty times. However, Hatterrall Ridge puts that claim firmly and fully in the bin. To my right, you see, and looking straight down, I could see the small village of Oldcastle, which meant that just a little further ahead was the point where Offa's Dyke path would actually follow the border exactly for around five or six miles as it ran along the top of the ridge. This meant that we would spend the next couple of hours constantly straddling and regularly crossing the border, which, when you think about it, made it actually impossible to calculate how many times you really do cross from one country to the other when doing the walk. Rob, however, said I was being stupid and none of those border crossings counted. In reply, I just hopped across it a couple of times more, dancing a little jig as I did so.

Regardless, we would only be following the ridge for another mile or two at the most today, but it was a most enjoyable couple of miles, and we all enjoyed the views on either side very much. The Welsh Vale of Ewyas stood below to our left, while to our right was the Olchon Valley in English Herefordshire. I must say that up here, I felt that I could see half of the country, and perhaps I could.

I was distracted from the spectacular view a few hundred yards further on when I came across a herd of wild ponies. I stopped and thought for a moment, wondering if herd was the correct collective term for them, but shrugged my shoulders when I was unable to come up with anything better, although the proper term is actually a string, but then you learn something new every day.

I wandered pretty close to them, though this was purely out of necessity as I wanted to stay on the path rather than fall off the side of the mountain. While they seemed moderately friendly, I sensed that they definitely kept one eye firmly on me as they continued their grass-munching activities along the crest of the hill.

Sheep would usually dot this hillside, too, but there were none today, so I presumed it to be perhaps the wrong time of year, and as I left the ponies behind, the rough grass and gorse promised many more hours of dining for my four-legged friends.

A track to our left soon took us temporarily off the route of Offa's Dyke path and instead led us along the Beacons Way, and it quickly began the slow descent to LLanthony, one which was quite steep in places. The views were still spectacular, and I could clearly see the ruins of LLanothy Priory far below me, which, of course, was our destination for the day. We still intended to camp tonight, and so far, the weather gods were being kind to us, which was good, as Llanthony was a tiny place and did not offer much of a choice should conditions take a turn for the worse. Thankfully, the weather stayed fine, and we soon found ourselves in the heart of the village.

Llanthony is a little beauty of a place which nestles right on the edge of the Black Mountains at the eastern end of the beautiful Brecon Beacons National Park.

It is not hard to understand why anyone would choose to come here, as the location is peaceful, idyllic and absolutely stunning, and one of the first people who ever settled here was a man called William de Lacy, who stumbled upon the place whilst out hunting one day. However, it is said that the patron saint of Wales, Saint David, once lived here, too, living the life of a hermit, which is what initially inspired William to do the same. He actually came to devote himself to a life of solitary prayer and study, which sounds like my worst nightmare if I am being truly honest. Furthermore, what he did was actually very untypical of his time, as he abandoned his old life of war and adventure and wholeheartedly embraced a much simpler life of religion instead.

Luckily, hordes of others soon joined him, all seeking the same solitary and peaceful life that William had so yearned for. Apart from defeating the object of coming here, of course, on a positive note, it did mean that he had lots of help when it came to building that beautiful abbey.

William had originally inherited the land around here when his dad died in what must be said was a tragic but slightly funny accident, and who was called Walter, by the way. Walter was a Norman nobleman who came over after William the Conqueror had managed to secure the island, and he later served under him in a military capacity. As a reward for his efforts, he was given lands in Shropshire and Herefordshire, and once the fighting finally stopped, he supervised the building of various castles and the like, all of which were intended to prop up the new king's regime in one way or another.

It was while Walter was inspecting the building work going on at Saint Guthlac's Abbey in nearby Hereford that the tragic but slightly funny event unfolded. Walter had climbed the scaffolding to give things a bit of a closer look, you see, and at some point, he took a step back in order to take in a broader perspective. Unfortunately, however, he somehow managed to step back off the scaffolding and immediately fell to a swift and messy end, which reminds me of one of those silly selfie deaths we heard about earlier. His remains were presumably swept up and put in a bucket, and he was later buried in Gloucester Cathedral, and that was the end of that.

Nowadays, Llanthony Priory consists of some fine ruins that are truly impressive indeed and which are best summed up in the words of Gerald of Wales, who wrote about it in the 12th century and who you may remember previously gave us the first Welsh account of the dyke. He said that this place *"was truly suited to the monastic life . . . in a wilderness far removed from the bustle of modern life".*

This still rings true, and today, Llanthony Priory sits abandoned and alone, but ironically, this only makes it even more beautiful. I can only think that knowing this, William de Lacy would be a very happy man, especially as the place now has a pub, which is precisely where we went next. We actually had a choice of pubs, which was unusual for such a small village, and while we could have chosen to eat at the priory itself, where the cellar has quite cheekily been turned into a bar, we instead made our way to the Half Moon, just a short stroll away.

The pub was reasonably busy when we burst through the door, and we really did burst through it. Robin, being what we call a big unit, put a little too much effort into opening it, you see, and as he stumbled in, heads turned in our direction, and all conversation ceased. I, for one, could feel my face quickly turning red, but thankfully, this lasted mere seconds, and then everyone simply carried on as they had been, presumably after realising that we were merely a bunch of English simpletons and that our actions probably couldn't be helped.

We soon found a table where I peeled my backpack off, which was an absolutely fantastic feeling, and after grabbing a local beer, mine made by the lovely people at the Wye Valley Brewery, we perused the menu for what seemed like several hours before making our choices. I was incredibly adventurous and went for the chicken.

I wanted to take my shoes off but didn't for two reasons. One, I didn't know if I would be able to get them back on again, at least not today, as my feet felt swollen, and two, I didn't want to kill anyone. Let's just say that my feet were probably not at their most pleasant after walking around fifty miles in three days.

As I waited for my food, I discovered a couple of leaflets and books lying around, as pubs often tend to have, of course, which told me all about the Brecon Beacons, or more specifically, the national park going by the same name.

They told me that the armed forces are regular visitors to the park, who use its bleak and barren landscape to tickle, train and torture their toughest recruits, including the elite Special Air Service. And covering over 500 square miles, with a mix of mountain and moorland and everything in between, there are plenty of places in which they can suffer.

And while the park might be new, the area is obviously ancient. Originally carved out by massive glaciers during the last ice age, an intricate landscape awaited the first brave human inhabitants.

First of all, they cleared small areas of scrubland for farming. By the New Stone Age, this work was already advanced, and by the Bronze Age, most of the forests were gone, being the efficient eco-vandals that our ancestors were. The Iron Age was next, leaving a scarred landscape of hillforts and earthen banks like those we had seen at Pentywyn, followed by the Romans, who quite frankly and somewhat surprisingly didn't leave much of an impression, though the Normans, who came next, had a huge impact on the area.

The Middle Ages profoundly affected farming here, and the black death affected it even more, and by the time industry came along, this landscape was changed forever. More modern changes include the inevitable urban expansion, as people have to live somewhere, of course. Reservoirs have also appeared here, there, and everywhere to supply drinking water for all those people, as Wales is blessed with lots and lots of rainfall, although, to be honest, I'm not sure that blessed is necessarily the right word. And finally, huge forests have recently been planted to replace the ones our glorious ancestors so efficiently destroyed. Unfortunately, however, these were usually coniferous and non-native, though attitudes towards this are now beginning to change, and these invaders are slowly but very surely being replaced with native species.

On a brighter note, the park is also one of the filming locations for the awesomely magical fantasy movie *Stardust*. Made in 2007 and starring Hollywood icon and absolute babe Michell Pfeiffer, the film sees hero and all-round hunk Tristan, played by a young Charlie Cox, heading off into these hills in search of a fallen star. What he finds instead of a star, much to his surprise, is a woman, and one with magical powers at that.

Anyway, that star, in human form, treks right through these beautiful mountains with Tristan, just a few miles to the west of Offa's Dyke path, specifically near a glacial lake called Llyn y Fan Fach. And while it might just be a movie, that lake does actually have real-life magical connections.

According to legend, the lake, which I will not name again due to it being so hard to pronounce for us mere English types, was, in fact, the place where the Lady in the Lake handed the sword Excalibur to none other than King Arthur himself.

However, whether this is true or not, I'm going to have to reference and agree with the Monty Python team in general, and Michael Palin in particular, who once famously said, and I quote, *"Strange women lying in ponds distributing swords is no basis for a system of government".*

And if you think the name of the lake, Llyn y Fan Fach, is somewhat amusing, then apart from being incredibly childish, you are also correct. But that's just the start. Other place names around here include the somewhat hilarious Fan Y Big, a rather rude mountain just to the south that has recently seen its status downgraded to that of a mere hill after it was discovered the Victorians managed to get the measurements entirely wrong. Three Cocks is another one, a village to the north and, my own personal favourite, simply because it's funny, is Booby Dingle, a valley just off to the east.

It's a shame that this practice of amusing names isn't continued nowadays, with our new towns, for instance. Instead, the dreary town planners have come up with such delights as *Milton Keynes* and *Stevenage*, as well as the incredibly original *Newtown*, of course, right here in Wales, which presumably took them ages to think of.

In more modern times, the Brecon Beacons have been nominated as the first Dark Skies Park in Wales, and coincidentally, Llanthony Priory is apparently one of the best places to come and gaze up at them. Situated miles from the nearest urban centres and nestling in a secluded valley, it is easy to understand why, and being something of a stargazer myself, I vowed to have a look later.

Our food eventually arrived, which I took as a good sign, suggesting that it was actually cooked to order and not simply reheated in a microwave. However, the long wait did have something of a downside, as I had to order yet another pint of that lovely Wye Valley ale. I was more than willing to make this sacrifice, though, especially considering that I was also supporting a local business, which I find is an excellent excuse for having a beer and which works almost every time.

I declined the kind offer of dessert when the

waitress took away my empty plate and glasses, and figured that we had better make a move to the campsite, mainly because it was starting to get dark.

My body didn't want to move, though, as my choice of a whole chicken dinner, my second today, weighed heavily on my stomach and left me feeling blissfully drowsy, too.

Luckily, it was only a short walk to the campsite, and on the way, I reflected on the fact that we should probably have pitched our tents before stuffing ourselves silly in the pub, but we all make mistakes.

The campsite was compact and clean, and we had it more or less to ourselves, probably because it was still early in the season and the weather had been a bit hit-and-miss, to say the least. We had a quick chat with the lady who ran it, who was very friendly and told us we could pitch up wherever we wished, after which we then went to get set up.

Just half an hour later, after getting my tent up and putting my sleeping bag and mat in place, and after waiting for my somewhat slow friends to do the same, we all had a wander back to the priory, and when we got there, the sky was already a mass of twinkling stars.

I am always amazed, what with being a city boy myself, of the actual number of stars that can be seen in a clear wilderness sky. To be honest, and although I know the names and locations of a few major stars and constellations, whenever I see a sky awash with stars, I always lose my bearings. There are simply too many to be seen, and I simply cannot make sense of it all, though I did finally manage to locate the Great Bear or the Plough as it is also called, and from there, I found what I thought to be Polaris or the North Star, so at least I knew which way was up, so to speak.

We chilled out on a low wall for a while, letting our eyes adjust further, and as the glowing carpet that was the Milky Way slowly but surely revealed itself from the black void of never-ending space, a chill also began to settle around us, and I for one certainly began to feel the cold.

Having seen all I wanted to see, which, let's face it, was more or less the whole of existence, we made our way back to the campsite and, I must say, quite gallantly resisted the urge to pop back to the pub and further support the local economy, mainly because we were all pretty much knackered. There was one minor hiccup when I got into my tent, however. I saw a bloody great spider, though it was gone before I could whack it with a mallet. However, whoever said *"out of sight, out of mind"* never had a giant spider disappear in their tent.

WHERE WEREWOLVES WERE

Llanthony to Hay-on-Wye

Dawn broke to an absolute chorus of birdsong in the trees above. Apparently, the birds had kindly and spontaneously decided to congregate directly above our little collection of tents. I had also become aware of a cockerel doing its best to wake everyone within five miles some hours earlier, but that problem had soon been resolved when I stepped out in my pyjamas and strangled the bloody thing.

I was probably going to need a scattergun for the birds, however, and despite rummaging through my entire rucksack, my search proved futile, which is probably why I woke up with a headache. Long story short, I must have packed the wrong pills, and as a result, I took the wrong tablet. The good news is that I'm now protected from fleas and ticks for up to twelve weeks. When I did finally find my headache tablets, I noticed that on the side of the box, it says that alcohol may intensify the effects of this medication. I never know if this is a warning or a suggestion.

Packing up camping gear was next, which is always a chore, especially when trying to make sure that everything is dry. I didn't know when I would have the tent out again, as I certainly wasn't planning on camping every night, so I hung it over a picnic bench in the hope that the early morning sunshine would help the process along. The others had done the same, and our tents hung on every available object around, which, I must say, really gave the campsite something of a classy look.

While we waited, we brewed ourselves a quick coffee on Rob's little stove, and I made sure to add sugar, which would hopefully give me the boost I would need to get back to the top of the ridge carrying Offa's Dyke path, which I had so happily bounced down yesterday. Now, however, I wished we had camped at the top.

I sat for a while listening to the birds and enjoying the various animals that kept stopping by, which included a small and exceptionally friendly robin as well as a slightly more skittish rabbit that almost had a heart attack when it realised I was an actual person and not, as he had presumably thought, a tree.

Keen to make a move, I repeatedly tried to burn my mouth with the coffee, but eventually, it cooled enough to become drinkable, after which I was pleasantly surprised to find that my tent was more or less dry.

However, when I tried to pack it, I realised the underside was still damp, which meant I was reduced to wafting it around in the air in a final attempt to get the thing dry so we could finally move off.

The wafting never really helped, but the sun had come up a bit more and felt to be offering a certain amount of warmth, so I simply stood there instead, acting almost like a human washing line, and angled it towards the sun's rays, simultaneously enjoying bathing my face in those exact same rays of golden loveliness.

This mad method actually worked, and in no time at all, I was packed up and ready to go. After a final inspection of the campsite confirmed we had not left anything behind other than square patches of flat grass, we made our way back from where we had come, passing the abbey and heading towards that massive hill.

The abbey looked even more splendid than I remembered it yesterday, presumably because of the brilliant sunshine that was all around and upon it, and I wished I could have stopped a while longer to have a proper look around.

And while Henry VIII had famously dissolved most monasteries and priories in the early

1500s, Llanthony had already been more or less finished off a few years earlier by Welsh folk hero Owain Glyndwr, who we came across earlier, although he probably wasn't considered a folk hero by the people of the monasteries he constantly raided. Thankfully, the English and Welsh seem to be on slightly better terms today.

A couple came the other way, and I stopped to talk to them, grateful for the chance to catch my breath. They said they were doing a circular walk from Abergavenny, which made me wonder about the ridiculous hour they must have set off at, though I decided not to ask out of fear of shaming myself.

In the field next to the abbey, I spied a few dozen sheep, all of them enjoying the finest breakfast of grass and all of them covered in magnificent layers of mud. A fingerpost directed me to the left, and it was good it was there, as otherwise, I would have gone straight ahead. Going off course is not something I want to do today, particularly while going up a massive mountain, and as the others were already far ahead of me, I was on my own for now.

This climb was not the ideal way to start the day. I had to keep stopping to get my breath, but when I did, I at least enjoyed the spectacular views back down into Llanthony, which only got better with every step.

I caught up with Rob, who was struggling a little, so for encouragement, I told him I believed in him and that he could do it. But then I also believe in Bigfoot, so he probably shouldn't get too excited.

After a quick hop over a gate, on the assumption that I was far too much of a serious walker to worry about things such as opening that gate, I felt a twinge in my knee and decided that I should probably not be so foolish and figured that I was definitely too old for such hijinks, so I slowed considerably, and Rob moved off ahead.

The uphill became even more uphill, only slightly steeper, though I did enjoy walking through what was effectively a vast meadow. Cows stared wearily at my passing self, though they were thankfully entirely disinterested. While you may laugh at the discovery that I am not particularly fond of these bovine beasts, they can be quite the killer, especially of chubby and ageing hikers such as yours truly.

Thankfully, I soon left them far behind me, and after turning a corner, the open fields turned into a forest of ferns which were just beginning to really shoot up.

I stopped once more to take a look back, wanting to get a good look behind me, as the view really was outstanding, but this also gave me another chance to rest, if only for a minute.

Getting steeper still, the path actually took in some natural steps carved out of the earth itself, and it was here that I chose to stop for yet another rest beneath a small copse of stunted and windblown trees. I say chose, but what I mean is that I had to stop, as I was simply out of breath.

I sat and enjoyed the views for five minutes or so, which still included Llanthony Priory as well as a vast swathe of countryside and valleys in all directions other than east. I tried to figure out where I had come from the day before, but I think it was just out of view.

The higher the path went, the steeper it became, until I thought it could become no steeper, after which it did just that. I huffed and puffed at this early morning struggle and wished I had been able to get breakfast in Llanthony, a luxury that would have to wait until we got all the way to Hay-on-Wye. I did have a couple of cereal bars, which I decided to sacrifice immediately, but they did not quite do the job, and I still felt famished, which in turn left me totally lacking in energy.

As a result, my rate of climb was slow, and I found myself taking little baby steps, barely putting one foot in front of the other. As I did so, the path began to take twists and turns, and on more than one occasion, I thought I had reached the top, only to discover I could merely see a false summit.

A considerable drop to my side offered an immediate way out of the misery should I choose to take it, although, in my present state, I felt

I might have dropped at any moment anyway. I knew I must be near the top, though, as I could see the ridge extending to my south from where I had come, and it was not all that much higher than where I was now, or at least that was how it looked. On the top, I could see some far-off figures and reckoned the others had probably stopped to wait for me.

Looks can be deceptive, though, and it was some twenty minutes before I finally reached the actual top, something that had been hinted at by those tiny stick figures I could just about see ahead of me. I knew I had made it when my muddy track finally turned into a gravelly path, after which I joined the main route at a spot marked out by a pile of stones. I say a pile of stones, but it might really have been the final resting place of some poor, unfortunate backpacker who had recently done exactly what I just did up that bloody hill.

The others were here and were already brewing up coffee and food, which consisted of some ration packs kindly donated by a friend of ours. And while porridge would never be my breakfast of choice at home, I must say that it was the nicest treat imaginable when you have just dragged yourself one thousand feet up a mountain on an empty stomach.

On a side note, I recently tried changing my morning drink from coffee to orange juice, and I felt much better for doing so. My doctor said it was the Vitamin C and the natural sugars, but I think it was the vodka. More seriously, by replacing your morning coffee with green tea, you can lose up to eighty-seven percent of what little joy you still have left in your life.

We didn't stop for long, as it was still pretty cold at this early hour, and the path was good along the top and offered a much firmer and probably drier surface than the area to either side of it, which was covered in gorse and looked to be a bit boggy. Occasional small ponds confirmed this, and every now and then along the path, someone had built little rocky bridges across the countless streams that criss-crossed the top of the ridge.

The path also marked more of the border between England and Wales, so as I walked, I was once again jumping between the two repeatedly, even as I moved from one side of the path to another, which I childishly enjoyed for the next few miles.

The wind dropped at some point, at least for a short while, and it dawned on me how quiet it was, too. There were no other people around other than our motley group, and I couldn't see any animals either, not even birds. Occasionally, I stopped, if only to savour the silence for a while, which was actually quite unnerving.

At one point, the gravel path turned into one made from large flagstones, which left me feeling sorry for whichever poor soul had dragged them up here. The work was still ongoing, with large builders' bags dotting the path ahead, and I figured these could only have been brought up by the likes of either a helicopter or perhaps Superman.

We soon found ourselves dodging puddles that stretched from one side of the path to the other and which looked too deep to risk stepping in. I hopped and skipped across and around them quite expertly for a while until I came to the mother of all puddles, which looked set to beat me, though across which I somehow managed to walk without getting wet at all and which must have been some sort of miracle.

After this unwelcome distraction, the path once again alternated between gravel path and flagstones, though luckily there were no further floods, and our walk was thankfully distracted by the tremendous views which alternated between east and west, along with the occasional wild horses that somehow managed to survive up here.

Eventually, we spied in the distance a trig point marking the highest part of the hill and, with it, the highest point of the Offa's Dyke path too. We saw it long before we got there, though, and for a while, it didn't seem to get any closer until, of course, we were suddenly and without warning directly upon it.

Incidentally, if you look due west from here, you can see Lord Hereford's Knob, which is not actually an aristocrat's member, but is instead another one of those funny placenames, and in this case, it is a hill.

We stopped and took advantage of the chance to rest our legs for a minute, still enjoying the solitude and peace of the area, though I was really wishing that I was sitting in a café stuffing myself silly with a full English breakfast instead. I enjoyed a good drink of water, for that was all I had left, and after five or ten minutes, we plodded on once again, only to stop after a few seconds when we bumped into a couple of walkers coming the other way.

They were father and son, and were walking to the priory at Llanthony and back, and were local. They were a mine of information and confirmed what I knew about the high point of the walk being on Hatterrall Ridge which we had just passed, but they also told us its height, which was 2,306 feet. They also told us there was a crash site nearby and that a military aircraft had once flown straight into the side of the mountain. I later did some digging, not literally, of course, and discovered they were right on both counts. However, I also found out that the aircraft in question was a Lockheed P38 flown by an American airman called Coleman Richards. He is said to have hit the ridge due to poor visibility in 1944 and was a mere 23 years old at the time.

The father and son were called Gareth and

Dan, they told us, and they became our new best friends when they pulled out a bag of food that included sliced beef as well as cheese and chocolate. Perhaps my questions about how far it was to Hay-on-Wye and where would be a good place to grab lunch had dropped a slight hint at my semi-starved state, but anyway, they willingly shared their supplies and gave us each a small chocolate bar to eat on the way, which we gleefully accepted, thanking them profusely as they moved on with their walk.

We carried on, too, newly invigorated by what had been a substantial intake of calories, and on top of that, the views got better, which I hadn't thought was possible. In fairness, though, I had certainly had enough of Hatterrall Ridge, and my mind went into a trance-like state as I wandered along its endless course, once again gradually falling further behind the others.

How pleased was I, then, when I finally came to what looked like the end of this section of the walk. This was Hay Bluff, a steep but immediate and long-awaited exit from this long mountain trek, with the town of Hay-on-Wye clearly visible on the plains below.

I stopped at the trig point at the top of the hill, where I caught up with the others, which marked the 2,221-foot-high summit and which was adorned with an impressive Welsh dragon of the brightest red. The car park was visible far below, with what looked like little dinky toy cars parked across it with ants scurrying between them, and after enjoying the impressive all-round panorama for a moment or two, we began the slow descent along this zig-zag section of path.

I am pretty sure we must have strayed from the actual route here, but it didn't really matter as we still came out at the road where we intended to, though a little to the left of where we had aimed for. This was actually a good thing, as I had wanted to take a slight detour to see a point of interest that might not be everyone's cup of tea but was certainly mine. There was a photo opportunity here that I did not want to miss, which was yet another filming location, this time for one of the 20th century's most iconic horror films.

If you haven't already guessed, the film in question is *An American Werewolf in London*. As far as horror movies go, it's probably quite tame by modern standards, but my memories of watching it as a young child are memories of absolute and sheer terror. This briefly made me question the wisdom of my parent's decision to allow me to watch it in the first place until I quickly remembered that they said I couldn't, but I watched it anyway, and what I saw was harrowing.

The film starts relatively calmly with two Americans, David and Jack, backpacking through Britain, pretty much as we were now doing. All is well until a large wolf attacks the pair, which sees Jack submit to a gruesome but relatively swift death, while David escapes with merely a bit of a bite, though one serious enough to see him admitted to hospital.

As he slowly recovers, David is visited in his dreams, or perhaps nightmares, by his good friend Jack, who is apparently trying to warn him of his upcoming appointment with fate, which, by the magic of stop-motion animation, will see him definitely and most positively turn into a werewolf.

The scene in question is filmed at a road junction just a couple of hundred yards or so from where we joined the road, so it is well worth the brief diversion, and is the spot where David and Jack are dropped off after hitching a lift on the back of a farmers tractor and trailer.

There was no one around, so we had to make do with taking a selfie in more or less the exact location where the clip was filmed, and as there was no one around, we didn't feel silly at all, which was a bonus.

The film will tell you that they are on the Yorkshire Moors, but they were, in fact, sneakily hiding out right here in beautiful Wales. And while, in the movie at least, the boys head off looking for the beautifully named pub *The Slaughtered Lamb*, which is a made-up pub in Crickadarn, just a few miles to our west, we turned around and headed due north, back towards our destination for the day, the beautiful little town of Hay-on-Wye.

We followed the road for a while, which was pleasantly devoid of traffic and, compared to what we had just walked, was relatively flat. A tiny acorn on a somewhat larger rock instructed us to turn left across a field, which thankfully took us gradually downhill, following what looked vaguely like a short section of Offa's Dyke or might have just been a lump in the ground.

Briefly turning around, I had one last look at Hay Bluff and wondered how on earth we had managed to get down it in one piece, as from my current vantage point, it looked just like a cliff.

Open fields led us next to the edge of a wood, where the footpath turned into a river, most literally. We splashed warily and carefully up a rocky riverbed, which thankfully was relatively dry given the time of year. Luckily, it only lasted for a few yards, and we then passed through a rather smelly farm, where a seemingly generous sign advised anyone who wanted water to knock on the farmhouse door. This was probably a trap, I thought to myself, as farmers have to feed their pigs somehow, and what better food than a nice, fat backpacker. Anyway, I still had ample water in my rucksack, so they weren't going to trick me that easily. We then followed a pleasant nettle-lined track before heading once more across-country, before finally emerging onto a narrow lane just outside of Hay-on-Wye, where I was almost squashed by a bus.

Thankfully, it was only a mini-bus, so I would only have been a little squashed, and after one last diversion across fields that could politely be described as well-composted, I emerged with shitty-smelling shoes in the beautiful little market town of Hay-on-Wye. They should have been clean, as a small herd of cows took an immense interest in me just outside of the town, or more accurately, they took an interest in my bright red rucksack and forced me to back up into a stream. My feet got wet, and while the level of wetness was apparently enough to soak my feet, quite paradoxically, it wasn't enough to actually clean them. Sometimes, I just don't understand this universe.

The first thing to say about Hay-on-Wye, and which incidentally is somewhat hard to miss, is that there are rather a lot of bookshops. This is largely down to the efforts of one somewhat eccentric man, Richard Booth, who, in 1962, opened the first bookshop here in the old fire station.

In 1977, he went one step further and declared Hay-on-Wye to be, of all things, an independent kingdom, which he ruled from his very own castle in the centre of the town, with him conveniently nominated as the head of state. If you think that's odd, he nominated his horse to be the prime minister, though come to think of it, that's probably much better than the bunch we've actually had to put up with in recent years.

Since then, the town hasn't looked back and has held an annual book fair every May, with the rich and famous turning up from far and wide. And although Booth recently died, his bookshop and castle are now in the hands of a trust, so things should hopefully continue unchanged for years to come.

While I love books, when I first came across Hay's book fair, I couldn't help but feel that some people get perhaps just a little too excited. For instance, none other than Bill Clinton, the 42nd President of the United States, who absolutely did not have sexual relations with that woman, described the Hay Book Festival as, and I quote, *"The Woodstock of the Mind"*. Another politician, though one slightly less famous called Tony Benn, once said of it, *"In my mind, it's replaced Christmas"*.

And the town's links to literature are actually quite extensive. Many famous authors are closely associated with the place, most notably Terry Pratchett, author of the Discworld series of fantasy novels. While he was indeed a fascinating individual and was undoubtedly good with a pen, he was also pretty handy with a smelter, so much so that when he was knighted by the late queen, he forged himself a sword using iron taken from meteorites especially for the occasion.

We're not going to talk about him, though, as there is someone far more interesting who came from here, and that would be Herbert Armstrong, who I mentioned earlier. Most people have never heard of him because the powers that be try not to mention his name.

Although Armstrong wasn't born in the town, he settled here early on, and by 1906, he was a well-respected local solicitor. A year after moving in, he married his lifelong sweetheart, Katharine Friend, who went by the name of Kitty, and together they had three children, two girls and a boy. From the outside, at least, their lives looked perfect.

Armstrong's stature in the town rose rapidly, and he served his country well during the First World War. He was promoted to the rank of Major whilst in the trenches of northern France and, quite predictably, in the post-war years, and after returning home, people began to call him *The Major*.

After the end of the war, beginning in 1919, just after Armstrong had returned home, Mrs Armstrong began to experience some health problems, which her doctor initially diagnosed as inflammation. Initially, the symptoms came and went intermittently, but by 1920, they had worsened considerably, and Mrs Armstrong was finally admitted to the local hospital.

She remained an in-patient for some months, and as her condition slowly improved, her doctors were hopeful of a full recovery. Finally, in January of 1921, they were able to discharge her. Once home, Mr Armstrong went to great lengths to care for his wife, often leaving work early to look after her, helped by his local physician, Doctor Hincks. Despite all of this, however, her condition once again worsened, and she passed away on the 22nd of February 1921, just one month after going home.

Herbert Armstrong was, on the face of it, absolutely distraught. Nevertheless, he concentrated on caring for his children and running his business, and he is said to have greatly impressed those around him by maintaining his focus in the face of such tragic events.

Just a short while later, Armstrong was back at work, and he was soon attempting to agree to terms with the only rival solicitor in the town, Oswald Martin, over a property deal which had not quite worked out as planned.

Armstrong invited Martin to his home, ostensibly so the two could finalise some sort of deal, but when Martin arrived, Armstrong talked only of his personal life and how much he missed his wife.

To cut a very long but nonetheless interesting story short, Armstrong tried to poison Martin, which raised suspicions, to say the least. Furthermore, Martin's father happened to be the local chemist, and he had suspicions of his own that everything was not as it seemed, mainly because he had previously sold some rather big bags of arsenic to none other than Armstrong.

And when Martin senior, in his capacity as the town chemist, happened to discuss his son's symptoms with Doctor Hincks, with whom he had close ties, Hincks identified several similarities between Martin junior's illness and that of the late Kitty Armstrong.

Much digging was done, some of it in the most literal sense, and after an exhumation and a somewhat belated post-mortem, it was formally suggested that Martin had, in fact, murdered his poor late wife, Kitty.

His claims of buying lots and lots of lovely arsenic from his local chemist just so he could solve a presumably quite serious dandelion problem were soon dismissed, especially after the local police constable was sent to count the dandelions in Armstrong's garden but had run out of things to count by the time he got to two. In no time at all, Armstrong found himself on trial in nearby Hereford, and after a lengthy court case that gained national notoriety, he was found to be as guilty as it was possible to be.

Sentenced to hang, which happened at Gloucester prison in May 1922, it was reported by the executioner, John Ellis, who you may remember also dispatched the famous Doctor Crippen, that just before his death, Armstrong cried out, *"Kitty, I'm coming to ya!"*

And incidentally, the executioner, Ellis, originally started out life as a hairdresser, but he clearly can't have been any good when you think about it, not if he ended up as an executioner.

We wandered around the town, just for a bit of a look around more than looking for anything in particular, and just around the corner from the castle, we discovered that Richard Booth's bookshop still very much exists.

Anyway, his bookshop is more than just that. It is also a cinema and events venue, as well as an artist's studio that also happens to sell books. It was incredibly busy and seemingly rather popular when we popped by, although there was no sign of the great man himself. This was a shame, though it did, of course, probably have something to do with the fact that he died in 2019. Still, it's worth a look inside just for the sheer quirkiness of the place.

Suddenly remembering I was incredibly hungry and conscious of the fact that it was probably too late for breakfast, we made our way to the Black Lion Inn before deciding almost immediately that it was too expensive, so we went to the Rose and Crown instead, which was closed.

Almost despairing as I wasted away literally in front of everyone's eyes, I checked my map and suggested we should head for Angie's, a small café I had heard about. Surprisingly, the charming ladies cooked us all an all-day breakfast, saying it wasn't too late after all, though whether it was a Welsh or English breakfast was never specified anywhere throughout the transaction. I dared not ask anyway because a huge sign across their window promised *"Teacakes and Insult's!"* although, to be honest, I did have quite a problem with the needless apostrophe towards the end of insults, though I dared not to mention that either.

In all actuality, I wanted neither teacakes nor insults, with or without a useless apostrophe, and I just wanted my bloody breakfast. I'm glad to say that my appetite had soon been very much obliged. I was a very happy man once again, although after I had finished eating, I made a new discovery in that I had apparently lost the ability to walk. This was not surprising, as although I was merely indulging in breakfast, albeit quite a large and late one, I did have a quick look at the menu while I was waiting, which offered such mysterious items as a cholesterol bomb and a coronary, which should serve to give you a good idea of what our meals had been like.

As our food settled, we had a decision to make, which was where to stay that evening. I had envisioned finding a small hotel or guest house but had come to the realisation soon after arriving in Hay-on-Wye that it was not a town for peasants.

Don't get me wrong. It's a very nice place, and in fact, it's lovely. However, wherever you go in the town, you will probably end up paying premium prices for everything. The idea of booking a bed for the night soon went out of the very expensive window. Luckily, a quick chat with Angie solved our problem, who fulfilled at least half of her windowed promises when she threw an insult at me regarding my chubby cheeks. She also told us of a campsite just over the bridge on the other side of the River Wye but added that judging by my current state, I probably wouldn't make it. At least she never threw a teacake at me.

We bade our new friends goodbye and told them we would probably be back one day when our bodies had finally digested our enormous meals, perhaps in three months or so. As a final parting gift, whenever I leave a restaurant, I always tell the people coming in, "*I recommend the squirrel*", and today was no exception, at which point the owner told us we should probably leave.

Waddling through the town like a flock of obese ducks with hangovers, I am sure we garnered at least some attention from tourists and locals alike, no doubt as they admired my new physique, especially around the waist, and as they also admired my unique way of carrying a backpack that no longer fitted, which was at an angle that almost defied gravity.

Luckily, we made it through the town and over the river and across the bridge, and after a short but significant fight with my rucksack, which I lost, by the way, we finally made it to our campsite, which was Radnor's End.

A few tents dotted the grass, along with a couple of motorhomes, which probably cost more than my house, and after a quick chat with the owner, we soon had our tents pitched. Rob had suggested that we put them away from all of the normal people, if you know what I mean, which was probably a good idea considering his snoring problem. James, Mark, and I once more insisted that Rob pitch his tent several yards away from us for the same reason, although, to be honest, it was such a short distance that it would probably not be far enough to make any difference.

I looked at my watch and figured it was maybe a little too early to go to sleep, so we brewed up some coffee and watched the world go by, which mainly involved watching new arrivals struggling to put up their tents, along with the occasional bird stopping by to say hello, one of which kindly pooped all over my tent.

We did our housekeeping, washed our clothes, and had another chat with the owner, who told us we had timed our trip perfectly. If we had come along a couple of days later, he said, we would not have been able to camp here. In fact, he said we probably wouldn't be able to camp anywhere within twenty miles, as the Hay Festival was due to start.

Thanking our lucky stars, we sat outside for a while, listening to some music and looking up at the actual stars on what was a clear and cloudless night. I was beginning to think our trip was blessed, apart from Rob almost breaking his ankle, James getting bitten by a dog, and me being chased into a river by a herd of cows, of course, but these things happen.

Eventually, I dozed off, though I was rudely awoken by Rob whispering something to James about whether or not he wanted any more lubricants for the sheep. I'm not sure where he learned to whisper, but I'm guessing it was inside a helicopter surrounded by chainsaws.

MAD DOGS AND ENGLISHMEN

Hay-on-Wye to Kington

Just think, every morning when you wake up, you break your own personal record for consecutive days lived. Every. Single. Day.

But what do they say about not counting your chickens before they've hatched? I very much enjoyed sitting outside last night and watching the stars for a while and had only ventured into my tent when I eventually began to feel the cold of the night. And as I climbed into my sleeping bag, I thought that the day had been perfect and that our trip really was blessed.

Well, I should have waited for a while, as in the early hours, I was awoken by the snapping of a twig right outside my tent, followed by the strange sounds of some type of animal.

I dismissed it all, however, and reminded myself that I was in Wales and not the Rocky

Mountains or deepest Siberia, so it was probably something harmless like a deer or perhaps a badger.

Unfortunately, presumably because of my little visit to a certain filming location yesterday, my subconscious mind told me it was a wolf, or possibly even a werewolf, so when I went back to sleep, I dreamt that it really was a monster, which woke me up once more, after which I struggled to get any sleep at all. Soon after this, Rob suddenly began to snore somewhere off to my left, though this did at least serve to scare off whichever monster had been schnaffling around outside.

And to top it off, a short while later, I began to hear the patter of rain upon the tarp of my tent, which slowly got louder and faster, which woke me up even more, and when it then started to get light, I knew that the game was up.

So, after probably getting only around four hours of sleep, I found myself packing away as much as I could from within my tent, which was easier said than done, as it was a tent of the tiny one-man variety, or woman if you so wish, and was therefore immensely small. Furthermore, I tried to pack my things into various plastic bags due to the ongoing rain outside, which now sounded like a downpour, after which I sat wondering how on earth I was going to get my tent dry during such a shower.

Luckily, rain always sounds much worse than

it actually is when you're in a tent. The same is true of caravans and conservatories and various other structures with things like metal roofs, and when I came outside, I discovered that the torrential downpour that I had heard from within was actually just a little shower.

Don't get me wrong, my tent was still wet, very wet, in fact, but the important thing was that we didn't get absolutely soaked as we packed our things away, which is what I had been concerned about.

Once packed. I strapped the tent to the bottom of my rucksack and figured I would have to stop and dry it out later, hopefully when the weather was a bit better, or if not, I would keep an eye out for a barn along the route where I might be able to hang it out for half an hour.

When we were all ready to go, I looked at the map and realised there were not many towns for quite some miles, so we decided to double back into Hay-on-Wye to grab some breakfast and a couple of drinks, where we ended up at a supermarket getting food we could eat on the go.

Before we moved off, though, I had to ask the guys to wait a moment while I made a call. Apparently, there had been some suspicious activity on my bank account, and my card had been blocked, which was not ideal when you were two hundred miles from home. The text message itself had annoyed me, as being the grammatical perfectionist that I am, its use of entirely lowercase letters had almost tipped me over the edge. Capital letters are incredibly important and are, in fact, the only thing that stands between helping your Uncle Jack off a horse and helping your uncle jack off a horse.

Autocorrect is not much better. It probably helps to imagine autocorrect as a tiny elf in your phone who is trying so hard to be helpful but is actually quite drunk and who, for some reason, thinks I want to say "*duck*" twelve times a day.

Anyway, the first hurdle was getting past the so-called security in the first place, which always leaves me puzzled. I have to do this whenever I ring up to pay my bill, which is odd. I mean, why do I have to prove who I am when I just want to pay my bill? Are random strangers ringing to pay my bills when I am not around? And if they are, why doesn't the bank just let them pay it? Perhaps the biggest joke on mankind, though, is that computers have started asking humans to prove they are not robots. And while we are talking about banks, why does it take 7-10 business days to refund my money when it took 5-9 seconds to take it out of my bank account?

Anyway, fifteen frustrating minutes later, we were ready to roll. I say roll because I really do need to get in shape. If I were murdered right now, my chalk outline would probably be a circle. I've always struggled to lose weight, though. Perhaps I would be more motivated if the weight I lost went to one of my enemies, of which I have many. And why is it that people cannot lose weight as easily as they lose their keys, pens, phone, temper and nowadays, their minds?

I even signed up for an exercise class once and was asked to wear loose-fitting clothing. If I had any loose-fitting clothing, I wouldn't have signed up to begin with. And while we are on the subject, it amazes me how exercise and extra fries sound so much alike.

In fairness, exercise does make you look better naked, but so does wine. Furthermore, a banana is 105 calories, and a shot of whiskey is 80 calories. Case closed.

And it is all probably pointless when you think about it. Eat right. Exercise regularly. Die anyway.

On top of that, my stomach is actually flat. The L is just silent.

With that little rant over, we were on our way and heading downstream, variously stuffing our fat little faces with a selection of lovely, sugar-infused pastries and the like. We wandered past a tree house, and while it looked great, I always think that a tree house is actually the biggest insult you can inflict on a tree. Here, I killed your friend. Hold him.

The path soon turned away from the River Wye, and I wondered if this would be the last time we would see what had become an old friend, having followed it and crossed it on and off since the beginning of this walk at Chepstow.

It wasn't quite the last time, however, as we saw it briefly about half a mile later after crossing some non-descript farmer's fields and joining an uncomfortably busy road that took us northeast for a quarter of a mile, after which a signpost graciously directed us left and down a much more pleasant and probably somewhat safer country lane.

That lane skirted a wood before it became a track and then a path. I enjoyed the late springtime birdsong in the trees above my head while a couple of rabbits darted across my way, seemingly startled by my presence despite the fact that the others were just a few yards ahead of me.

The path edged carefully along the side of a wood, where the birds were quite happy to keep me company, and I went slowly uphill, with the path dumping me unceremoniously and without warning on yet another tiny country lane where the little acorn directed me to the right.

My map told me we now had a mile or two of road walking to contend with, which continued to take us slowly uphill while the road narrowed as it did so. It was so narrow, in fact, that I nearly took a wrong turn into a farm, as their track was better than the actual road.

Fortunately, no traffic came until we crested the top of whatever hill this was, and we were lucky that this was the spot where we encountered a rather muddy tractor, as there was a small gap in the hedge. This meant we had around two inches of room in between some rather prickly plants where we could secrete ourselves while we were coated head to foot with the finest Welsh sludge available to man.

We carried on and eventually came to a junction where a sign pointed left towards Newchurch, which was our next destination, and which told me our road walking wasn't over yet. While it's nice to have variety when out and about walking, being on a road is not my preferred choice, as the tarmac can soon begin to pound against your feet, so I generally prefer being off-road, so to speak. Anyway, we turned left and followed the road as instructed, just as a postman drove past us from our front and gave us a little wave as he turned onto a farm track.

After a few hundred yards, however, I had my doubts about this road, and although I could not quite put my finger on why, I felt as if we had taken a wrong turn.

Indeed, upon checking the map, we really had gone the wrong way, as while we were heading for Newchurch, we should nonetheless have turned right at the last junction. As I was muttering unprintable words under my breath as we turned around and retraced our steps, somewhat bitter and angry about the extra mileage, the postman whom we had just seen emerged from the farm track and drove past us once again. I could see the puzzled look on his face as he no doubt wondered what these idiots were up to, wandering aimlessly up and down country lanes as we were. We didn't even get a wave this time.

A half a mile or so further on, we finally came to the junction where we really did have to turn left, but for a while, I wondered if we were actually on the right path. Passing a small cottage, I figured we probably were because I saw one of those lovely little acorns on a fingerpost, just after which, near a line of trees that hid a small stream, we crossed the border once more, this time from England into Wales, though there was no sign for that.

The path twisted and turned, still heading steadily uphill, and I almost missed another fingerpost directing us north down a tiny lane. To say this was muddy would be an understatement, and as I hopped along from one dry point to another, carefully dodging countless puddles which steadily grew larger and larger, I knew my luck would run out at some point. Ironically, it happened just as I neared the gate at the end of this bridleway, mere seconds before a nice, dry path. This was probably my own fault, I mused, as I had, of course, just been moaning about tarmac and had wished to be back on softer ground. Well, this was certainly softer ground, only it was wetter too, I thought to myself as I jumped across one last puddle that must have been five feet wide, confident that I could make it. I did, too, more or less, and made it approximately eighty percent of the way, but it was that last twenty percent that got me.

Splashing back onto the tarmac, I realised the water had at least washed some of the tractor mud off my shoes, and for a moment or two, I wondered why on earth I had chosen to do this walk in the springtime, when everything was so very wet.

I had pondered waiting until the summer to do it, but this week had been the only one when everyone had been free. Furthermore, at the time we had planned it, which had been over a pint in our local pub in front of a roaring fire, we had figured it would be fine. Someone had even said out loud, specifically, what was the worst thing that could happen?

Well, as it transpires, the worst thing that could happen was animal attacks, car crashes, getting covered in cow shit, losing yourself among the highways and byways of rural Wales, and then falling into the world's deepest puddle, apparently. And I'm not one to point fingers, but it was Rob who asked what the worst thing that could happen was.

I trudged on just as it started to rain again, but it was only very light. However, I still put my hat back on, as I didn't want to get any wetter than I already was, and while I could cope with damp feet and muddy trousers, I didn't want to get hyperthermia and die.

The others had disappeared off ahead of me once again, so as I trudged along in silence, enjoying the tranquillity of the countryside, I figured that the funny smell that I could smell must be me. Luckily, I quite enjoy my own company anyway. In fact, I can even be somewhat antisocial at times. For example, when people come up to me and say I look familiar, asking them if we were in the same prison together is usually enough to get rid of them.

This road, by the way, was another one that marked out the border between England and Wales, though I couldn't tell whether it ran down one of the sides or along the middle. This didn't matter for long anyway, as after a few more yards and a very pretty section where branches formed a nice little canopy above it, the road ran out and became a mere track.

Unfortunately, after even less yards this time, the track also ran out, and the path became merely a muddy field, at which point I felt like giving up altogether. Parts of it looked impassable, apart from some recent footprints hopefully left by my team-mates, and after checking my map and figuring that there was no real alternative that wouldn't involve a diversion of several muddy miles and a rather pissed-off Englishman, I carried on regardless and made a point of stomping through each and every puddle, just because I could.

My splashing plan worked, as the puddles eventually gave up, and the field became much more amenable, particularly after passing a farm, where the track became an actual track again, which meant only one thing, I must be near Newchurch.

I was not only heading for the village, but I was specifically heading for the thing in the name, basically the church, though I didn't really care if it was new or not. I had heard good things about this church, mainly that you could get a cup of tea or coffee there as well as a refill for your water bottles and other essential things. I was particularly hoping that I might be able to dry my tent there, as it was still hanging soggily off the back of my rucksack, and come to think of it, it was probably wetter now than when I had actually set off this morning, which meant it was also heavier, of course.

The track spat me out right in the centre of the village and more or less next to the church, and I wasted no time in heading up the steps and straight past the sign promising me it was open, genuinely hoping that it really was and that the sign hadn't simply been left there at the end of last summer, which it looked like it had, to be honest. And almost on cue, the sun came out.

Luckily, the door swung open, meaning I didn't have to break it down, which quite frankly had been plan B, and I ventured into the darkened interior, which was only darkened while my eyes slowly adjusted. I was delighted to find my fellow adventurers already inside with the kettle half-boiled.

While I waited for the kettle to finish, I removed my tent from its bag and took it outside to hang on the porch, and then spent the next twenty minutes enjoying a coffee and rubbing my sore, wet feet, which had been pounded by tarmac today, apparently, at least according to the throbbing I could currently feel. I also found a small stone which had been painted by someone who was quite artistic, and while he wasn't looking, I popped it into James' bag. I'm not sure why I did this, but perhaps it's because I'm a bit of an idiot. Anyway, I was sure he would appreciate the extra weight.

A few people turned up whilst we were there, the first one being an incredibly old and odd-looking hobbit type. I know they say that people who live in glass houses shouldn't throw stones and that I myself am not perhaps the most normal person in the world, but this guy really would have looked right at home in Middle Earth.

He was very friendly, and he told us he was also walking the Dyke, though he was doing it the wrong way, north to south. He had been on the go for roundabout two weeks, he went on, so he was certainly taking it steady, but then he could, because he said he was a retired teacher, which probably explained his odd looks. I wanted to mention to him that because he was really old, he should perhaps concentrate on finishing it sooner rather than later, but I feared that if I did, he would probably put a curse or a spell on me, so I kept schtum.

Have you ever looked at someone and thought that the wheel was turning, but the hamster was dead? Well, that was this guy. There was just something odd about him, and as I tried to engage in conversation, he certainly seemed to listen. He nodded at all the right times, too, but when he replied, he had seemingly changed the subject to something completely different and wholly random. He did this on several occasions, so in the end, I simply gave up on the conversation. Trying to understand the behaviour of some people is like trying to smell the colour 9.

When we told him we were heading in the opposite direction and aiming to finish the walk in ten days, his smile turned into a laugh, but it was more of a laugh of pity, in my mind anyway, though it also suggested an air of superiority. Sometimes, you meet someone, and you immediately realise that you want to spend the whole of your life without them.

Next came a couple of elderly ladies, all the way from New Zealand, though they were not walking along the dyke as such. They told us they were doing a road trip instead and were revisiting some of the places they had passed through when they did the walk way back in the 1970s, before they had emigrated. I will be honest, after dealing with the little hobbit, I probably was not best equipped for another conversation, and I did not listen to much of what they said. I can be quite inattentive at times, you see, and usually concentrate on other things, though, in fairness, this is mainly in meetings at work, where I am often asked to take notes. By the time anyone says anything worth writing down, I've already taken my pen apart and lost the spring. Even when I am paying attention, things tend to go wrong. At a recent safety meeting just before this trip, I was asked, *"What steps would you take in a fire?"* Bloody big ones was the wrong answer, apparently.

Anyway, they were very nice, though they were a bit loud and more than a little bit fussy. Whether or not they were actually on speed or some other drug, it is hard to say. I definitely found them quite overwhelming, however, and possibly a little bit mad, although eccentric is perhaps a more polite way of describing them. Maybe I am just a crazy magnet, I thought to myself, but I was definitely starting to believe that, for these people at least, the wheels on the bus do not go round and round, which meant that it was time to leave.

I should confess that if I have given the impression that I am normal myself, I might have exaggerated slightly. For instance, I tend to tell people different stories about my life, so when they get together and gossip about me, they end up arguing. And whenever someone asks what I did over the weekend, I squint and say, *"Why, what did you hear?"* Not surprisingly, some people call me crazy. I prefer the term *happy, but with a twist*. In reality, it is probably just a matter of time before they add *"syndrome"* after my last name. And if I really had to describe myself, I would have to say I am a free spirit, but only because it sounds better than out-of-control nutjob.

Anyway, we told them that because of the sheer volume of traffic, we were vacating the church to give them a chance to enjoy it, so we tidied up our mess and moved on, bidding all the lunatics goodbye and good luck.

Unfortunately, my tent had not dried as planned, certainly not in the half hour or so we spent here. In fact, it now seemed even harder to repack it for what was the second time today, though this might have been because I was merely a beaten shadow of my former self, and if I am being completely honest, I was on the verge of throwing the towel in.

I managed to squeeze it back in, though, and after saying goodbye to the church and leaving our thanks in the form of some loose change in the donation box, we moved on, which meant heading up the seemingly giant-looking Disgwylfa Hill behind the village, which was about as difficult to climb as it was to pronounce, at least for a simple Englishman such as myself.

I sighed to myself at my own apparent foolishness in thinking I could do this walk, but nonetheless set off behind the others with one foot in front of the other, simply looking at the ground and trying to concentrate purely on the next step, as opposed to the next ten thousand of them.

I sometimes find this helps me keep moving when I really don't want to, and today, I really didn't want to. I had briefly considered bedding down in the church until tomorrow, purely and simply because I was shattered, but had quickly rubbished the idea, and anyway, Rob, Mark and James seemed to be full of beans and ready to go on indefinitely. Halfway up this hill, however, I found myself wishing I really had stayed down there after all.

A farm track took us only so far, after which it gave way to a muddy path that led up and across a field, but it was at least considerably drier than some of the paths I had been on earlier. The rain was holding off, and a gentle breeze was actually helping to dry me, or at least my outer layers, which had, until now, remained damp all day.

I didn't realise how high we had climbed until I realised I was at the top, and I was pleasantly surprised when I also realised it had not taken that long to get up after all. After enjoying the view for a moment or two, I carried on along my way, far behind the others, but nonetheless, I suddenly felt wholly reinvigorated. Perhaps the caffeine was kicking in.

When the route took on a decidedly downhill nature, I felt even better, and then, to top it all off, the sun came out, and, for the first time today, I actually felt rather warm.

Crossing a couple of minor roads, the going stayed good, with the ground underfoot firm and solid, and there were more signs of sheep, though most of those signs consisted of piles of poop.

As I caught up with the others at the next road, we decided to take advantage of the sunshine. We stopped next to a metal gate where we all hung our tents haphazardly here and there in one final attempt at drying them.

We chatted about our progress while we waited, and the intense sunshine certainly seemed to do its job. After turning the canvas over every few minutes, mine soon felt completely dry. As a result, I found it much easier to pack, and there was a bonus because it also felt a little lighter.

Unfortunately, while we still had everything out, an elderly couple turned up. I think they thought we were going to camp here, as they suggested a much nicer spot a little further on, one which was away from the road. We must have looked funny because when I told them we had merely been drying our gear out, they simply laughed and moved on.

A short while later, we were once again setting off on our merry way, following our couple of lengthy but much-needed stops. As a result, I definitely felt one hundred percent better, and my pack really did feel ever so slightly lighter. This might have been psychological, however, as I don't really think a wet tent would weigh all that much more than a dry one.

With a new spring in my step, I tackled the next few ups and downs with absolute abandon, though I was, as always, still behind the others. In no time at all, we were heading down into Gladestry along a hedge-lined lane of the type that kills hikers when any kind of vehicle comes the other way, which, of course, was something that happened almost as soon as I got to the bit where there was absolutely, positively, nowhere to hide.

It was a truck too, a fairly big one that presumably belonged to one supermarket or another, and while the driver did his best to slow down upon seeing me, he was still going uncomfortably quickly, so I secreted myself into the hedge in a manner that you might expect would typically see you end up in Narnia.

When that danger had passed, I emerged back onto the road and waited for the noise of the engine to die down so that I could check if any other vehicles were coming. There was no point in moving on if there was anything coming, as the stretch ahead looked even narrower, but as a hushed silence descended all around me, I decided it was safe to continue.

When the hedges receded a little, I enjoyed occasional glimpses of a uniquely double-humped hill to my right and spent a second or two admiring it until it almost immediately dawned on me that I would probably soon find myself scrambling up its forbidding slopes.

Thankfully, no other vehicles came, and I soon caught sight of houses that signalled my imminent arrival in Gladestry, which was welcomed if for no other reason than I now had paths to walk on rather than bushes to hide in when traffic came.

There was not a lot to Gladestry other than a pub, but then what more do you need. The others had waited for me on a bench, and while we were tempted to stop and support the local economy, time was getting on. Anyway, we were all eager to destroy our legs by climbing up the hill that I had just seen, which was called Yewtree Bank and which now sat right in front of us, taunting us to come and have a go if we thought we were hard enough.

A sign soon led us onto a minor road, which inevitably took us up what were the beginnings of the hill, and for a few hundred yards, we enjoyed walking beneath a canopy of trees before emerging at a junction where we actually had a choice of routes.

The Offa's Dyke path, a sign kindly informed us, led left and up the hill, presumably Yewtree Hill, while a different option also tempted me.

Offa's Orchard was a mere 150 yards ahead of us, which called me for two reasons. The first was that the distance really was given in yards, and because I am an old dinosaur, it is my preferred unit of measurement. Metres, on the other hand, make me confused and unable to guess how far away something is, as do kilometres, because my mind works in miles, I am afraid.

Anyway, the second reason was that the orchard was not one for apples but for people. Offa's Orchard, you see, is a green burial ground where you can plonk yourself in the earth at the end of your ever-so-exciting life and revert back to nature, so to speak.

So the temptation to give up on Yewtree Hill and to go and lay in a nice warm hole in the ground was actually quite an attractive one.

Unfortunately, this would probably cause more problems than it solved and would certainly annoy my wife, so with at least some reluctance, I followed the others up the hill after all and began my slow and steady ascent, with the emphasis being most definitely on slow. However, I could quite easily have stopped there, as the plans for my ultimate death are already worryingly advanced, thanks in part to my wonderful wife.

At my funeral, you see, which will probably be

a cremation, I want someone to take the bouquet off my coffin and throw it into the crowd to see who is next. Afterwards, I'm going to get Rob to grab my phone and text everyone, *"Thanks for coming".* Oh, and right before I die, I'm going to swallow a bag of popcorn kernels just to make things interesting.

The lane followed a line of trees which sheltered me from a stiff breeze, and after having an argument with a gate half a mile later that seemed reluctant to open, which was creatively solved by myself with just a hint of vandalism, I soon left the trees behind. I emerged onto the final climb that would take me to the top of Hergest Ridge, where I discovered that Rob, James and Mark were now variously off ahead of me, but not considerably so, which at least gave me the motivation to keep on going. That kind of motivation can be dangerous, however. Think about it. Every single corpse found on Mount Everest was once a highly motivated individual. Stay lazy, my friends.

Hergest ridge, which, when correctly pronounced, rhymes with *hardest*, is actually home to some spooky goings-on. A ghost has been spotted on its slopes on several occasions, which is said to be the restless spirit of Sir Thomas Vaughan, who was killed at the Battle of Banbury in 1469. And if that wasn't enough to get you a bit unsettled, perhaps the Black Dog of Hergest will. If you are lucky enough to see it, then you should probably get your affairs in order pretty sharpish, as any sighting of the beast is said to foretell a swift and gruesome death. This news made me once again ponder my decision not to stop at Offa's Orchard and made me wonder if I would, in fact, end up there anyway.

Apparently, the beast is also the inspiration for the Sherlock Holmes story *The Hound of the Baskervilles*, which came about when Sir Arthur Conan Doyle stayed at Hergest Court, an impressive Tudor framed timber manor house on the outskirts of Kington, our next stop, shortly before he put pen to paper on perhaps his most disturbing masterpiece ever.

In fact, there is also reason to believe that the stories of Vaughan and the beastly dog may actually be linked. When I said that Vaughan died at the battle, it turned out that he was actually beheaded at Banbury just after the end of the fighting by forces loyal to the evil Earl of Warwick.

His headless body was then brought back to Kington and buried in Saint Mary's Church, after which a strangeness like no other was said to have taken over the town and the surrounding hills. Black Vaughan, as he was now known, possibly because he was not exactly the nicest man on earth, was said to have taken many forms, the most obvious being the black dog, but he also took the form of a fly that annoyed horses, which is as strange an incarnation of a ghost as I have ever heard of.

He also appeared in the form of a black bull that ran amok in the church, scaring the parishioners. However, as far as I am concerned, the only bull in this story is the story itself, if you know what I mean.

Anyway, Black Vaughan, which I have to admit is a much better name than Sir Thomas, now rests for all eternity in Saint Mary's, as mentioned earlier, and he is laid to rest right next to his wife in a rather fancy and elaborately carved tomb which must have cost a tidy sum of money, even back then. And at his feet, incidentally, lies his faithful dog.

His wife, Ellen, is also of some interest, as her nickname was *Terrible Helen*, and by the sounds of it, this was a reputation well-deserved. Following the death of her brother, who was said to have died at the hands of their own cousin, she cold-bloodedly fired an arrow at point-blank range into said cousin, and for him, that was the end of that.

And as for the dog in question, Sir Thomas is said to have really and actually owned his own pooch, which he looked after better than his family, apparently, and it even had its own room at the top of the house. This dog is known as the *Black Dog of Hergest Court*, which was the Vaughan family home. As we have heard, it is supposedly the one where Conan Doyle spent some time and where he perhaps got the idea for his beastly hound. While there, it is probable that he was also introduced to or at least heard of the Baskerville family from nearby Eardisley, which implies some truth in the possibility of this particular origin story being true, although, without a time machine, I am afraid we will probably never really know for sure.

In its more recent history, Kington served a somewhat surprising role in the Second World War, and in particular, the evacuation of Dunkirk. I say surprising because the town is nowhere near either the sea or France, at least not when I last checked.

Just on the outskirts of the town, in fact, just beyond Hergest Court, the War Office built what later became known as Kington Camp. In June 1940, the camp suddenly found itself full of thousands of troops after they had been evacuated from the continent in what has since become known as one of the most significant rescue operations ever, one which Winston Churchill memorably called a *miracle of deliverance*.

Later on in the war, the Americans arrived and built two giant hospitals here in anticipation of the mass casualties that the 1944 invasion of France would inevitably incur. As well as hospitals, the Americans also threw up chapels, barracks, cinemas and warehouses, much of which survives today in the form of, wait for it, an industrial estate.

As all this ran through my mind, I put myself into some kind of standby mode as I negotiated each step upwards and onwards, though I did stop halfway up to enjoy the spectacular views behind me. To be honest, the stop had more to do with getting my breath back than enjoying the views, and when I felt my heartbeat slow down to a mere 300 beats per minute, I carried on along my way.

Spectacular is a much-overused word, particularly along this path, but the views really had been consistently good since day one, and just when you thought they couldn't get any better, boom, they got better.

This was the case for Hergest Ridge, and once at the top, the panorama went in all directions, for while I had been expecting a ridge as such, Hergest had more of a flat top, if you know what I mean. The path was great too, a spongy layer of the finest grasses, kept short by a wandering tribe of ponies or donkeys, although, to be honest, I cannot tell a horse from an ass, which anyone who knows me will know is true simply by looking at my circle of friends.

Years ago, those crazy Victorians would come up here for a bit of horse racing, and they built a full-sized racecourse that ran up and across the ridge, which can still be seen today. The horses of today, however, were not at all interested in racing, and in fact, they weren't all that interested in me as I passed by, which pleased me immensely and meant I would not have to run away shrieking like a banshee when one of them approached me.

I had been consistently behind the others, and I had presumed they had just carried on until, ahead of me, I saw a small copse of trees. I could see tiny figures sitting on a bench, but their profiles seemed to match that of my friends, as I could clearly see that one of them was bald whilst another had ginger hair, and the last had a beard. In my mind, however, I saw three monkeys, one with their hands over their eyes, one their ears, and the other covering their mouth, which suggests I was perhaps dehydrated or had inadvertently ingested some magic mushrooms. Also, surprisingly, the trees turned out to be monkey puzzle trees.

Rob had the kettle on and offered me a choice of coffee or soup as I collapsed into their neat little camp, so I naturally went for the coffee. Perhaps it would give me the energy I needed to go on, I pondered, though I did make sure it wasn't decaffeinated first. Decaffeinated coffee is like a hooker who only wants to cuddle. I mean, what's the point?

I sat and enjoyed the calm of the day and could feel my calf muscles almost throbbing after the torment of the latest climb. We talked about the walk so far and how it had been more challenging than we had imagined, particularly for me and Rob. James and Mark, though admittedly finding it somewhat challenging, were nonetheless faring far better than us oldies.

Luckily, there was no more uphill, for today at least, and as we moved on and began the long descent into Kington, I could feel my legs using different muscles on the way down, which was a welcome relief.

Unfortunately, the way down was as long as the way up had been, and by the time we got to the gate, which presumably marked the end of the common land and which kept the horses from going on a bit of a shopping trip into Kington, my calves were once again just as painful as before, though in a slightly different way.

The gate also meant we would be hobbling along on tarmac now, something which didn't exactly thrill me with joy. However, the prospect of walking into a town where I could buy some greasy and incredibly unhealthy junk food filled me with absolute delight, as did the thought of following said greasy infusion with some kind of diabetes-inducing sugar rush, and to hell with the consequences. I mean, why be healthy? All you're doing if you're healthy is dying as slowly as possible.

A sign soon welcomed us into Kington, declaring it the centre for walking apparently, after which some incredibly considerate drivers had done their best to block the entire road by parking in apparently random patterns and in all directions, presumably to stop those pesky horses from invading the town.

I navigated my way between these cars, being ever so careful not to accidentally bash them with my walking poles or to inadvertently remove any wing mirrors by repeatedly kicking them with a booted foot that had walked more miles than I cared to think about.

Almost immediately after this randomised parking, we came across an oasis of absolute calmness as we arrived at the welcome distraction of Hergest Gardens, where we took the welcome opportunity to rest our weary legs.

Luckily, the garden was free to enter, as otherwise, we would have been scaling fences and digging tunnels to get in. I'm not the type of person who pays to go in gardens, you see, mainly because I still have a pulse and don't yet qualify to live in some kind of care home. Judging by the cohort of people wandering around the garden today, all of whom were using either walking sticks, zimmer frames or even wheelchairs, I suspected there were a lot of folks here on day release, if you know what I mean. This probably also explained the terribly parked cars on the lane outside, many of which now coincidentally and quite mysteriously sported numerous dents and scratches, as well as an odd number of wing mirrors, with that odd number generally being one.

I must admit that the garden was exquisitely kept and very beautiful, if you like that sort of thing, but I still wouldn't have paid to get in. Maybe that's something that will come as I get older, and perhaps in twenty years or so, I will be more than willing to part with my precious pounds to see such fanciful flora. In fact, because this garden was free to enter, it did beg one question. How on earth did it manage to stay open, as the upkeep must cost a fortune?

Fortunately, this eternal and enduring mystery was solved soon enough as we all stumbled into the small café. I had desperately needed some food and grabbed myself a cup of tea, a sandwich and a rather nice-looking, calorie-laden giant slab of cake. Come to think of it, it might have been a whole cake.

Unfortunately, I also had to grab myself a mortgage to pay for it all. I failed to look at the prices beforehand, mainly because I was still in pain from today's long walk but also because I was on the verge of starvation, though fortunately for me, the risk of actually dying of starvation receded completely when I got the bill, replaced by a sudden and imminent danger of death from a heart attack induced solely and entirely by the prices of the items I had just invested in.

Of course, being English and polite and all that, I said nothing about the considerable shock and trauma I had suffered when I realised how much I had been charged for what was essentially a snack, but determined to get my money's worth, I may or may not have stolen extra sugar from the vast array of condiments on offer to whatever oldies generally frequent this place.

I certainly got my money's worth, too, and ate every last speck and morsel of my food, and when a small bird landed at my table and gave me a quizzical but cute look, a quick *meow* was all it took to get rid of it, as this food was far too expensive for a mere white sparrow to munch on, no matter how rare and endangered he may be.

Unfortunately, my over-priced food did not even come close to filling me up, so after stealing some more sugar and after considering then dismissing the thought of also taking my table and chairs, mainly because I couldn't carry them, I moved on. Technically, this would not have been theft. I had paid so much for my food that, in my mind at least, I had also paid for the furniture.

I hadn't even been sure what country we were in, but it turns out that Kington is in England, and therefore, we had been ripped off by our own brethren. Still, it's a lovely place to be robbed, even if it is by your own countrymen. In fact, anyone walking Offa's Dyke path is sure to be very happy indeed with their arrival in Kington, a pleasant little English market town situated just a mile or two east of the Welsh border in the beautiful county of Herefordshire.

And I learned that a very long time ago, it was known as *Chingtune*, a strangely satisfying name that the town would do well to start using again, in my opinion anyway, not that anybody listens to me.

Heading into town, the first thing we passed was the church, Saint Mary's, so we popped in to pay our respects to Sir Thomas Vaughan, whom you may remember is interred here with his crazy, murderous wife deep within a fine alabaster tomb. It was very impressive and must have cost a pretty penny, so it is perhaps a shame that he was apparently buried without his head, which had probably been left somewhere in Banbury when it fell off.

We moved on, heading further into town, and we all had accommodation firmly on our minds as we had done enough walking today and simply wanted to lay down and sleep. Furthermore, the weather forecast suggested that several million gallons of water would soon be falling from the sky, so camping was out of the question.

I thought we were in luck when I discovered that Kington had a youth hostel, but unless I was willing to pay over four hundred pounds and hire out the entire building for the night for my sole use, this was never going to be an option, not that it would have been, as unbeknown to me, the hostel had actually closed months before. So much for the centre of walking, I thought to myself.

I have stayed at many youth hostels in my time, so I was pretty sad when I discovered that there is not actually a single one of them serving Offa's Dyke, though there is one near Newcastle at a place called Clun, approximately three miles off the track, which I made a mental note of for later.

Not having much luck with finding somewhere to stay, not at a reasonable price anyway, our thoughts turned to food, as we all agreed that our previous snacks back at the garden centre had totally failed to hit the spot.

There was certainly a lot more choice in this regard, with the Royal Oak, the Swan and the Oxford Arms all vying for our attention with signs offering home-cooked food and fine ales available from dawn till dusk.

Alas, it was the Royal Oak that won. We variously enjoyed whopping great big plates of fish and chips or steak and ale pies while some of the locals enjoyed a whopping great quiz which was apparently raising money for lifeboats, which was a bit odd so far from the sea. They also offered rooms at reasonable prices, a sign said, but when I checked, they clearly failed to understand the meaning of the word reasonable.

I should have had a go at the quiz myself, as I knew the answers to at least ten percent of the questions that came up, so I might well have come in last place had I done so. Unfortunately, we were just too late to the party, so as it was, we simply ate our food, charged our phones, and enjoyed our pints.

At some point, we got talking to the people at the next table after they had asked me if we were enjoying our walk, and I guessed our rucksacks, muddy boots, and walking poles were a bit of a giveaway. I told them that I was enjoying my dinner more, and it turned out that this particular quiz team were also avid walkers and had done the walk themselves just a couple of years before. They had had the added advantage, they said, of various members of their group living up and down the Wye Valley, with a couple also living a little further north, so had been able to enjoy things like comfortable nights at one another's houses where they could wash and sleep and the like as well as poo in a proper toilet. We, on the other hand, explained our predicament about tonight's accommodation, or lack thereof, and were delighted with the news that one of them gave us next.

Apparently, the youth hostel was no longer what it said on the box, and the information on their website about having to rent the entire building was all poppycock and balderdash. Soon enough, a phone number was provided, and after a quick chat with the new owner, Rachel, who told me it was now a private hostel, I had secured a room for four smelly men, and off we went. However, before we shuffled off, I should mention that one way to find out if you are old is to fall down in front of a lot of people. If they laugh, you are young, and if they panic and run to you, you're old. They panicked and ran to me.

The hostel was paradise. Comfy beds, a huge kitchen and dining room, and, to top it off, flushable toilets. What more could a bunch of stinky blokes want or need? I did, however, have one brief moment of absolute, sheer horror. Let's just say the most terrifying moment in life is when the toilet refuses to flush at someone else's house.

The priority was the shower, obviously, so we took turns using the two that were available to us, and we were soon slightly less smelly, if not actually clean. We explored the building like giddy school kids, which had originally been a hospital, by the way, and in the dining room, we found a map of Offa's Dyke, and discovered that we were almost, but not quite, halfway along. By the looks of it, we would probably get to the halfway point tomorrow, which, if I remembered correctly, was somewhere near Knighton, the next town along, which confused me immensely, sounding so similar to Kington as it did.

We quizzed Rachel's local knowledge, and as a result, we were soon a few yards up the road at a homely little pub called Ye Olde Tavern, which was indeed both old and a tavern, enjoying one last beer and making friends with Ralph, an octogenarian dog, in doggy years anyway. I think he was after my pint, but the only thing he got from me was a good belly rub, and in return, he was equally generous, happily sharing his fleas with me, or at least some of them. Not to worry, they wouldn't last long, not on a smelly hiker.

We had one last little treat, too, when a dozen or so Morris dancers turned up on the street outside and started performing some jingly moves to the delight of everyone. Apparently, it's making something of a comeback. As we went outside to watch, pint glasses in hand and enjoying the last of the evening sunshine, I thought to myself that it didn't get much more English than this, but then it actually did, because it started to rain.

BELLS AND BALLS

Kington to Knighton

The sleep I had in that hostel last night was possibly some of the best sleep I had had in the previous twenty-four hours. Strange sounds awoke me every now and then, alternating between the constant snoring and occasional farting of a bunch of smelly hikers, though I should confess that some of it was probably my own. Other than that, it was great, and I was probably asleep for a good percentage of the night. Eleven percent, perhaps, maybe even twelve.

The sound of the early morning traffic outside was not unbearable either, and it only woke me at the absolute crack of dawn, but every cloud has a silver lining, as we were ready to go by 7am, even if we were all in something of a foul mood. Oh, and did I mention that it was raining? Not just normal rain either, but more of a downpour.

I was still aching this morning, as well. While I really don't mind getting older, my body is certainly taking it badly. One minute, you're young and fun. The next, you're turning down your car stereo so you can see better. In fact, the older I get, the less surprised I would be if some random part just fell off one day. I am making efforts, though. I did a push-up this morning. Well, actually, I fell down and had to use my arms to get back up, which was close enough. I sometimes wonder if all this is happening because I didn't forward that email to ten people.

Anyway, every day is a gift, apparently. So far, however, today was socks.

The first thing we did was wander back into the town centre, hoping to find a sandwich shop open at this unearthly hour, but our efforts were in vain. We did, however, manage to find a supermarket, and in fact, we found a couple. After a quick look in both, I managed to get myself something of a breakfast in the form of a sandwich and some milk, which was better than nothing but was not quite a bacon and egg McMuffin, if you know what I mean. Rob copied me, while James went for something more civilised in the form of a pain au chocolat, as did Mark.

We sat in a shelter in the car park, munching on our early morning feast and enjoying every single scrap of it. Once I had chugged the last of my milk, I took advantage of the toilet facilities, as did we all, before heading off once more through Kington, though this time it was definitely for the last time.

According to my map, we were only 66 miles into this walk, though it felt like much further, and while we were in no rush, I knew for sure we were not going to set any records for walking Offa's Dyke Path, other than perhaps the one for the longest time taken to do it and most idiots walking it at once.

We left Kington for the very last time after crossing a narrow wooden bridge over Back Brook and emerged at what was presumably the town's bypass. It was probably the height of the rush hour now, though I should point out that Kington is kind of in the middle of nowhere, so after all three cars had gone by, we crossed the road en masse at our most leisurely pace, confident that all of the day's cars had now gone past. Unfortunately, there should have been four cars today, not three, apparently. A BMW came screaming around the bend from our left and almost managed to nip my heels as I scurried across the road, what with me being the last one, as usual. I just managed to get myself to safety at a sign that thanked me for visiting the place, which I thought was a really nice touch and which had probably been put there by the lovely people of Knighton, sorry, Kington, especially for me.

I stopped for a moment to get my breath back and to give the BMW driver my verdict on his driving technique by using a unique but intriguing combination of my middle fingers, and then immediately ran up the hill to catch up with the others when I saw his brake lights come on.

I don't think he was stopping because of me, though. He probably just realised he was heading straight into the bushes at the next bend because of his speed, but you never know.

The hill we found ourselves going up was uncomfortably steep for a chubby little Englishman with a full stomach who was in a bad mood at such an early hour in the day. I had to stop and wipe my brow once or twice in an ever-so-dramatic fashion that I imagined made me look like Lawrence of Arabia but, in reality, probably made me look like a chubby little Englishman with a full stomach who was in a bad mood.

Onwards and upwards I went, still behind my somewhat fitter friends for what seemed like an eternity, but in reality was probably less than half a mile, and at the top, I was forced to stop when the path ended at a small cottage. After having a very rude wander into the garden of whoever lived there, I realised my mistake and made my way around the side of the house instead, where I found a track heading further uphill. Luckily, nobody was there to witness my ignorance.

The track was firm underfoot but uncomfortably steep once more, and I made slow progress for the next twenty minutes or so until I finally emerged into the open just after a small collection of houses that apparently formed the hamlet of Bradnor Green, which lived up to its name because of all the fields and trees, which were indeed mainly green. Rob, James and Mark were waiting for me here, and Rob magically produced a bag of sugary but surprisingly sour sweets, which momentarily confused my taste buds.

For the next half a mile or so, we risked life and limb, as on the hill in front of us was Kington Golf Club, home of golferists galore. I don't mind golf as such, although I cannot understand the attraction of whacking a ball as far as the eye can see, but each to their own. Anyway, I expect golferists probably say the same about us walkerists and wonder silently or perhaps even occasionally loudly as to what on earth is the point of walking miles and miles if you are not going to whack a ball as far as the eye can see.

Anyway, as I said, it's not the game that is the problem per se. It is the possibility of dying. On more than one occasion in the not-so-distant past, I have crossed golf courses only to find myself uncomfortably close to incoming projectiles that seem to have the accuracy of cruise missiles and apparently target chubby old men in hiking boots.

Anyway, just before the golf course, just on our right and behind a small row of cottages, was a house called The Beacon, which itself has something of a fascinating history to tell. Had you popped by in the early 1970s, then you may well have heard the sound of keyboards and drums, and in particular, guitars, for this was another little place, similar to Rockfield Farm, where a musician decided to hole up and concentrate on his life's work.

This time, the artist in question was Mike Oldfield, him of *Tubular Bells* fame, a song which pretty much surprised everyone when it rocketed straight to the top of the charts back in May of 1973. This was surprising for two reasons, the first being that Oldfield was relatively unknown at the time. What was more surprising, however, was that it was the first album released by a new and obscure record label that nobody had ever heard of but was called Virgin Records and which went on to become something of a big banana itself. In fact, it was because of Tubular Bells that Virgin Records even came into being, as its founder, Richard Branson, who was also then relatively unknown and, it should be said, somewhat skint, had been unable to find a record label willing to release Oldfield's new but risqué sounds to the world at large, so he simply started his own and did it himself.

And it's a good job he did, as it went on to become one of the biggest-selling albums of the decade and was even the soundtrack to the movie *The Exorcist* due to its unusual and, if you pardon the pun, rather haunting introduction, a movie which incidentally scared the bejeezus out of me even more than *An American Werewolf in London* did a few years later.

Back to Oldfield, though, and it is also worth mentioning that he was heavily influenced by the beautiful hills and valleys in this part of the country, so much so that his next album was called *Hergest Ridge*, and bizarrely, it was this album that paved the way for *Tubular Bells* to become so successful. Upon its initial release, Bells never actually reached the number one top spot, but when Oldfield released *Hergest Ridge*, which went straight to number one, it reinvigorated sales of Oldfield's first album.

In fact, it was actually *Tubular Bells* which knocked *Hergest Ridge* off the top spot in October 1974, cementing Oldfield's place in chart history forevermore and making him one of a select club of very few artists who have managed to overtake themselves in the charts in such a manner. And it all began here, in the humble hills of Herefordshire. I'm not exactly a superfan of Mike Oldfield, although I do enjoy his work from time to time, and I can state that while I don't always listen to *Tubular Bells*, when I do, so do my neighbours.

And finally, it is probably worth mentioning how Oldfield ended up here in the first place. As already mentioned, Bells never achieved number one following its initial release, but it was still very successful. This unexpected and somewhat instant fame threw Oldfield out of kilter, so to speak, and caused him to give up on the idea of touring and to come and hide out here instead, far away from the press. And in all honesty, he couldn't have picked a more beautiful spot, as it is absolutely perfect, or at least it would be if it wasn't for all the bloody golferists.

We somehow made it to the other side without being pummelled to death in the head by lumps of heavy rubber encased in hard white plastic, mainly because we stuck together as a foursome for this stretch of the path. Soon enough, we found ourselves following a very prominent stretch of the actual Offa's Dyke as we turned left to follow the path around a couple of prominent hills, Rushock Hill and Herrock Hill, and we were more than happy to see our old friend once again. The sheep seemed to like it too, variously munching, sleeping and shitting atop the priceless, historic mound, and I wondered how much longer the dyke would last, as it already looked to have lost most of its height hereabouts.

We followed the path around these hills, which thankfully traced the contours rather than trying to ascend them, and emerged onto a road devoid of everything other than a squashed squirrel who looked to be doing some form of yoga, after which we passed almost immediately back into Wales, where a sign welcomed us to Powys.

This road was lined with hedges once again but was thankfully wide, meaning we didn't have to secrete ourselves into it when the inevitable bus came along almost immediately. It must have been a school bus, judging by the small child who gave me an interesting two-fingered salute as they passed, so I did the only thing I could and returned the compliment. I can be childish like that.

The road looked to be heading towards a forest, as indeed it was, and in no time at all, we were leaving the main road behind us and heading onwards and upwards towards the lofty heights of Burfa Wood.

After that, a long straight stretch followed what looked like another section of the dyke, but this was overgrown, though thankfully, because it was still so early in the year, the plants had not yet had the chance to hide it entirely.

Next came a few miles of trance-like walking, which involved some pointless ups and downs, although the views off to the hills in the north were outstanding.

I finally emerged out of my trance and found myself alone as I crossed a small wooden bridge just near Dolley Green, where I had to briefly contend with a busy main road. This was only for a hundred yards or so, whereupon I turned back on myself, sort of, and headed up yet another hill. Unfortunately, this time, the path took me almost to the very top of the hill, which was Hawthorn Hill, and which, at around 1,200 feet high, did not exactly enthral me, though I did catch up with Rob, James and Mark.

Whilst at the top, we took the opportunity to remove our backpacks and enjoy the view, but I also took my shoes off to get some air to my feet, which almost caused the others to flee for their lives. It was as I peeled my sock off that I realised I had a massive blister on the heel of my right foot, which was odd because I had not felt a thing.

After airing it for a while and making sure it was well and truly dry, I applied a blister plaster to it, holding it in place for a while to give it the best chance of sticking, after which we moved on.

One final hill stood in our way before Knighton, which momentarily confused me when I thought I was back at Kington for a minute, and I wondered why they had put the two so close together. I realised it must be a different place, though, when we had to skirt yet another bloody golf course on our way into the town, though this time, the path was luckily sheltered by a protective screen of trees.

Knighton is a cross-border town that sits a few miles north of its dyslexic namesake and derives its name, not surprisingly, from *Knight's Town,* which suggests that Kington must have come from *King's Town.* Most of it lies within Wales, but if you want to catch a train from here, you will need to cross both a river and a border, though luckily a bridge takes care of things, as the train station is over in England across the both of them.

Not that you will want to leave, however, as it really is a little gem of a town with everything you might need and much more besides. For example, and you might not believe this, but high on a hill overlooking Knighton is something called the Spaceguard Centre, which is basically a place where lots of bespectacled boffins sit staring into space, looking for asteroids and comets along with countless other things that might threaten to spoil your Monday morning.

I watched one of their promotional videos, which was alarmingly depressing and warned of the possibility of human civilization being wiped, dinosaur-style, off the face of the earth in the blink of an eye, never to bother this precious little planet of ours again, not that there would be much of it left if that happened, of course. The gentleman in the video, who was very polite and immensely likeable, also suggested that we should all have an interest in saving this world of ours. However, he further went on to say that all those who didn't should probably, and I quote, *go out the back with a twelve gauge and simply end it all now*, which I thought was just a little bit harsh and a little bit worrying if I am being brutally honest.

Thankfully, there are other things in the town which don't necessarily involve blowing your brains out, including the number one attraction, in my mind at least, which is the Offa's Dyke Visitor Centre, an absolute must-see when passing through, especially on this walk. And as a little bonus, it is built at the site where John Hunt, Baron of Llanfair Waterdine, whoever he was, first inaugurated this path way back in 1971.

And finally, there is an excellent market here every Thursday, and back in the day, anything could be bought here. In fact, wives were even bought and sold, with the last recorded instance being as recent as 1854. Apparently, the going rate was a mere shilling, which was twelve old pence, though I have a word of warning for anyone who thinks that this sum would represent a bargain. It is not the purchase price that is the problem, you see, it is the upkeep.

On the way to the centre, by the way, we walked past a football field, upon which were around a dozen or so children playing five-a-side football, and I wondered if they knew that Alfred Edwards, the founder of world-class football club A.C. Milan, also came from this tiny little backwater of a town, as unlikely as that may seem. He was not only one of the founders of the club, by the way, but was their first chairman, too.

Lunch was calling us, so we all tumbled into the Little Black Sheep Café. The place was full of locals, and as we were in Wales, I had to remind the lads not to tell any jokes about sheep, certainly not black ones.

We built a scruffy but impressive sculpture in the corner consisting of backpacks, raincoats, hats, and sticks, after which four breakfasts were quickly ordered, one of them of the vegan type for Mark. In truth, when they arrived, they all looked identical, so every time he took a bite of something, we made the appropriate animal noise, taking turns to variously snort and bleat and the like, with Rob doing a rather good impression of a cock, which is not difficult because he really can be one at times.

The locals chatted amongst themselves, and I'm glad to say that despite them speaking in Welsh, I still knew full well that they were talking about us, mainly because they kept laughing, probably at our damp, sorry state.

Luckily, they slipped into English at some point, though I'm not sure they even realised it, but at least this gave us the opportunity to eavesdrop, and the conversation was more interesting than you might expect. One old man was trying to persuade another to look after his cat, which was called Kevin, while he went on his holidays to Ponty Pandy or wherever. However, the other was objecting on the grounds that the cat was racist. In fact, the conversation became so heated that, at one point, it looked like it was going to end in fisticuffs. This had us all excited, and we were fully prepared and ready to follow the fight out into the street to see how it all progressed. Fortunately for them, however, but unfortunately for us, it didn't. And worst of all, I never did find out if the old man said he'd look after Kevin the racist cat or not.

I'm not sure how I feel about cats. I do own one, a small, moody little black and white thing that my wife stole from one of the neighbours many moons ago. It's not much use as a pet, other than perhaps being a paperweight, as it does its own thing and is only friendly when it wants to be. I could probably best describe it by using one of the very first dictionary definitions of such an animal, carefully written down by Noah Webster a couple of hundred years ago, who first produced the now-famous Webster's Dictionary. He stated that a cat needs no description, adding that it is a deceitful animal and, when enraged, is extremely spiteful. Yup, that sounds exactly like Noodles. And no, I didn't choose the name.

I mean, in fairness, his description isn't wrong, though when I checked the historical record, he mentioned nothing of their racist tendencies.

Incidentally, Webster was incredibly influential in the development of American English following the country's somewhat impressive escape from the madness of King George and his evil empire, and this is one of the main reasons that Americans spell so many words wrong to this very day, bless them, mainly because they wanted to distinguish themselves from their oppressive overlords.

Back to the café, though, and the lady who ran it was very nice, and she kept us topped up with tea while she apologised about the locals in a manner similar to how our wives apologise about us whenever we all go out together. She asked us if we were enjoying our walk, but a quick look out of the window at the still persistent rain probably told her all she needed to know about that. I sometimes wonder, if we start telling people their brain is an app, perhaps they'll want to use it?

With lunch well and truly done, it was time to move on, and as we unwillingly changed once more back into our waterproofs and wandered solemnly off down Knighton's main shopping street, I discovered that I didn't need to worry about getting wet, because I hadn't really dried out from this morning.

Incidentally, on the hill just to the north of Knighton is Kinsley Wood, where, to mark the coronation of the queen in 1953, some green-fingered enthusiasts planted some trees in the shape of the letters E.R.

Unfortunately, due to today's atrocious rain, visibility was poor, and I could barely see my feet, never mind a hill almost a mile away, so we trudged off instead up the high street towards the Offa's Dyke Centre. I can confirm, however, that I later checked a satellite photo, and you can indeed clearly see our late queen's initials within the forest.

Alas, when we arrived at the visitor centre, everything was in darkness, and a sign on the door told us it was only open on weekends, which was a shame. I had to think for a minute while I tried to figure out what day it was, and I counted the days back to when we had set off and decided it was probably Wednesday, while Rob said it was Thursday. Both of us were adamant that we were right, so we asked James to adjudicate, but he was no use because he thought it was Tuesday. We all looked at Mark, hoping for a referee's decision, but he just shrugged his shoulders. He said he had no idea but added that we would probably find out if we got home. What do you mean *if*, I shouted after him as he walked off, but it was too late. He was gone.

An exciting sculpture awaited us around the back of the Offa's Dyke Centre, as someone had taken a litter bin and placed it on top of what was either a smoking shelter or somewhere to leave your bike. Admittedly, it was vandalism, but it was nonetheless quite creative and, therefore, entirely impressive. Perhaps if whichever nefarious miscreant was responsible for this put as much effort into other aspects of their life, however, then maybe they wouldn't be spending their evenings around the backs of buildings being a cretin.

A short downhill path took us to a small stream, which was the River Teme, where we found something even better than the vandalism. Someone had built a small bridge, sort of, although it did not cross the river. It did, however, cross an international border, once again sort of, and that border was between England and Wales. How did I know this, I hear you ask? Well, someone had put a sign up saying so, and furthermore, they had painted not only a bright yellow line to mark that border but also painted two footprints, with one on either side of the border.

Well, this was too good a photo opportunity to miss, despite the rain, so we all immediately dumped our backpacks and formed an ever-so-British queue to have our picture taken. Rob took one of me, then I took one of Mark, then Mark took one of James, and so on. Then we all had a picture together, as best as we could manage, with Rob holding his phone at arm's length, basically because he had freakishly long arms.

Well, this was the most fun we had had all day, I thought to myself, as the rain persisted all around us, and as we put our rucksacks back on, water trickled down the back of my neck, sending a shiver down my spine in the most literal sense.

One solitary bead of water didn't stop there, though. It somehow managed to breach my trousers and slid in between somewhere rather cheeky, if you know what I mean, after which it slowly slithered down my leg and ended up in my right sock. I swear that I felt it every bit of the way, and it was as if my body had been turned into a human waterfall. After that initial drop had paved the way, you see, other slightly less original but still highly persistent drops followed course, and I was soon getting very wet indeed. It was time to find somewhere dry.

The canopy of trees didn't help, either, and in fact, it was probably raining more in this wood than it was outside, which was Kinsley Wood, by the way, and is the one that the queen's initials are in.

I had more or less accepted the fact that I was going to stay very wet for very long, as had the others judging by their silence, when a minor miracle occurred. The rain stopped.

Almost immediately, another miracle happened, and the sun came out, literally from out of nowhere. Miracles come in threes, I thought, and lo-and-behold, just a few minutes later, we came across the biggest one of all, Panpwnton Farm.

If you still haven't got the hang of Welsh

pronunciation, fear not, because I am at hand, and it is pronounced Panpunton. The place was very nice too and had, of all things, a camping barn, and within seconds we were in it.

We stood dripping for a minute or two, hardly believing our luck, when a young man came over, and this was Will, the cause of our saviour. The campsite had been around as long as the Offa's Dyke Path had, he told us, and he said that we would probably have the place to ourselves tonight as he had no bookings and did not expect anyone else to turn up, partly down to the time of year but mainly because, once again, most people were not stupid enough to be out in such conditions.

Anyway, we soon settled into our new home for the night, though we did have to play rock, paper, scissors to decide who got to sleep on the comfy mattress that sat atop some wooden pallets. I lost, although I wasn't particularly bothered, as I did wonder what critters might have been living in it.

We hung our gear here and there to dry, and Rob and James then decided to act as our chefs. Various tins and bags appeared from the darkest depths of their rucksacks, and, in no time at all, we were enjoying the finest chilli con carne I had ever had. Mark had some vegetables.

HALFWAY

Knighton to Forden

When dawn broke, I was happy to be able to report that the rain had stopped. This was a welcome surprise, as when I awoke in the night, I had heard it lashing down all around us. I remember sticking my head out of my sleeping bag and looking around in the darkness and wondering if perhaps the roof was going to blow off and kill us all, such were the winds of the storm raging outside, but whoever built that barn thankfully did a professional job. And because that storm was so noisy, I couldn't hear Rob snoring either, which was an added bonus.

We didn't see anyone as we left, but then we were setting off early, as we wanted to take advantage of the nice weather that had descended upon us. Unfortunately, however, we were heading skywards, which meant a rude and unwelcome uphill walk, as our first obstacle was Panpunton Hill, which I assumed was the English spelling of Panpwnton.

A couple of memorials dotted the route, both dedicated to hikers who had died, which momentarily alarmed me and left me contemplating whether or not this stretch of the walk was particularly dangerous. Just in case, I decided that we should probably stay in single file for now, with James up front and on point, seems as he probably has the most experience with such things. I made sure Rob was at the back, though, just in case any dangers approached us from the rear, such as out-of-control cows, bloodthirsty badgers or rabid rabbits and the like. I wouldn't have to outrun them necessarily. I'd just have to outrun Rob, which, bearing in mind his current ankle situation, would probably not be all that difficult.

Once we had finally managed to drag ourselves to the top, the path became much more enjoyable, although I still wouldn't call it flat. The views were outstanding, too. Because of the improved weather, we could see much further today, and this included a fantastic vista back towards Knighton, as well as a beautiful view along the Teme Valley, with the River Teme winding its way along the valley floor in what could only be described as a snake-like manner.

That little river, by the way, is one of the fastest-flowing rivers in Europe, which surprised me immensely, as from my viewpoint, it just looked like a meandering little stream. It also forms the border between England and Wales for much of its length.

A bridge was visible, too, and this was the Knucklas Viaduct. Carrying the Central Wales Line to Swansea, the viaduct is said to be one of the most picturesque in Britain and was completed in 1864. It has thirteen arches, which is my lucky number, though it is said to have bankrupted those who built it, probably because they built what looks like a medieval castle at one end. Still, it was worth it.

If you look carefully at the area behind the viaduct, by the way, you will see a hill upon which is all that is left of Knucklas Castle, which, it should be said, is not a lot. Knucklas Castle does have one claim to fame, however, as it is said to be the place where England's most famous King, Arthur, married the love of his life, which was, of course, Guinevere. I must stress that this is only a legend, but then most of the stories attached to Arthur are legends anyway.

Another interesting little snippet about this castle, though, is that it was built by a child. Not literally, of course, but anyway, it was commissioned in the early 1200s by the Mortimer family, in particular, by Ralph Mortimer. Ralph, however, went off abroad, probably to kill people and chop them up and the like, which was very popular back then, and it is said that he left his 11-year-old grandson Roger in charge of the building works, as you do.

Just behind the castle is another little delight

worth a brief mention, the small village of Heyop. For decades, people disposed of millions of old car tyres in a forest there, not knowing what else to do with them. Unfortunately, some cheeky little toad decided to set fire to the tyres in 1989, by which time there were an estimated ten million of them. If I asked you to guess how long that fire burned for, a few of you would probably say a week. Some might say a month, whilst others would probably say a year. That fire, believe it or not, burned for fifteen years, which is crazy, and it is thought to be the longest-burning tyre fire in history.

We couldn't stand and stare at the views all day, though, no matter how nice they were, so we plodded on, following the ridge line until we came to a hill with a difficult-to-pronounce Welsh-sounding name, for me at least, which is odd, because it is in England. Cwm-Sanaham Hill is not the highest mountain in the country, but the effort to get up it certainly made it feel like it was. In fact, for anyone who may be interested, which is perhaps nobody, I checked, and it is, in fact, the 1,054th tallest peak in the land. In my defence, I can only say that I have too much time on my hands.

A pleasant path followed the edge of a small wood at the hill with the unpronounceable name, after which Offa's Dyke Path began to follow the actual dyke for much of this stretch, which was a welcome treat. It's pretty impressive hereabouts, too, and is easy to make out, even for a layman such as myself who couldn't tell a dyke from a ditch.

In a similar vein, I remember walking the Hadrian's Wall path a few years ago, which distinctly lacks any kind of wall for much of its length if my memory serves me correctly, and parts of this walk have been equally lacking in dyke. Not so for this stretch, however, as it was fantastic.

I briefly checked the map and noticed an unusually named village just a couple of miles to the east worth mentioning, which was called New Invention. Apparently, the name stems from a farrier, which is someone who fits shoes to horses, who, possibly during the Civil War, decided to shoe a horse backwards to confuse the enemy. A variation on the story suggests the shoesmith did this to the horse of King Charles when he was trying to escape. If so, the plan didn't work out too well, as Charlie ultimately had his head quickly but very thoroughly removed by something rather sharp when he was deposed in 1649. Anyway, I digress.

Moving on, the dyke stretched for as far as the eye could see across rolling green hills, a scene that could not have been more English even if you had dropped a red phone box, a London bus and a cup of tea in the middle of it.

Somewhere up ahead was the village of Newcastle, a popular name apparently, but before that, we dropped down into a steep-sided valley dotted with farmhouses, where we found a small summerhouse made of recycled windows, which made a great place to stop to brew a quick cup of coffee.

I had a quick look at my map and wondered where the halfway point of the walk would be, as I reckoned we were almost there, or at least I hoped we were. We should be, as it certainly felt like we had walked the best part of ninety miles, and anyway, we deserved it.

It was inevitably uphill when we moved off once again, and we had already decided that we were not going to go into Newcastle as it was about a mile off the path. We had everything we needed anyway, although we would need to top up with water at some point, though we could probably get that from a friendly farmer.

A footbridge took us across the River Clun, which hereabouts was more of a stream than a river, though it would flow into the River Teme several miles downstream, which would then eventually flow into the River Severn just south of Worcester, meaning that all of this water would eventually flow past the exact spot where we started this walk back at Sedbury Cliffs.

And water certainly was in abundance around here. Just after crossing Church Road and beginning to head up Graig Hill, we came across something entirely unexpected in the middle of a field. A water tap stood lonely and alone but was never more welcomed than it was by us, so we all took the opportunity to drop our packs and refill our various water bottles and camel packs and whatnot. I had a big, long glug, too, just to be on the safe side. One thing was for sure, I was definitely not going to be thirsty for quite some time.

And as if that wasn't enough excitement for the day, as soon as we moved on, we came to a sign that proclaimed we had finally made it to the halfway point of the walk. Chepstow, it stated, was eighty-eight and a half miles to the south, while Prestatyn, it promised, was the same difference to the north. Obviously, another photo opportunity was immediately grabbed by the proverbials, and while I momentarily considered bailing out, going home and having a nice cup of tea, with perhaps a return visit sometime next year for the other half, we moved on.

I was beginning to think that today was going to turn out to be one of the hardest sections of this walk, as the path had now decided to go up and down hill after hill for no other reason than it could. I huffed and puffed my way up each one as my fitter friends strode ahead of me, but I always seemed to catch up with them at the tops. A quick chat on top of one unnamed hill gave me the opportunity to tell them not to wait for me anymore and to go ahead and save themselves. We could meet up, I suggested, at the next church, which, funnily enough, was at Churchtown.

Within minutes of moving off, I was on my own, my so-called friends having left me for dead. Still, I enjoyed the silence, and the only sound was the birds in the trees and my overworked heart.

The small village of Mardu proved to be a non-event, although, after that, the path continued to closely follow the earthwork of the Dyke, so I did at least have some company. Small birds darted in and out of the bushes, probably alarmed by my sudden appearance, though one of their cousins sought appropriate revenge a little later on when a pheasant flew out of the undergrowth, causing my already over-taxed heart to miss a beat and leaving me wondering whether my underwear might possibly need changing.

One particularly steep hill threatened to give me yet another coronary event, but stops and starts allowed me to slowly move on, and as I did so, I wondered why I had not passed by the cold, dead corpse of one of my walking buddies, probably Rob. They must have made it alive, I pondered.

A small wood was a bit of a surprise, and the map told me it was Churchtown Wood. Beyond this, a hop across a small meadow and a bridge finally had me at Churchtown itself, which certainly lived up to its name as it was basically composed of not much more than a church, although you could hardly call it a town.

My friends were huddled in the porch of the church, and I could see that they had a couple of gas cookers on the go. In no time at all, I was being handed a piping-hot cup of sweet coffee in one hand and a bowl of porridge in the other. Life doesn't get much better than this, I thought to myself as I dropped my backpack onto the floor and also collapsed onto that tiny little bench.

The church is dedicated to Saint John, who incidentally is the patron saint of love, loyalty, friendships and, of all things, authors. It was nice enough, but there was little to keep us here for more than a few minutes, so after we had finished our refreshments, we moved on.

It was uphill, of course, and the hill in question was Edenhope Hill, after which the path dropped down into a small valley and crossed a footbridge over the curiously named River Unk. There's not much to say about this tiny little river, which is more of a stream, really, other than that it is one of the few places in the country where you can still find freshwater pearl mussels, but please don't tell anyone, because it's supposed to be a secret.

Next up was Cwm, pronounced *Come*, which is entirely appropriate because when you zoom the map out for this part of Wales, which is called Powys, by the way, the shape of the border looks a bit like the end of a willy.

The path got busier here, but it wasn't walkers

we met as such, but holidaymakers, by the looks of it. Several people passed us by, all causally dressed, and not one of them was wearing walking shoes or carrying any kind of backpack, and none had any waterproof gear either.

All was explained a few minutes later, however, when we spotted lots of caravans through the trees, and a quick look at the map told us we were at Mellington Hall, and even better, there was a sign that welcomed walkers. We decided to take a look, and although we didn't need anything, we wondered if there might be a shop. Sometimes, you see, you just don't realise you need anything until you actually stumble into a shop. When you do go in, however, you then realise that you really do need a multipack of chocolate bars, a big bottle of something borderline illegal, and an inflatable banana.

We wandered through the park, which was very civilised and full of normal people, and we must have looked entirely out of place, what with our massive rucksacks and unshaven faces. We literally stumbled out of the woods, too, and I'm pretty sure that we actually scared some people, as kids ran this way and that when they saw us.

Refreshments were indeed available, so we variously treated ourselves to chocolate, drinks and ice creams and parked on a nearby bench to enjoy them, though I wholly resisted the urge to buy the inflatable banana.

Rob, doing what he does best, then went off to find a toilet, and a few minutes later, he came back all giddy and excited. The source of this excitement was soon revealed to be a gleaming toilet block complete with showers, and as soon as he said this, we all had the same idea. Showers had been scarce on this walk, to say the least, so off we trotted, hoping that no one would see us and throw us out.

I took advantage of the toilet facilities, too. In fact, it was while I was in there that I had quite a deep and philosophical thought. You never appreciate what you have until it is gone. Toilet paper, for instance.

Well, the shower was glorious. Clean, hot water splashed all around me, and I used half a bottle of shower gel in the process, and I almost came out clean. Luckily, I had one of those compact micro-fibre camping towels that served to wipe off whatever dirt was left behind, and I came out of that shower feeling as fresh as a daisy. Rob and Mark soon followed, but James was in there for ages. Eventually, we figured that we would soon have to regard him as missing in action and finish the walk without him, but then he too appeared, also looking as fresh as a daisy. A big, stupid, ginger daisy.

And while we did our best to clean the showers afterwards, we may have left some mess behind, but this was probably inevitable. And I never heard anything on the news about the place having to be decontaminated or anything, so we can't have been that bad.

Before we left, there was also a vast stately home here, hence the name of Mellington Hall. The house was built in the Gothic style and looked to be some kind of high-class hotel, but despite our recent pampering, we still dared not go in.

The hall was built in the 1800s by Philip Wright from Derbyshire, who was presumably looking for somewhere nice to spend his weekends. He had made lots of money first through coal mines and then with an iron foundry, and if you have ever been to London and have perhaps passed through Saint Pancras Station, then you have certainly seen some of his work.

Nowadays, the hall is said to be haunted, and several people have reported ghostly carriages crashing through what is now the billiards room, presumably late at night and after lots and lots of drinkies.

Philip Wright is said to haunt the place as well, particularly up in the tower, and other so-called witnesses have reported seeing apparitions of children variously playing in the woods or peering through the windows. Maybe, though, this is just actual children playing in the woods and peering through the windows, as, after all, it is a bloody holiday park.

Unimpressed with the crappy ghost stories,

we finally decided to move on as the hour was getting late, and as we left, I saw some children playing in the woods and peering through the windows.

A small bridge took us over yet another river with an unusual name, this one being the River Caebitra, which sounds a bit Roman if you ask me. It was here that we crossed the border back into England and came to Brompton Crossroads. I had heard of this place, and quite frankly, I had expected bigger things, but it really was just a crossroads. Although there was a pub and a petrol pump, there was no café, no sauna and not even a McDonalds, all of the stuff you would expect to find at any decent crossroads, so we simply plodded on. And even the petrol pump looked like it no longer worked, while the pub, the Blue Bell, was closed.

Heading due north on a small track, the next few miles of walking was a straight line, more or less, and much of it followed the exact border between England and Wales. We were following the course of the actual dyke too, which was a bonus, and for many miles, it was pretty easy to see. Progress was swift, and in no time at all, just off to our left was the small town of Montgomery.

While technically a mile or so off the route of Offa's Dyke path, it would be remiss of us not to include it in our little walk, and anyway, we were hungry, so after a short deviation, we soon found ourselves in this smart little town.

We grabbed some food, which for me meant a stunningly fat cheese salad sandwich, and I had originally intended to go and eat it in the shade of the churchyard. I particularly wanted to see something called the Robber's Grave, which is exactly what it sounds like.

In 1821, John Davies, a plasterer from Wrexham, was sentenced to death by hanging for the crime of highway robbery. He vigorously contested his innocence, however, and boldly decreed that after his death, God would not allow any grass to grow upon the site of his grave for a hundred years. This, he told the townspeople, should be taken as proof of his innocence.

With insufficient evidence to stop his hanging, Davies was soon pushing up daisies, after which locals started reporting ghostly sightings. Apparently, the restless spirit of John Davies was not as easy to get rid of as the mortal man had been.

This story had actually started with a robbery on the road from Welshpool to Berriew, just a few miles to the north, where evidence incriminating John Davies was found, rather conveniently, right at the scene of the crime.

However, evidence later emerged that two men, one called Robert Parker along with his acquaintance Thomas Pearce, had actually fabricated the whole affair. Apparently, John Davies had successfully turned around the fortunes of a struggling farm and, in doing so, had caught the eye of the farmer's daughter. But why did these two men decide to frame poor old John Davies for murder? Well, it turns out that Thomas Pearce ran a rival farm and was jealous of John Davies, while Robert Parker was in love with the farmer's daughter. Davies, it seems, had been their mutual enemy, totally unbeknown to him.

When we actually got to the grave, a cold wind blew through the trees over the still bare grass. For some reason, I decided I didn't want to hang around, and anyway, I had already eaten my food.

Perhaps the town's most famous resident, however, is Oscar-winning actress Julie Christie, who starred in everything from Doctor Zhivago to Harry Potter, and who enjoys the quiet life in this beautiful little back-water of a place, so if you see her in the street, please pretend you don't know who she is.

Montgomery Castle is also pretty impressive, but it sits on the top of a hill high above the town, so we chose to admire it from afar. Even as a ruin, the castle was impressive, and I couldn't help but wonder what it would have looked like before it was destroyed.

Originally built on the orders of English King Henry III in the early 1200s, the castle was constructed purely and simply to counter the threat of one man, Welsh Prince Llywelyn the Great, which suggests he must have been regarded as something of a threat.

In fact, Llywelyn the Great dominated Wales for almost fifty years and was a wise statesman. Initially, he was on good terms with the English King John and even married his daughter Joan. At some point, however, the family had a bit of a falling out, and by 1215, Llywelyn was allied with the Barons, who forced the king to sign the Magna Carta, which was basically a charter of rights that limited the king's powers and established the rule of law. Essentially, in a nutshell, from now on, the king, or queen for that matter, would never be above the law.

The castle somehow managed to survive for hundreds of years, but in 1644, it became the site of the largest battle of the Civil War to occur on Welsh soil. It was finally destroyed in 1649, which is a real shame, and ever since, it has stood as an empty shell. It is worth mentioning, incidentally, that the English Civil War is often referred to as the Wars of the Three Kingdoms. Those three kingdoms, by the way, were England, Scotland and Ireland, and what is perhaps telling is that Wales was not even regarded as a country back then but was merely a province of England.

Done with the town, as lovely as it was, we shuffled off back up the road to rejoin our route, and to our delight, we were still able to follow the earthworks of Offa's Dyke. After another stretch of reasonably straight path, the hills became more pronounced, and our thoughts turned to looking for somewhere to pitch our tents for the night.

A spot suggested itself to us just outside of Forden, though it looked suspiciously like somebody's garden. Rob was keen, though, and went to knock on the door of a nearby house, which was immediately answered by a lady who looked like she had been baking. Covered from head to toe in what looked like flour, although it could have been cocaine, to be honest, she said that the land belonged to her dad but that we could happily camp there, which is precisely what we did.

Cookers were lit, coffee was made, and tents were erected. In no time at all, we had made ourselves truly at home, and Rob somehow magically produced scones, jam and cream, which almost made us civilized. He still snored all night, though.

VIKINGS TO VICTORIANS

Forden to Trefonen

The sound of rain once again woke me up, and when I unzipped my tent and stuck my head out, Rob was somehow simultaneously cooking us a full English breakfast and a cup of coffee on his little stove. He wasn't, of course, but it really was raining, and he did make me a coffee.

And coffee is incredibly important to me in the morning. If I don't have enough of it to properly help me catastrophize the day, I just feel somewhat off for the rest of it.

Our tents were wet when we packed them away this morning, but a quick look at the forecast, which simply involved turning around and looking north, suggested a brighter day ahead. All too soon, we were on our way, which inevitably involved going uphill more or less instantly, much to my dismay.

I was soon in my usual place, which meant I was at the back of our little troupe of performing monkeys. James was at the front, closely followed by Mark, after which there was a bit of a gap with Rob in third place, followed by a lot of a gap, which, of course, is where I came in.

Last, fourth, call it what you want, but you are never going to get any medals for coming in where I did. Still, I didn't want a medal. I just wanted to finish. For some reason, my mind turned towards those paralympian athletes, and I pondered the fact that they all probably have blue badges, which means they can park their cars anywhere they want. Yet all of them can probably run faster than me, jump higher, and throw further, as well as a lot more besides. This was just a fleeting thought, of course, as I slowly hobbled along with a rather strange pain in my leg, which I suspected was probably my shin splint.

We came to Nantcribba Castle, which is unfortunately on private land, and a plethora of signs told us this in no uncertain terms. The owners clearly didn't want to have to deal with peasants, and we couldn't even cross the field here, so the path took us along the main road for a while, where traffic roared past us at uncomfortable speeds.

Luckily, this didn't last very long, and a small path took us literally through somebody's garden and back to the safety of the fields.

Ahead of us were our first views of the long mountain, so named because it is, you've guessed it, long. While this was not a very imaginative name, it was certainly an accurate one.

We passed through Forden next, where the dyke formed the backdrop for the houses on a surprisingly modern little housing estate. I'm not quite sure how the construction company managed to get planning permission to build right up to the edge of a scheduled ancient monument, but I'm sure it didn't involve a bribe, I thought to myself, coughing as I did so, if you know what I mean.

Another short stretch of road walking followed, after which we turned left into the woods, which, for me, was going to be one of the highlights of this walk. Up ahead of us, you see, was the Leighton Estate, a secluded area of beautiful forest, within which is a rather special treat. And it is always good to go into the woods as it enables you to get away from it all. Lately, all you hear about in the news are wars, diseases and loads of other nasty stuff. Apparently, this decade is being written by Stephen King.

Anyway, Leighton is, quite surprisingly, home to some of the most enormous trees in Europe. These are, in fact, giant Californian Redwoods, otherwise known as Sequoia, a fiendishly difficult word to spell, if ever there was one. In fact, the full name is Sequoia Sempervirens, with Sempervirens meaning long-lived in Latin, entirely appropriate when you consider that these behemoths can live for thousands of years, and the word is almost as hard to spell as Sequoia is, never mind pronounce.

Not only can these trees live for a very long time, but if they fall or, dare I say it, are chopped down, they tend to re-shoot, with their lower branches taking root and their upper branches basically becoming new trees. There is an excellent example of exactly this within the grove of trees at Leighton, with one that blew down in 1936, and around ten trees now live off the fallen one, which is, appropriately enough, known as *The Mother Tree*. And as if all of that isn't enough, these trees are also incredibly resistant to fire.

We owe profound thanks for all of these trees to the Naylor family who once owned the hall, who, for whatever reason, sent their gardener off to America in the mid-1800s and told him to bring back some saplings. Apparently, they had a grand plan to create the largest redwood grove outside of America, and while they may not quite have achieved that particular goal, they did nonetheless plant rather a lot of them here. Some of them are now over 120 feet tall, and not surprisingly, many now refer to these woods as the *Cathedral of Trees*.

Interestingly, the scourge of many British suburban housing estates, the incredibly fast-growing Leylandii, was also developed right here at Leighton Hall. The name of that tree comes from Leyland, which was the original name of the Naylor family, and it was from this branch that the estate originated, if you pardon the pun.

Christopher Leyland first bought Leighton Hall in 1845, though he never intended to keep it. The following year, he gave it to his nephew John Naylor as a wedding present, which you have to admit was a pretty good gift when all things are considered. I think the best thing that my wife and I received when we got married was a toaster.

Anyway, Naylor commissioned Edward Kemp, a hitherto unknown gardener who was a student of none other than Sir Joseph Paxton. You may know who he was when I tell you that it was he who designed Crystal Palace for the Great Exhibition of 1851, which was a rather large and impressive greenhouse really, and which famously burned down in 1936, although how a greenhouse managed to burn down is anybody's guess. What Paxton is less known for, however, is bananas. I don't mean he went wild, but it is he who is responsible for the humble banana that you might have in your lunchbox right now. He spent years cultivating selected specimens and ultimately came up with the Cavendish banana, which is apparently the most consumed banana in the world.

Anyway, back to Kemp, who had shown great promise as Paxton's apprentice, and later on, he certainly lived up to it. While he was laying out the garden at Leighton Hall, you see, Kemp placed two particular conifers side by side, and this was quite deliberate. One, from Alaska, was a Nootka Cypress, and the other, from California, was a Monterey Cypress.

It is important to mention that California and Alaska are thousands of miles apart, so out in the wild, these two trees would never have crossbred in a thousand years, and proof of that is that they never had. That all changed in 1888, however, when Kemp intervened with his kinky tree swinging. Perhaps inevitably, later that year, the female cones of the Nootka Cypress were finally fertilised by pollen from the Monterey Cypress, the dirty thing. The result, if you have not already guessed, is the Leylandii, one of the fastest-growing conifers ever known and which has since, perhaps inevitably, become incredibly common throughout the land, and all can be traced back to trees from this very spot.

Fast forward a hundred years or so, and these things are everywhere. They can grow to incredible heights at remarkable speeds under the right conditions but, as an unfortunate side-effect, have become the cause of many neighbourly fallouts ever since. People have even been murdered in disputes over them.

Anyway, the Naylor family sold off the estate in 1931, and it was bought by someone called Charles Ackers, who cultivated and cared for it until 1958 when he passed it to its current owners, the rather fancily named Royal Forestry Society. Unfortunately, they don't allow common peasants like me and you onto their land, so if you want to see them, you will have to sneak on, just like I did. And when I did, it was clear to see that the giant redwoods were doing rather well, but as for those leylandii, well, don't get me started.

The path went straight through the forests of the Leighton estate, which also took us past Offa's Pool. It looked pretty empty today and was clearly past its best, but once upon a time, it would have been brimming with water and was, in fact, the uppermost reservoir in a string of four that powered a mini hydroelectric plant for the estate. The electricity it generated was used to power everything from lights to farm equipment to a funicular railway that once ran up these very hills.

All of that had gone, however, and all I could see were trees and the occasional squirrel. The estate has apparently recently introduced red squirrels into these forests and now run what they call a grey squirrel management plan, which sounds technical but basically means blowing the heads off any they see. I'm not sure what colour the squirrel that I saw was, but I didn't really care because I'm colour-blind anyway.

I caught up with the others as we cleared

the tree line. The path was steadily going uphill, and we were heading to Beacon Ring Hill, where there was, presumably, a beacon, and maybe even a ring.

I huffed and puffed in a vain effort to keep up with my erstwhile friends, but the gap grew anyway, and it was not until we got to the top that we regrouped once more. I met them at a gate that took us through a canopy of trees, and although the actual route of our path went around the hill, we decided to go straight across it, as there was also an iron-aged hillfort up here, and we wanted to see what we could see.

Well, other than trees and a modern transmitter, the answer was not a lot, although the place does have a long and interesting history. It had been occupied since prehistoric times, probably since around 1000 BC, and references to its occupation continued until well into the Middle Ages.

Much later on, in August 1485, Beacon Ring Hillfort was the spot where Henry Tudor gathered his army before going off to fight King Richard III at the Battle of Bosworth. The king was ultimately killed, and his body vanished off the face of the earth, and Henry Tudor became the new king, Henry VII. This finally ended 30 years of war between the houses of Lancaster and York and saw the ushering in of the Tudor dynasty, significantly influencing English history ever since. And unless you have spent the last few years on the moon, you probably know that Richard III was recently found buried beneath, of all things, a car park in Leicester. Well, that all started here.

It's called Beacon Hill, by the way, because those clever Victorians chose to site a beacon on the top of this hill to mark the golden jubilee of Queen Victoria in 1887, but the place also has another royal link. When Queen Elizabeth II was crowned in 1953, someone had the bright idea of planting a copse of trees up here consisting of pine and beech trees, similar to the trees back at Kington, which, when viewed from above, would spell out E II R, which represented Elizabeth II Regina. You can still see the effect today if you happen to be flying overhead in your hot air balloon or whatnot, but as I am a mere peasant, I had to make do with looking on the internet.

There was no way to tell from the ground, however, and as the trees and shrubbery gradually became thicker, we realised we probably should have stuck to the perimeter of the hill. By the time we managed to rejoin our path, and after taking more than a few wrong turns, I was absolutely covered in scratches, Robin had nearly lost a shoe, and James and Mark had vanished off the face of the earth. Perhaps they'd turn up in a car park in Leicester, I pondered.

When we left the woods, a long descent towards Buttington sprawled ahead of us, and as it turned out, James and Mark had not vanished at all, as we saw their tiny figures far off on the slopes below us.

We knew they would stop at Buttington, as there was a pub there where we intended to eat, so we trod carefully on. The descent was deceptively long, and we seemed to make no progress whatsoever. Furthermore, the often steep path put considerable pressure on parts of our legs that were simply not used to hard work.

Because of this, it was almost an hour before we reached the bottom of the valley, where we finally met the road into Buttington. We joined this road just after crossing a railway line that linked Welshpool with Shrewsbury, and judging by the speed of the train that nearly creamed us both, we deduced it was probably a main line.

It was here that Rob's phone pinged, and he told me that James had sent him a message telling us to meet them at the Green Dragon pub, which was to our right. Being good boys, we did as we were told, but when we got there, it was closed, and there was no sign of either James or Mark.

I tried ringing both of them, one after the other, but my phone wouldn't connect. Scratching our heads and looking around, we were perplexed.

Across the road was a small church, so we decided to go and have a look, just in case the boys had popped in there for a rest, but once again, there was no sign of them. While we were in there, however, Rob's phone rang, and it was James, but when he answered it, he couldn't hear anything. We did go outside to see if the signal was any better, but despite walking along the road, past the vicarage and to the end of the village, it was to no avail.

There was only one thing to do, we decided, and that was to move on. The phone reception here was clearly terrible, and considering the pub was closed, we concluded that James and Mark had simply done the same.

Popping our backpacks back on, we walked back to where the path had met the road, which was actually at Buttington Bridge. The bridge is a sort of checkpoint along the walk, and according to my guidebook, we were 111 miles in.

The bridge crosses over the River Severn, which you may remember is where we started, though obviously at the other end. The river bubbles out of the ground in the Cambrian Mountains in mid-Wales and is commonly considered to be the longest river in the country, at 220 miles in length. This is certainly debatable, however. According to some people in the know, there is at least an outside chance that the Thames, which officially comes in at 215 miles, is actually longer than the Severn. Others, however, claim that this does depend on how you choose to measure the rivers, although I imagine that from beginning to end would be a good start. I mean, it's hardly rocket science.

The path turned to the north just after the bridge, which was a bit of a problem. I had read that it can be challenging to cross the bridge as there is no path, but this is an understatement. A constant stream of traffic passed by in both directions, and there was barely room for the cars to pass each other safely, never mind a couple of fat, sluggish hikers.

We waited for what seemed like an age, becoming increasingly frustrated at the sheer number of cars passing by, but eventually, a small gap presented itself, and we went for it.

Unfortunately, almost as soon as we moved, a car towing a caravan appeared from behind us, but it was too late as we were already committed. Luckily, the car's brakes worked, although I'm not sure that the driver was all that impressed with us. Nonetheless, we continued across, jumping onto the grass verge once we got to the other side. I did offer the driver a quick bow and a wave of appreciation, but he must have thought I was deriding him judging by the two fingers he stuck up at me, and in fairness, I think I was.

It was here that a miracle happened. In the hazy distance, almost beyond view, the sunlight caught something. For a minute, I thought it was the golden arches of a McDonald's restaurant, although, in fairness, restaurant is always a stretch in this context. Regardless, I blinked my eyes once or twice and discovered it was, in fact, exactly that, so off we trotted, like the little piggies that we are.

After a couple more life-and-death situations crossing a busy dual carriageway, we hopped a low fence and dropped our backpacks to go inside, and discovered something very surprising. James and Mark were sat inside, and they looked like they had been there a while, as they had almost finished their breakfast.

Apparently, this part of Wales, just north of Welshpool, is something akin to the Bermuda Triangle when it comes to phone signals, they told us. They had been trying to ring, text and message us but without any luck whatsoever. Stranger still, the messages we had sent them had come through, often two or three times, but they had still been unable to reply.

While this was all very interesting, there was food to be had, and I nudged Rob to let him know that the breakfast menu was about to close very soon, so we had to decide if we were going to get McMuffins and the like, or were we going to wait and get Quarter Pounders and whatnot. Without a moment's hesitation, Rob simply said both, so that is precisely what we did. We had breakfast, then immediately had lunch, and I was absolutely stuffed.

Welshpool itself is worth a quick visit if you have time, and there are also lots of places to stay. And it even adds its own history to the dyke, too.

For instance, perhaps the town's most famous

resident was someone I had come across before, a certain William Boyd Dawkins, who apparently had many talents. When he was young, he became very interested in fossils, amassing an impressive collection in his formative years. His career then took him into mining and geology, and he was instrumental in the survey work done for a proposed tunnel under the English Channel.

Closer to home, it was also Dawkins who took a significant role in planning a tunnel in my neck of the woods, one under the Humber, just next to my home town of Hull, which is why I had come across him before. However, due to poor-quality clay, a high water table, engineering problems, opposition and a ballooning budget, these plans never came to fruition, although we did finally get a bridge.

Dawkins was also into archaeology, particularly at a place called Wookey Hole Cave. It was he who first proved that exotic animals had once lived on our lovely little island, which was considered by many to be an absolutely outrageous idea at the time. Among his discoveries were the skeletons of bison, hyenas, bears and even a sabre-toothed tiger, the earliest of which were dated to 35,000 BC. Later on, we found out that Dawkins had actually been born at the vicarage in Buttington, which we had wandered past just a short time before, waving our phones in the air like mad men. Such a small world.

We were stuffed up to our eyeballs with junk food, but it was, nonetheless, time to move on. We had a choice between going back to Buttington to resume the path, perhaps getting run over by a succession of cars on Buttington Bridge in the process, or following the path of the Montgomery Canal for a short while, which would actually be our route anyway in a few hundred yards. We chose the latter, although this did mean that we would miss the Buttington Oak, a tree that was planted to commemorate an English victory here over the Vikings in 893 AD at what has since become known as the Battle of Buttington.

The Vikings had sailed up the River Severn, raping and pillaging as they did so, but luckily for the English, this was the time of Alfred the Great. Very soon, he had gathered together his own army and chased the pesky Scandinavians right across the country. He finally caught up with them here at Buttington Bridge, though there wasn't a bridge back then, and it probably wasn't called Buttington either.

The Vikings, knowing full well that the game was up, built lots of fancy defences, and a siege began. After several weeks, and with the invaders slowly beginning to starve to death, they had no choice but to fight their way out. The incident is well-recorded in *The Anglo-Saxon Chronicles*, and it tells us that *some of the heathen died of hunger*, meaning the Vikings, of course, and that *having by then eaten their horses, they broke out of the fortress,* whereupon a great battle began.

Alfred the Great, being, well, great, was having none of it, and he had all the pagans put to the sword, though some did ultimately escape. At the end of the battle, it was said that the Christians, meaning the combined English and Welsh forces, were *the masters of the place of death*, which has quite a cheery ring to it and makes me wonder why the local tourist board doesn't adopt the term today. I'm sure it would be very popular for romantic weekend breaks and the like.

As it happened, our shortcut didn't cause us to miss much because I later found out that the tree had already fallen down during a storm. Bits of it were shipped off to various bespectacled boffins who confirmed it was more than a thousand years old, and it was also discovered that this tree was the second-largest in Wales, or at least it had been until it fell down.

The canal was a pleasant walk, and more importantly, it was flat. It was full of wildlife, too, with swans hissing at us and pigeons dive-bombing us as we disturbed their otherwise peaceful day. After perhaps a mile, though, the canal coincided with a busy main road, with heavy trucks lumbering by, threatening to lift us up as they sped past us, but at least this scared the swans and pigeons away.

The Montgomery Canal, or The Monty, as it is colloquially known, is oddly named. When we nipped into Montgomery for sausage rolls, you see, I recall seeing a castle and a hill and even a road or two, but there was not a sniff of the canal. Upon checking, it turns out that it does not, nor has it ever, gone to the town of Montgomery. Still, it's a good name, which, by the way, was only adopted recently.

It was built in the late 1700s, as were most canals. However, the Montgomery Canal is different from any other in that it was constructed to primarily bring things in rather than take products out of the area. There is lots of farmland around here, you see, but it was somewhat lacking in nutrients, so the idea was to use the canal to bring in lime for agricultural purposes, thereby significantly improving crop yields. Perhaps not surprisingly, then, most shareholders were also local landowners, and rather than receive share dividends on the canal, they benefitted from those increased crop yields instead.

We left the towpath behind and crossed the road where we almost got hit by a truck before heading into some fields, where we found ourselves following the River Severn slowly downstream. As for the dyke itself, it appeared that we had left it behind for now, as a quick check of the map told us it ran somewhere off to the east, on the other side of the river.

The Severn snakes and winds its way through the fields hereabouts, and for a while, we snaked with it, which I couldn't help but think must have added some distance to our journey. It was a nice enough walk, though, until we came across something of an obstacle.

A section of the riverbank was absolutely crowded with cows, and I mean crowded. For some reason, they had all congregated in one place and seemed reluctant to move, and they also looked a bit skittish.

The cause of their behaviour was soon revealed when a helicopter rose from behind some trees ahead of us. We had heard the sound of its engine but had assumed it to be a tractor, perhaps, or maybe a generator, or basically anything other than a helicopter. It was incredibly close, too, so there was no wonder the cows had tried to get out of its way.

Cows can be unpredictable when spooked and are, in fact, one of the most dangerous animals in the United Kingdom, statistically speaking. Sure, there are possibly more harmful things like adders, false widow spiders and people from Birmingham, but none of them are going to kill you, probably. We also have badgers, wildcats, and, as already mentioned, wild boar, which are potentially dangerous, but only if you're a bit dim. Anyway, they are so few and far between that most people go their whole lives without seeing one, even the dim ones.

Cows, on the other hand, are killers, especially if you happen to have a dog. We didn't have a dog, of course, but we did have Rob, who smelt like one.

A few minutes of pondering our situation got us nowhere, and the helicopter continued to hover in the field behind the cows, presumably doing some survey work on the electricity pylons or something. Eventually, James had had enough, and he just climbed the gate into the field of death and went for it. As soon as he did this, I followed him, hoping that either Rob or Mark would follow me. That way, I wouldn't be at the back. I've seen Scooby Doo, and while you should never be at the front, you should never be at the back, either.

By some divine miracle, we made it through the field of death, and as we approached the helicopter, it flew up and disappeared, which I thought was just charming. Perhaps they could have done that a minute ago, but oh no, they probably wanted to see what happened to those chubby hikers first.

As it turned out, it was actually a military helicopter, so what they were doing out here was anybody's guess. Mutilating cattle was my guess, trying to make it look like the work of aliens or perhaps the French.

We moved on and found a little delight just near Trederwen. Some kind soul had put a table and chairs on the riverbank, just beneath a canopy of willow trees. There were four chairs, too, and there were four of us, so it was probably fate.

Rob pulled out his trusty stove and soon had a pot of coffee on while I dispensed biscuits to the boys, and we had an almost-civilized afternoon tea, only with coffee, because we had no tea.

Beyond Trederwen, we left the River Severn behind and headed cross-country to Four Crosses. We were back on the actual dyke, albeit briefly, and while we hoped to find a pub or somewhere to eat, the place was unfortunately deserted.

There was a village hall, though, which had an impressive bell hanging on the wall. Beneath that, on a fence, someone had put a sign up advising anyone who wanted to get fit quickly to come to their yoga classes, but for us, at least, it was clearly too late for that. I have never actually tried yoga, though I have tried bending over to pick up my keys, so I am pretty sure it wouldn't be for me anyway. It was not yoga tonight, however, but dancing, and through the window, I could just see the dance teacher practising. She was dancing like nobody was watching. But somebody was watching, and it looked like bees were attacking her.

A quick perusal of the map told us our next eating opportunity would be at Llanymynech, which is as hard a word to pronounce as any. We briefly considered cheating and heading straight up the main road to the place but had a last-minute rethink and decided to stick to the path, not because we were purists or anything, but because we would probably die on the road.

I even considered going solo and trying to hitch a lift, but I quickly reconsidered because you never know which psycho is going to pick you up. I know because I picked up a hitchhiker once, and we had the usual friendly chat where he jokingly asked me why I picked him up and how did I know he wasn't a serial killer. I told him that the chances of there being two serial killers in one car were astronomical.

Within minutes, we were back on the canal towpath, and yet another glance at my map told me we could have stayed on it the whole way from Welshpool to here. It probably would have been a more pleasant walk, as it would have been quieter and wouldn't have involved crossing dangerous roads and navigating through fields full of dodgy cows, but hindsight is a wonderful thing.

Anyway, a great clockwise arc along the canal eventually took us into Llanymynech, and after regrouping at a flight of steps, we staggered up and into the village to go and find something to eat. The options were good, as well, with a choice between various pubs and takeaways, but a quick look at the weather made us choose the pub, as it was just starting to rain.

The pub in question was The Bradford Arms, and it was cosy indeed. Dumping our rucksacks, walking poles, coats and jackets in the corner by the door, we grabbed the only free table, which was in the opposite corner and was ideal.

I went to grab a menu from the bar to see what, if any, food was on offer, and it was here that I made a crucial mistake. No sooner had I picked it up than I saw a sign telling everyone, in no uncertain terms, not to take a menu without asking.

The barman, who had been quietly drying glasses, stopped what he was doing and just looked at me, and I felt like a naughty child. Questions were asked regarding my ability to read and my general level of intelligence, and I didn't quite know what to say, so I just lied and pretended I had not seen the sign.

This only made things worse, so I lamely tried to slide the menu back onto the pile, but it was too late for that. Luckily, the barman, who was actually the manager, told me he could probably squeeze us in, but let's just say I didn't get the friendliest vibe from him.

Orders were placed, drinks were bought, and we enjoyed a quick chat with some ladies at the next table who sounded like they came from Australia. Luckily, they were next on my list of people to offend when I asked them this, only for them to tell me they were from New Zealand. Well, that was the end of that conversation. Still, the beer was excellent.

James and Mark had managed to find an empty electrical socket and had plugged their phones in to charge, as had Rob, which meant there were no spare sockets for me. However, there was a restaurant at the back of the pub, so I wandered off, hoping to find another one, which I did. Luckily, the restaurant was empty, as I had to crawl under a table to get to the socket, and it must have been something of a sight to see my rear end sticking out as it did.

When I came back, the whole atmosphere had changed, and the manager was eagerly chatting with the boys while the Australians, sorry, the New Zealanders, had joined in, too. Apparently, the manager was a retired member of the Royal Air Force, and when he found out that one of our party had also similarly served, well, let's just say he was our new best friend.

Unfortunately, it soon dawned on me that he thought we were all in the RAF, which was a bit awkward, but because I had already offended everyone in the pub with my brazen menu stealing, blatant lies and my cultural assumptions, I thought it best to keep quiet.

Luckily, the food duly arrived, which served to end the conversation, and the barman went back to what he did best, which was drying his glasses, while we absolutely stuffed our faces. I had a meat pie with gravy and chips, while the others went for lesser foods. When we had finished, we decided that it had all been excellent, and we were all royally stuffed, but in a good way.

The barman told us some interesting things about Llanymynech, and it is a surprisingly historical place. Apparently, the English and Welsh border runs right through the village, north to south, more or less along the main road. I say more or less, as in places, it literally runs directly through buildings, and in particular through one of the pubs, The Lion Inn. Back in the day, when English and Welsh drinking laws were different, the border dissected the pub's three bars, leaving two in England and one in Wales. This meant that it was illegal to drink in the Welsh bar on Sundays, but it was perfectly allowable in the two English bars. Incidentally, a secret passage is said to run from a cave in the hills high above directly to the pub, which can also take you to the underworld of the fairies, but only after twenty pints, I expect.

In a similar vein, the two halves of the village are served by different councils, police forces, fire services and ambulances, and this caused chaos during the days of COVID-19 when entirely different laws applied to either side of the village, which referred to everything from going out, working, attending school or even going shopping. It sounded like absolute madness, which, of course, it was.

On a slightly saner note, just above the village,

on Llanymynech Hill, sits an 18-hole golf course, which, we were told, is the only one in Europe that straddles an international border. However, such a claim to fame is dubious at best, if only because it refers to the border between England and Wales as being international, which is a push, to say the least.

There are a couple of interesting people who came from the place, too, and the first one was a young lady called Kate Evans. She was born in the late 1800s and became involved in the suffragist movement, which campaigned for women's rights. Apparently, her parents were very disappointed at this outcome, but nonetheless, Evans spent her whole life dedicated to the cause, serving time in Holloway Prison and going on a hunger strike to promote the cause. The suffragists eventually won, of course. Women were finally given the right to vote on equal terms as men, but not until 1928, though by this time, Evans was sixty-two years old.

The other interesting character to come out of Llanymynech was engineer Richard Roberts. I mention him for one reason and for one reason only, which will become abundantly clear later on, but first, a little background.

Roberts was born here at the height of the Industrial Revolution, and he became one of the pre-eminent engineers of his time, though he has often been overlooked until now. He invented things such as the first reliable gas meter, as well as gear cutters, planing machines, and his most famous invention, the automated spinning mule, which was used to spin cotton and really did revolutionize the world, though none of this is why I chose to mention him.

He went further still, however, and next began inventing such things as turret clocks, road vehicles, steamships, locomotives and even fairground rides, though that is still not why I chose to mention him.

Obviously, Roberts was never going to come up with all of these inventions in little old Llanymynech, so he moved to the big city and soon found himself in nearby Manchester. He set up shop, so to speak, in his own home and built a huge lathe in one of his spare bedrooms, however, there was no electricity back then, so the question arose of how to power it. He must have looked around and decided to use whatever was at hand as he built some intricate gearing and powered his machinery by turning a big wheel in the basement.

And what, specifically, was the power source that actually turned the wheel? Well, I told you he decided to use whatever was at hand, and that power source was his wife. Imagine a giant hamster wheel, only with a human as the hamster. He actually chose to keep his wife down in the basement, powering his crazy inventions. That is why I decided to mention

Richard Roberts, and it is probably also why Kate Evans spent her life campaigning for women's rights, knowing that just down the road, her crazy neighbour was using his wife as a human hamster.

As we left the pub, I thought I would ask the landlord, who was once again busy drying his glasses, what the quickest way to Trefonen was, as we were considering a cheeky shortcut. He paused for a moment and then asked if we were walking or going by car, so I told him we were walking. It's definitely quicker by car, he said, and then carried on drying his glasses, with just a hint of a smile on his face.

I almost forgot to retrieve my phone and charger, but remembered at the last minute. Imagine how thrilled I was when I went back to the restaurant and found a young couple trying to enjoy a romantic meal at the table where I had plugged it in. I'm not sure if the sight of my rear end disappearing under it helped or hindered them, but you never know. People are into all sorts of weird stuff nowadays.

Luckily, as we went outside, we discovered that the rain had stopped, so we resumed our walk and headed north towards Llanymynech Hill. The path follows the western contours around it, though we somehow took a wrong turn and followed a minor road instead of the actual route. Thankfully, we still ended up at the same place.

Just as we rediscovered the path, a lady in a car pulled up and offered to let us camp in her garden, which was just at the top of the hill. The other three were, as usual, far ahead of me, so I politely declined her offer on this occasion but said we would certainly consider it the next time we were passing.

A series of left and right turns left me a bit discombobulated for the next couple of miles, and as darkness began to fall, our thoughts turned to looking for somewhere to camp for the night. Options were limited, and as we continued to clock up the miles, we began to wonder if we would actually find anywhere.

A couple of options presented themselves, with one being a disused railway line, which was the Tanat Valley Light Railway. A sign announced it was a restoration project, and it certainly was. It was overgrown in an almost end-of-the-world apocalypse scenario, so we moved on.

Eventually, we found a field, empty and devoid, with not a soul in sight apart from a single, solitary sheep. We sat outside for a while, enjoying the fresh night air and talking about this and that. I told the others that I hoped to see them in the morning, but if any of them had any last messages for their families, then they should tell me now. Nearby, you see, was a place closely associated with sightings of spaceships and the like, and that would be the Berwyn Mountains, just to the west of where we now found ourselves camping.

The most exciting stuff happened there in the 1970s when it was said that a UFO slammed into Berwyn Mountain itself on the 23rd of January, 1974. Local residents reported a loud noise and bright lights in the sky, and claims soon emerged that a flying saucer had crashed, which was immediately recovered by the government and taken to RAF Rudloe Manor, who then covered the whole thing up if you believe that sort of thing.

The clever tabloids quickly began calling it the *Roswelsh Incident,* which I thought was pretty snappy, although the official explanation for all this tomfoolery was simple. Apparently, there had been an earthquake and a meteor at precisely the same time, which makes perfect sense. I mean, both are incredibly rare around these parts, but I guess it was all they could think of.

Wales, in fact, has lots of links to things like aliens and UFOs, and quite recently, Darren Millar, an opposition minister who was a member of the non-ruling Conservative Party, officially asked the Welsh Government, run by the Labour Party, to disclose details of alleged UFO sightings around Cardiff Airport as well as across the rest of the country.

The minister who responded played an absolute slam dunk, it has to be said. Instead of replying in either Welsh or English, which are the two recognised languages when it comes to doing business in Wales, she chose to respond in Klingon, which is the native language of Star Trek's Klingon race, the arch-enemies of Captain Kirk. I'm not sure how long that took her, but I do love it when taxpayers' money is well spent.

Millar had the last laugh, though, and told the press that he had always suspected that government ministers were from another planet.

Being abducted by aliens might just be the vacation I need at this point, to be honest, though it's probably not very likely. With the state of our world nowadays, I bet aliens ride past the Earth and lock their doors.

Anyway, the tents were eventually put up as the temperature started to drop, kettles were boiled and, having thoroughly exhausted myself, I was probably the first one to go to sleep. The lads stayed awake a bit longer than me, though, or at least I assumed they did. And I'm not sure what they did to that sheep, but it sure was noisy.

Unless, of course, it was the aliens.

HOMICIDAL TENDENCIES

Trefonen to Pontcysyllte

I slept like a baby, meaning I kept waking up, and I had to go to the toilet twice. Still, I woke up feeling somewhat refreshed, although I could feel a twinge of pain in my left shin, and I wondered if my shin splint was going to erupt again. If it did, that would be the end of the walk, for me anyway.

Rob had the coffee on when I crawled out of my tent, and a low mist hung over the valley of trees that lay below us. It had been pitch black when we had rocked up last night, so having a glorious view to start our morning was something of a treat.

There was no time to waste, though. Damp tents were rolled and packed, and I waited on the tarmac of the road for the others, mainly so I didn't drench my shoes on the grass, which was heavy with the morning dew.

I did have a bag of rubbish to dispose of, which would have to wait until we found a bin, as the eco-brigade would probably go nuts if I tied it in a tree again. Normally, when I want to get rid of unwanted junk, I simply put it in an Amazon box and leave it by the side of the road. It is usually gone within minutes. None of that today, though, as we found a bin at the next farm, though their dog did go barmy when I slammed the lid.

Eventually, having woken up the entire valley, we were off, and just as we began our daily walk, the sun decided to pay us a visit, which was good. Unfortunately, however, the path immediately went up a steep hill, which was bad.

A small village greeted us after less than a mile, which was Nantmawr, and was where I spent a minute or two stroking a very friendly pair of black lambs who seemed intrigued by our presence. Perhaps it was the smell because, as I said, those showers had been few and far between.

We passed a group of hikers coming the other way here, though they were only out for the day. They had come from Trefonen, they told us, which was where we were heading, and they were doing a circular walk of around ten miles or so.

It was only a couple of miles to Trefonen, but it felt like more because the path twisted this way and that and took us up and down hills in what I could only describe as a random manner. We got there eventually, though, and when we did, the village was apparently still asleep.

There was no reason to stop here, and the only memorable thing about the place was the rather ornate hedgehog house someone had built into their garden wall and a small sign which read *Watch for Children*, which I thought was a fair trade. In no time at all, we were once again back in the fields.

We edged Summer Hill, keeping to its eastern side but still climbing a fair bit, and when we dropped down into the valley at the other side, we landed in heaven.

Passing by the old mill, someone had put a sign on the path welcoming hikers to the Kettle House, where apparently drinks and cakes were available. Well, as we do love to support local businesses, we did not hesitate at all in dropping our backpacks and diving into the little barn that was the Kettle House, and what we found inside was truly terrific.

There was indeed a kettle, but there were also sofas to sit on, tables to use, cakes and biscuits to eat, and lots more besides. That kettle was on before you could say hungry hiker, and I also took one for the team and sampled a big fat piece of flapjack.

And just when we thought things couldn't get better, Neil appeared, who owned this little bit of paradise. We had a little chat, which turned into a long chat, and when he told us that he could arrange for some bacon and egg sandwiches to magically appear in exchange for a few coins of the realm, well, we had no choice, really. Rob and James went for bacon while Mark chose egg, and after a moment of hesitation and indecision, I asked if bacon and egg were a possibility, and apparently, it was.

We enjoyed a cup of tea while we waited and decided to unpack our tents to dry them out in the sunshine, hanging them on whatever bits of gate and fencing we could find. Because the sun was out, we also decided to move outside so we could sit on a picnic bench, soaking up the early morning rays. As we were doing so, our food appeared.

I smothered mine in tomato sauce and dived straight into it, and it hit the spot perfectly. I may or may not have had a combination of ketchup and egg yolk running down my chin at one point, but I didn't care, as that sandwich was heavenly. If only I had ordered two, I thought to myself as I took my last bite.

One last cup of tea washed it all down, and as Rob washed our pots, I packed my tent away, happily noting that it was now about as dry as it was ever going to be.

We never saw Neil again, so we didn't get the chance to thank him for his hospitality, but we did leave a good lump of cash in the donation box in the Kettle House in exchange for our drinks and snacks. I could have stayed there a while longer, just sitting in the sun and sipping tea, but alas, we had miles to cover, so off we went.

After a quick hop across the River Morda, it was, as usual, uphill, this time into the woods. The path through the trees followed the actual dyke for a while, and at one point, I stumbled across a small deer, which surprised me as much as I surprised him. I was once again at the back of our little group, and I thought they would already have scared away anything within a hundred yards, but this brave chap just stood and stared at me, munching on the foliage as he did so. I did reach for my camera to take a picture, but as soon as I did so, he was gone.

The woods seemed to go on for ages, but the path was good underfoot, and I enjoyed the change of scenery. It was mainly pine trees in this forest, with the occasional oak, and all the pinecones on the floor had given me an idea. If I live to some crazy age, like a hundred, and everyone starts asking me what my secret is, I am going to make up something stupid just to mess with people. I think I will tell them I ate a pinecone every day.

When the forest finally ended, I was almost blinded by the bright sunshine as I stepped out onto what a sign told me was Racecourse Common. It didn't take Sherlock Holmes to work out what once went on up here, and the path follows the route where horses once galloped. Unusually, however, the racecourse is in the shape of a figure of eight rather than just an oval. Some remains of the grandstand survive to this day, and there is a rather interesting sculpture of a horse that invites children to sit on it, so obviously, I had a go, though my rucksack nearly unbalanced me.

Apparently, there were once lots of these provincial racecourses about, and they enabled local landowners and the gentry to socialise and show off their best beasts. Some of them were very fast, as well, but bearing in mind that a lot of them were Welsh, it is said that the horses were only fast because they had seen what the farmers do to the sheep.

Anyway, with the introduction of the railways, people were able to travel further afield and seek out better racecourses. It is perhaps not a coincidence that Oswestry last hosted racing in 1848, which was the same year that the railway arrived in the town, and ever since, this site has been a haven of tranquillity.

Impressive sections of Offa's Dyke escorted us on and off for the next few miles to Craignant, a name which once again led me to believe we were back in Wales. However, the village actually sits more or less bang on the border and is technically in England.

At one point, when the others were ahead of me, I took a moment to have a rest and sat down on a bench in the middle of nowhere. After a few minutes, a strange man appeared out of nowhere and sat down right next to me. I say strange because, despite me probably being the only person for miles around, he never said a word. Fear not because I have a top tip for you in case you ever find yourself in such a situation. If this ever happens to you, just stare straight ahead and say, *"Did you bring the money?"* They'll soon be gone. Similarly, when you get a call from an unknown number, answer it by whispering, *"It's done, but there's blood everywhere".* Alternatively, you can also answer the phone with, *"Hello, you're live on air"*, and most telemarketers will hang up immediately, trust me.

A couple of pointless switchbacks led us down and then up again, after which we were following the actual dyke once more, and unusually, for the next mile or so, the dyke also exactly followed the English and Welsh border.

This was so all the way to Bronygarth, and when we arrived in the tiny village, we were still straddling both countries. Once here, the border turned abruptly east and followed the River Ceiriog to who knows where, while we would head north, but not before a quick stop.

There was one reason and one reason only to stop in Bronygarth, and that was because of the Bronygarth Heads, a supposed pair of ancient carved heads, possibly of Celtic origin.

So-called Celtic heads have been found all over

the British Isles, and it is thought that their origin dates back to our ancestors' belief that the head was both the centre of the soul and the link to the afterlife. Indeed, warriors would lop off the heads of their enemies and attach them to their horses' necks to ward off evil, which obviously makes perfect sense.

The Bronygarth heads were found hereabouts in the 1960s near a spring and next to the dyke. Villagers immediately recognised their potential importance and contacted the British Museum, which soon sent an expert to retrieve them.

Renowned Celtic scholar Doctor Anne Ross and her unfortunately named husband, Dick, subsequently turned up to collect them on a day that she described as beautiful and sunny with a clear sky, yet when the pair picked them up and carried them to the car, an almighty thunderclap and a terrible storm blew out of nowhere. Furthermore, they had three accidents on their way home, with one of them nearly killing the pair after the car's brakes failed.

Later on, and we should remember that this comes from a qualified individual with a scientific background, Doctor Ross even went so far as to describe one of the heads, and I quote, *as having an evil expression and a homicidal tendency*. I do love a good quote, but it is only fair to mention, however, that the same Doctor Ross had earlier reported werewolves and the like wandering around her house.

Anyway, the heads somehow eventually made it to the British Museum, where they remain to this day, and Doctor Ross lived happily ever after, only dying in 2012 at the grand old age of eighty-seven, presumably of natural causes and nothing whatsoever to do with either haunted heads or werewolves.

Unfortunately, we were unable to pinpoint the spring near the dyke despite spending several seconds looking, as it was a somewhat vague description, so we moved on. It was uphill, too, which James didn't seem too happy about, and as a result, he looked like he had an evil expression and a homicidal tendency.

We crossed the river, leaving the border behind, and a quick look at the map surprisingly informed us that we had left that border for the last time. The rest of this walk, some forty miles or so, would be in Wales, which was a shame, as one of the only Welsh words I had learned so far was *araf*. I had only learned this because it was written in bold white letters across many steep downhill roads, and I presumed it to mean slow, which, appropriately enough, described my walking speed when compared to that of my buddies.

I had learned a couple of other words, but they probably weren't going to be very useful. The first was the Welsh word for microwave, which quite hilariously, and without absolutely taking the mickey out of someone's culture, is *popty ping*. The second word is more tricky to convey, and I am probably going to have to resort to using asterisks for this one. Jellyfish, you see, when translated into Welsh, is *Cont y Mor*, which quite literally means cu*t of the sea, so unless I'm going to want to quickly cook a jellyfish at some point in the near future, my knowledge of Welsh is more or less useless.

The path took us west, edging around a large hill which we presumed to be a part of the Chirk Estate, as Chirk Castle stood somewhere to the east. We had seen it from the higher ground earlier, though only from a distance, but now, either the trees blocked the view, or I had simply missed it. I was concentrating on not slipping to my death, however, so I can probably be excused, as apparently, some recent rain had left this part of the path in a bit of a mess.

Chirk Castle was built in 1295 by Roger Mortimer, who started out in life with a lucky roll of the dice simply by being born into a noble Welsh family. However, it is pertinent to mention that Welsh nobility back then was only tied to England by virtue of vassalage, which means they were classed as inferior to the English nobility.

This presumably upset old Roger, and he must have been somewhat bitter as a result, to the point that those around him described him as lecherous and violent, which basically means he was a rapist.

He did warm to the king, though, which was Edward I initially, or Edward Longshanks as he was better known, due to his unusually tall height for the times. Roger fought for the king many times, at the Battle of Falkirk in 1298, for instance, a crucial battle of the First War of Scottish Independence, which was, in fact, the one where William Wallace was famously defeated.

Later on, Roger fought with the king once again, this time at the Battle of Bannockburn, but things didn't go so well, and Robert the Bruce and the Scots took great revenge on the English. The Scottish were victorious, and Longshanks fled into the castle to save his life. It is said that Edward was so incensed with the humiliation of this defeat that he vowed to crush the Scottish once and for all. As a result, he later became known as the Hammer of the Scots, such was his hate for the North Britons.

On a side note, however, if you think you have ever visited the battlefield of Bannockburn, then I am sorry to tell you that you probably haven't. While historians are split on the actual location of this most famous fight, they are all firmly on the same page and agree that the traditionally accepted site, where the visitor centre and statue are located, is definitely not the correct one.

Anyway, when Longshanks died in 1307, he is said to have succumbed to the gruesome effects of dysentery, meaning he basically bled to death through his bum hole, about as un-noble a death as you can get. As a result, Edward II then came to power, and Roger Mortimer suddenly found himself no longer on the royal Christmas card list. To cut a long story short, he died in the Tower of London in 1326, far removed from his comfortable home at Chirk Castle, such was the king's displeasure with him. Apparently, Edward II had totally forgotten about such trivial matters as the laws of the land and the Magna Carta and spent much of his life fighting the powerful barons. While he was ultimately unsuccessful, it was too late for poor Roger Mortimer.

It was getting late for us, too, and thoughts turned to where we would be staying tonight. I was aware of a small guesthouse at Froncysyllte, which, much like you probably, I could read but not say, and I had heard that they allowed camping in the garden.

Unfortunately, when I phoned them, a terribly lovely lady told me they had just retired and were now too busy spending the kids' inheritance and had much better things to do than let smelly English blokes sleep on their grass. I thanked her profusely, and despite my generous offer of temporarily pausing her retirement to accommodate said blokes, it was not to be.

And by the way, I never did learn how to pronounce Froncysyllte. I tried many times and spent several days on the project, but even my best attempt still sounded like I was barfing up last night's dinner. Anyway, the locals simply call it Fron, apparently, so that's that problem solved.

We wandered on almost aimlessly, and sometime later, I spied what I thought was the Pontcysyllte Aqueduct through the trees. When it failed to materialise, however, and fearing we were lost, a quick check of the map told us we had instead passed the Newbridge Viaduct, which, despite its name, is rather old and was built in 1848, and is presumably how those trains got to Oswestry.

Soon enough, though, we joined the towpath of the Shropshire and Union Canal, and after a final sharp right-hand bend, we were almost at the aqueduct, which was just a few dozen yards ahead of us. Unfortunately, however, we made one crucial mistake. In following the signs for Offa's Dyke Path, we now found ourselves on the western side of the canal. This was a problem because, when it got to the aqueduct, the path only carried on along the eastern side of the canal, and there was no bridge because, of course, the aqueduct was the bridge.

For some reason, it was just Rob and me at this stage, as James and Mark had fallen behind, which was odd. As we stood and waited, I couldn't help but be reminded that my good friend is incredibly tall, a thought which made me wonder if we should call him Longshanks from now on. Anyway, because of his height and because the canal is only a few feet wide here, I naturally encouraged Rob to jump across it.

He wasn't having any of it, however, probably because he didn't want to end up three feet deep in stinky canal water, and anyway, he had a better plan.

Quite cheekily but admittedly rather cleverly, he started a conversation with the captain of the next canal boat that came trundling along. Almost instantly, my sweet-talking friend had negotiated permission for the pair of us to use his craft as a sort of moving bridge, which quite appropriately was called the *Genie in the Lamp*, appropriate because it made our wish come true.

Alas, we needn't have bothered, as just a few dozen yards further on, we realised we could have ducked under the aqueduct anyway. Still, our way was more fun, and by the way, if Rob had attempted to jump across, he would definitely have gone for a swim. I later found out that the canal was eight feet wide, far too wide to jump across, but still, it would have been fun watching.

It turns out that the Pontcysyllte aqueduct is an absolute marvel of Georgian engineering that carries the Llangollen Canal over the River Dee just near the ingloriously named but sweet little township of Trevor. For those illiterate, uneducated English folks among us, Pontcysyllte is pronounced *pont-ker-sulth-tay*, and it means simply *Bridge of Csysllte,* which is the small town that sits at its southern end, which I presumed was the same place as Froncysyllte.

If you look at the website that promotes this bridge as a world heritage site, however, you will see outlandish and controversial claims being thrown around that the name actually means *the bridge that connects.*

This turns out to be a somewhat contentious issue, as others out there violently disagree and say that any such claims are the result of recent misguidedness linked purely to the fact that the name is similar to another Welsh word, *cywllt,* which really does mean connect. I can't pronounce either of these, so this is one argument I'm staying out of because, quite frankly, I've got bigger fish to fry.

Anyway, generally regarded to have been designed by famous civil engineer Thomas Telford, the aqueduct was first birthed into being at the turn of the 19th century, and it has been delighting canal-goers, walkers and tourists alike ever since. Amazingly, the canal bit, known as the trough, is actually constructed of iron, of both the wrought and cast variety, and it is this mix that enabled the aqueduct to be built with arches that were both light and strong and also incredibly beautiful. And perhaps not surprisingly, it is the longest and highest aqueduct in Britain.

And when I said that it was generally

considered to have been designed by Telford, he actually took much of his instruction from a man called William Jessop, who did all the hard work.

Originally, the canal was supposed to be a part of a much grander scheme that would ultimately have linked the River Severn with the great port of Liverpool. However, sufficient funds to complete the dream were somewhat lacking, so most of it was never built.

Thankfully, however, this aqueduct was built, which is good, for it is probably the most interesting part of the scheme anyway.

In fact, its construction was even more unlikely than we can imagine, as the original design never actually included the viaduct. Instead, the scheme envisaged a series of locks on the hills up either side of the valley, and it was solely down to Telford, who, despite much scepticism, came up with his idea for the uninterrupted waterway that we see today. It was recognised as something quite exceptional very early on, too, with its proponents including famous poet Sir Walter Scott, who once described it as *a stream in the sky where the fish swim above the birds*, which is actually pretty cool when you think about it, even for us non-poetic, Neanderthal types.

The fact that it was built at all was even more of a miracle, as Telford was relatively unknown at the time and was more or less at the beginning of his career when he came up with his grand plan. Furthermore, the construction was incredibly difficult and expensive, and it cost a staggering sum of money, equivalent to one percent of the national economy at the time it was built. It is comparable to the modern-day equivalent of something called HS2, which was basically a giant white elephant of a railway line up the middle of England that was designed to shave twenty-six seconds off the time it takes to commute from London to Birmingham but which now won't because nobody even wants to go to Birmingham. At the time of writing, it probably won't actually go into London, either, which kind of defeats the point of the whole thing anyway. In fact, I suspect, just like the canal, the train line will also probably never be finished, and I also suspect that whichever people come along in a couple of hundred years will certainly not be marvelling at whatever engineering was built, if any.

Anyway, once completed, the aqueduct was well used for many years; however, a general lack of maintenance gradually saw it slip into a poor state of repair, and by the 1930s, serious problems began to develop, which not surprisingly mainly involved lots and lots of water leaks.

In fact, by 1939, it had become impossible to sail a boat across the aqueduct, although there was still a little bit of water running across it, but only enough for a paddle.

And in 1945, disaster struck. The nearby canal finally breached its banks just east of Llangollen, which in turn washed away the railway line that ran alongside it. The subsequent torrent of water was enough to derail the first train of the day, and the engine driver was killed instantly. All sixteen wagons of the train were also derailed, but as it was a goods train, the only other casualty was the fireman, though luckily, he survived and suffered just a broken wrist and a surprise shower.

The manager of the local pub, the Sun Trevor Inn, had heard the kerfuffle and immediately summoned the fire brigade, but by the time they arrived and despite the millions of gallons of water that had just washed everywhere, cinders from the locomotive's fire still managed to ignite the wreckage, as was common back then. Thankfully, someone took some rather interesting photos of the disaster, and while I am not sure if it was the landlord who was in them, those photos can now be seen in the pub, which is as good an excuse as any to call in if you are ever passing.

And as for one last fact on the aqueduct, quite bizarrely, Telford used animal blood, in this case, blood from an Ox, in the mortar used to build the thing, which is not as unusual as it might sound. For centuries, you see, blood has been routinely added to mortar as it makes it more resistant to damage during freezing weather, which is not something I had ever heard of.

We waited for James and Mark to catch us up, and eventually, we saw them coming up the path. They had done the same as us and were on the wrong side, so we dropped our backpacks and walked up to meet them, as a little trick was in order.

With perhaps more urgency than was required, we shouted to the pair of them that the footpath ended up ahead and that they simply had to use the next canal boat as a bridge. The only alternative, we added loudly, was to walk a mile back to use the actual bridge, thereby adding two miles to the walk.

I am both delighted and ashamed at the same time to mention that they fell for it, hook, line and sinker. Mark immediately began talking to the driver of the next and only canal boat approaching, but he clearly didn't have as much luck as us. The captain, if that is the correct term, looked simultaneously puzzled and worried, and I think he even put the throttle on full to get away from the two crazy Englishmen now bearing down on him. As it passed us, and as we gave the driver a cheery little wave, we noticed this boat was called *Carry On*, which is once again appropriate, as that is precisely what it did, all the while pursued by two wild and desperate looking unwashed human beings of dubious origin.

For a moment or two, our friends looked crestfallen and were undoubtedly contemplating that two-mile walk to the previous bridge and back. However, when they realised that they could, in fact, simply duck under the viaduct just ahead of us, they instead took on an evil expression and a homicidal tendency, at which point Rob and I thought it best to move on.

It was awkward, to say the least, crossing the aqueduct. There were lots of people coming the other way, and one or two rather rude individuals tried to push past us. While I knew I couldn't throw them over the side as such, I did consider beating them with a stick. Anyway, this meant someone had to step to the side and that someone was generally us. Choosing whether to fall into a cold canal or whether to disappear hundreds of feet over the side of the aqueduct was not the best choice, but we repeatedly did so and somehow got across without getting splattered into a pile of broken bones and oozing blood out of every orifice, or even worse, getting wet.

On a positive note, we did see Thomas Telford's house as we crossed, which he allegedly had built so he could keep an eye on the lazy navvies who were doing all the hard work. However, we should remember that while Telford took the credit for much of the work, it was actually William Jessop who was the man on the ground, so to speak.

Because of his modesty, however, most people have never heard of Jessop, and much of his work is traditionally attributed to his so-called assistants. Examples of this include the Caledonian Canal, which bravely connects the east and west coasts of Scotland, as well as the appropriately named Grand Canal of Ireland, and, of course, the Pontcysyllte Aqueduct.

William Jessop was born in Devon in 1745, the only son of lighthouse keeper Josiah Jessop, who was responsible for the old wooden lighthouse that once stood on Eddystone Rocks, which later became famous for being the location of the first stone lighthouse in the world.

When the original wooden lighthouse burned down in 1755, aspiring civil engineer John Smeaton was brought in to build a new one. I had come across Smeaton before, on the Yorkshire Coast Path, as he had also been responsible for the lighthouse on Spurn Point, and I vaguely recalled a reference to him in a Kaiser Chiefs' song, *I Predict A Riot*, made because the Chiefs went to the same grammar school as Smeaton, but anyway, I digress.

When Smeaton started work on the lighthouse, he hired Josiah Jessop to be his wingman, so to speak, with his son William helping out by running errands, as children love to do. Progress was slow, as they could only work on the lighthouse during the brief summer months, but this gave Smeaton and Josiah a chance to get to know each other. They became good friends, so when Josiah died in 1761, Smeaton became William Jessop's guardian, and, to cut a long story short, this is how William Jessop ended up building bridges in Wales, and thank goodness he did, because this one is fantastic. It's not just me who is saying that, either. Because the aqueduct has recently been designated a World Heritage Site, it sits alongside the likes of the Great Wall of China and the Pyramids of Egypt.

The aqueduct has something that the wall and the pyramids don't have, however, and that is a pub, which is where we went next. We were soon hogging a table at the Telford Inn, which should, of course, be called The Jessop.

Still, the food was good, and so was the weather, so we sat outside in the sun and discussed our next move. We had all had about enough for the day, but a quick check of the map did not reveal any campsites along the next few miles of our route. Instead, we would get a few more miles under our feet and then look for somewhere to wild camp just before sunset, and as far as sunsets go, it looked like it was going to be a glorious one.

Getting moving again after a heavy meal is always difficult. Especially when it's uphill. Especially when you've had a pudding. And especially when you've washed that all down with a couple of pints. So it was with a bit of a struggle that we made our way through Poncysyllte heading west, where I had a thought. When this walk is over, which meeting do we attend first? Weight Watchers or AA? Probably the latter, if my wife had any say in the matter. She says I have a drinking problem. The other day, she asked me to toast some bread, and I raised my glass and said, *"Here's to the bread".*

Immediately after leaving the unpronounceable town, the path entered a wood, and as we wandered along, we could just make out a big house through the trees to the south. This was Trevor Hall, which actually sounded more like a television presenter than a country house. Now a luxurious hotel for people with more money than sense, I had heard that the hall was once reduced to nothing more than a cow barn after a fire left it in ruin and a farmer put a tin roof over what was left of it, which wasn't all that much. Well, those days are long gone, and if you ever happen to win the lottery, this is probably the place to come to.

The forest gave way to a smooth tarmac road just after Trevor Rocks, which, similar to Trevor Hall, sounded more like a statement than the name of a geographical feature, so for a while, all four of us walked as one, something of a rarity along this route. We chatted about how near the end was and reckoned that, barring any interesting or fatal developments, we would probably be walking into Prestatyn tomorrow or possibly the day after.

This gave me a familiar feeling, but unfortunately, it was one of sadness. I always feel like this when nearing the end of a walk, and this one was no exception. We had certainly had some fun along the way, such as watching Rob stumble into the earth and then witnessing James being mauled by a vicious dog, but soon, all of that would be over, and we would be back at home.

I was brought out of my melancholy by the appearance of an impressive conical hill ahead of me, upon which was something exciting indeed, and that something was Castell Dinas Bran, the remnants of a once-mighty medieval castle. But as well as being a remarkable hilltop fort, Castell Dinas Bran is also a place of legend. It is said that during Arthurian times, one of the kings of England, Bran the Blessed, allowed his sister Branwen to marry the King of Ireland. Unfortunately, as sometimes happens at weddings, everyone had a bit too much to drink, and the two families fell out. To smooth things over, Bran offered the Irish king a spare magic cauldron that he happened to have lying around, as you do, one that could apparently bring the dead back to life, and after everyone calmed down a little, the Irish king returned home with his new wife.

Unfortunately, Branwen soon found herself mistreated and banished to the kitchen, where she was beaten every day, which, in fairness, was probably just called marriage back in medieval times. Anyway, she wasn't exactly thrilled with her new-found domestic arrangements, so she befriended a starling and sent it back to her brother, who immediately raced off to Ireland to rescue her.

To cut a long story short, a big battle ensued, and almost everyone in this story was killed. On his deathbed, King Bran ordered his surviving men to cut off his head and take it back to England, and they duly complied.

Presumably because Bran had at some point stuck his coconut in the magic cauldron, his head stayed alive after his death, and he is said to have entertained his men for seven years, after which he finally ran out of jokes and really did drop dead.

Upon his actual death, his loyal subjects buried his head on White Hill, which is supposedly the modern-day site of the Tower of London, and they made sure he was facing France. Legend has it, you see, that as long as his head remains in situ, England is protected from invasion.

Incidentally, this image of the talking head is said to be derived from the Celtic cult of the head that we last heard about back at Bronygarth, which made me wonder if there was a connection, given the similar spelling and the fact that heads are common to both tales, though we'll probably never know.

That's not all, though. In Welsh, bran means crow, and there have been attempts to link the practice of the keeping of ravens at the Tower of London with that of Bran the Blessed. Ravens are still kept there today, living on the south lawn and paid for by the government, which employs someone called the Yeomen Warder to look after them. There are six of them, and they even have names and have been officially cared for since the time of Charles II. His Astronomer Royal, John Flamsteed, wasn't too happy, however, and he is said to have complained vigorously, mainly because of the fact that they were constantly shitting all over his telescopes, apparently.

Nowadays, the ravens are, quite bizarrely, classed as enlisted soldiers of the kingdom. As such, they can be dismissed for unsatisfactory conduct, and believe it or not, this has actually happened. Raven George, who served between 1977 and 1986, lost his appointment to the crown because he kept destroying television aerials and was retired to the Welsh Mountain Zoo.

Another raven, appropriately named Grog because he was partial to a bit of alcohol, deserted his post in 1981 and went to live in a pub, which doesn't sound all that bad an idea, to be honest.

The last story concerns two ravens, who were named James and Edgar. James died, and Edgar must have been smarter than the average bird, as when he noticed the commotion surrounding his colleague's death, he decided to play dead himself in order to elicit a bit of attention. When the raven master came to pick up his so-called corpse, Edgar bit his finger and flapped away while croaking huge raven laughs.

Another recent raven, Merlin, is said to have copied this trick. When she was bored, because apparently, Merlin was a female, she was said to have laid upside down with her legs in the air until one tourist or another eventually screamed and raised the alarm, at which point Merlin would hop off laughing.

On a serious note, ravens are said to be exceptionally intelligent, mourning their dead and sharing their resources with selected friends. At the Tower of London, for instance, they have regularly been seen chasing seagulls away whilst choosing to share their food with their cousins, the crows.

Finally, similar to the folklore surrounding Bran's head, if the ravens ever vanish, so says the legend, then England will fall. In fact, during the dark days of the Blitz of the Second World War, when there was only one raven left, Winston Churchill ordered that more should be brought in immediately. This all makes me wonder if our national security really does depend on some spooky corvids and an old bloke's magic head, though quite frankly, I sincerely hope not, and I much prefer nuclear-tipped missiles if I am being brutally honest.

Resisting the considerable temptation to deviate from our path and take a closer look at Dinas Bran, we kept moving, all the while keeping an eye out for somewhere to pitch our tents, and all I can say is that the gods must have been shining on us tonight.

Rock Farm greeted us just before the path took a turn up into the hills, and James went to find someone to ask if they had a patch of grass where four dishevelled blokes could pitch their tents for the night.

He was gone a while, which made me both hopeful and anxious at the same time, but when he returned, he told us that, unfortunately, there was nowhere to put them.

There was, however, a barn we could sleep in, which made us all smile, and we immediately shuffled off to find it.

Perhaps *barn* was an overstatement. Open-sided shack would have been more accurate, though probably still overly generous a description if I am brutally honest. Various murder weapons dotted the walls, some of them rusted and seemingly ancient, and I momentarily wondered which one the farmer was going to use to chop us all up in the dead of the night.

Still, we were tired, and it was getting dark, and on top of that, it now looked like it was going to rain.

There was a little picnic table, too, which we all sat at while Rob brewed us a special coffee, one with a little something in it. Well, this was one of our last nights on the trail, after all, so we could afford to treat ourselves, so for once, we had a late night, chatting about this and that, but mainly about the trip and how we all unanimously agreed that while we were ready to go home and enjoy such civilities as a bath and a hairbrush, we still didn't actually want the walk to come to an end.

As the evening went on, Rob somehow magically conjured up some more little bottles of delight that had been secreted somewhere deep within his backpack, one of which was spiced rum, while the other was my absolute weakness, Jack Daniels.

Music found its way into the merry mix as well, courtesy of Mark's phone, and as we sat there enjoying the steadily cooling evening, rain began to fall, which made us doubly grateful for our night under this shelter. We should do this more often, James suggested, and he was right.

And to top it off, I had made it through the day without beating anyone with a stick. I'd say my people skills are improving.

THE END IS NIGH

Pontcysyllte to Ruthin

There was nobody around as we packed our little camp away, but it was a welcome change not to have to dry our tents for once. This meant we were soon on our way, walking uphill, of course, and almost immediately, we left the smooth road for something which could only be described as rustic.

A rocky path took us into a desolate land of rocks and stones, with loose-looking scree slopes all around us. The path itself was pretty good, however, so we stumbled steadily on, passing an old limekiln that was now home to a huge tree and several noisy birds.

The hillside soon became ever more impressive, culminating in the vast rampart that was Craig Arthur, a vertical rock face towering far above our heads. There was even more excitement to be had, though, as two people had escaped from a nearby lunatic asylum and were now climbing up it, though for what reason, I could not fathom. We waited in anticipation for a while, but after a few minutes, when nobody had fallen to an incredibly splatty but rather entertaining death, we moved on.

Thankfully, there weren't many ups and downs here as the path followed the natural contours of the hill. After passing a couple of streams, we eventually found ourselves back on the same road we had been on earlier, though we were now at one of the best-named places along the whole walk and one which I had been looking forward to immensely, as we were in the forests of World's End.

The woods proved to be truly beautiful, utterly enchanting and almost magical. The gently undulating road slowly snaked its way up the mountain, leading us through a scene that would not look out of place in a fantasy novel, and in many ways, it also reminded me of the Wild West, with steep hills full of Sitka spruce totally engulfing the valley, which was topped off by yet more slopes of loose, rocky scree beneath impressive limestone outcroppings of rock.

The top of the valley is even more picturesque, to borrow a word we heard many times in the Wye Valley. Here, the road has switchbacks and fords, which were thankfully not entirely out of control today, and it also has that wonderful name, World's End, though I have no idea why.

As we passed the farm, which funnily enough was called World's End Farm, I caught a quick glimpse of an old manor house but only really saw the gable end, which is a shame. Built almost 500 years ago, this timber-framed little beauty has a lot of history of its own, and if walls could talk, those walls would probably sing.

Firstly, it was built on the site of a hunting lodge that stood here around a thousand years ago. The lodge was used by Owain, the Prince of Powys, in the 1100s, and it is fair to say that his story gets somewhat spicy. Legend has it, you see, that Owain kidnapped a princess known as Helen of Wales, although, for some unfathomable reason, everyone called her Nest.

Anyway, given that she was the wife of Gerald FitzWalter, one of the most powerful Welsh Lords of the time who ruled over much of South Wales, kidnapping Nest was probably not the best idea that Owain had ever had.

Nevertheless, it is said that Owain ended up right here at World's End, along with Nest or Helen or whatever she was called, and furthermore, she may actually have gone with him willingly. Other accounts claim that she was indeed kidnapped but then suffered from an incredibly early version of Stockholm Syndrome, where the victim begins to relate to their kidnappers, which was odd because Stockholm had not then been founded as a city.

Anyway, one important clue that suggests one of these possibilities is that on the night of the kidnapping, it is said that she had encouraged her own husband to escape down something called the garderobe, which was basically the medieval toilet, presumably so she could run off with Owain, the Pervert of Powys.

Anyway, the historical record is far from certain on precisely what happened next, and while some say Owain raped Helen, others say they willingly had two children together. What is certain, however, is that the so-called kidnapping was a lengthy one indeed.

Eventually, however, the game was inevitably up, and after Helen was ultimately returned to FitzWalter, with a couple of presumably hard-to-explain youngsters strapped to her waist, Owain was forced to flee to Ireland, where he spent the next few years hiding from Gerald, the jealous husband.

Many years later, however, and after being pardoned by none other than the king, Owain finally thought it safe to return to Wales, and he did so around the year 1112. What's more, the only reason he returned was to fight on behalf of the very king who had so generously pardoned him. Unfortunately, on the way to the battle, he happened to run into, of all people, Gerald FitzWalter, who, not surprisingly, was still ever so slightly displeased, to put it mildly, that Owain had borrowed his old lady for a couple of years for a bit of hide the sausage. And while the king might have pardoned Owain, Gerald certainly hadn't, and things got a bit nasty.

While they had initially both been heading for the same battle, where they would actually have been fighting on the same side, they chose instead to fight each other and, to cut a long story short, Gerald finally got his revenge for the rape of his wife, and chopped Owain into tiny little bits, probably starting with the sausage, and that was the end of that for poor old Owain.

Several hundred years later, intrigue once again visited this house when it became the home of a man called John Jones Maesygarnedd in the 1600s, who happened to be a judge. However, because I'm merely an illiterate and ignorant Englishman, I'm going to call him John Jones, but don't judge me because I bet you couldn't say his surname either. Anyway, he lived here during the Civil War and was a powerful figure in military and political circles, and he threw pretty good parties, too.

When the war ended in 1651, John Jones was selected as one of the judges at the trial of King Charles, and when they found him well and truly guilty after what was absolutely, positively and definitely a fair trial, Jones' signature was one of those that could be seen at the bottom of the king's death warrant.

Unfortunately, once they had dispatched the king by lopping off his head, the new people in charge, namely Oliver Cromwell and his cronies, let the power go straight to their heads, and Cromwell became the new king in all but name. He wasn't very popular, either, particularly when he told everyone they had to go to church or else, and even more so when he closed all the theatres and, perhaps quite foolishly, shut all the pubs, too.

When Cromwell popped his clogs in 1658 and passed his powerful position to his son, Richard, it became blindingly obvious to everybody that they had simply replaced one tyrant with another, which paved the way for the restoration of the monarchy, particularly as Cromwell junior had none of the charisma of his father. Perhaps tellingly, Cromwell senior's nickname had been *Old Ironsides*, while his son was not-so-affectionately known as *Tumbledown Dick*.

Hence, in 1660, the old king's son, also called Charles, returned to England and was proclaimed the new king, becoming Charles II on the 29th of May 1660.

Not surprisingly, the new king then took the opportunity to sort out all those who had deposed his dear old dad, and that notably and perhaps not surprisingly included anyone who had been foolish enough to sign the old king's death warrant. John Jones thus found himself plucked from the streets of London just four days after the coronation and, after spending a few months in the Tower of London, where someone locked him in a room and told him to take some time to think about what he had done, he was tried, convicted and sentenced in just a few short days, thanks once again to the absolute fairness and total impartiality of the English judicial system.

Some would say that this series of events really did represent the extraordinary efficiency of English justice, while others might call it a kangaroo court. Regardless, as per the custom of the time, after John Jones was found guilty of high treason, he was more or less immediately hanged, drawn and quartered, and that was the end of his story, though not the end of the story of World's End Farm.

The house then enjoyed some years of obscurity, where nothing much happened at all until the Germans stumbled across it in 1940. They had been looking for Wrexham, over the border in England, around 20 miles away, so how they ended up dropping a bomb on this charming little manor house in a wooded valley in an entirely different country is somewhat perplexing.

Anyway, on Saturday, 31st of August 1940, they did indeed drop a bomb on this very place, and, as shots go, it was a pretty good one, as it blew the house to smithereens. It was a farm at the time, and while the owner, Peter Morris, somehow managed to survive, his two sisters, Ann and Mary, were killed in the explosion along with his farmhand, Frank Jones, which made me wonder if John Jones had been his great, great grandad, but I digress. Anyhow, this story presents a problem in itself because accounts at the time suggested the house was utterly destroyed. Later reports, however, say the house was restored after the bombing, but by saying restored, they must surely mean rebuilt.

The others had continued onwards and upwards by now, so I was by myself, and as I was having a nosey at the house through the gate, an old man walked up the road from the opposite direction along with his dog, a scruffy and old-looking collie.

I said hello to him and we began talking, and I asked him about the house, mentioning how surprised I had been when I first read of it being bombed during the war. He said there was a reason for this and then, quite surprisingly, told me the whole story, which I later checked out and dug into a bit more, though I'll give you the condensed version.

Liverpool had been a strategic target during the war, particularly its docks. In order to protect them, men of the Home Guard, and it was men, by the way, ventured into the hills and valleys of North Wales and lit fires here, there and everywhere in order to fool the Luftwaffe, the German air force, and to lure them away from the real targets.

Unfortunately, their plan was a little too

successful, and on that fateful night in August 1940, the Germans dropped tons of bombs all across this area. One of them hit this manor house, and they also hit the tiny village of Rhosllanerchrugog, which is just a couple of miles or so to the east. And by the way, it's pronounced something like *Russ-lan-ek-ree-goak*, but when I attempted to say it, it sounded like I was vomiting.

Anyway, when the bombs dropped, all hell broke loose. The hillsides caught fire, lighting tinder-dry gorse and bracken at the end of a long summer, and almost 30 square miles of mountain went up in flames, and there were incredibly sad stories of sheep being roasted alive.

As I listened, I noticed a tear in the corner of the old man's eye, and I realised that for him, this was much more than just a story, much more, but I did not ask, as some things are simply personal. But I did ask him why this valley is called World's End, which made him switch back into the now, as he simply said, "*It's bloody obvious, ain't it*," and I guess it was when you actually think about it.

Before we parted, he also told me about a memorial on the hill above us. Over the years, hikers and walkers have contributed to a huge stone cross made of thousands of rocks that was built to remember the countless airmen who have died whilst flying in and around these valleys, particularly during the Second World War. The cross is quite impressive, he went on, and sort of resembles an aeroplane itself, perhaps because the aircraft that have crashed up there include Spitfires, Hurricanes, P-51 Mustangs and more. In fact, he finished, it is probably quicker to list the aircraft that have not crashed up there.

I bade my farewells and thanked him for his stories, and wandered up the road towards a bend and a stepping-stone bridge, but the weird thing is, when I turned around to give him one last wave, the guy had gone, and there was no sign of his dog either. He had simply vanished into the trees, and when I caught the others up and mentioned him, they looked blankly at me and said they hadn't seen anyone at all, never mind a dog, which was odd because he must have come from their direction.

The road became incredibly steep for a while, but as it evened off, a stone marker told us to make a left across the moorland towards Llandegla. We made good progress here, mainly because some kind soul had put excellent paths in, which alternated between heavy flagstones and timber sleepers.

Heather and bilberry plants surrounded us, and small birds darted at manic speeds here and there, making this stretch of the walk a pleasant one, and before we knew it, we were climbing over a ladder gate and entering the forest.

Llandegla Forest proved to be much more substantial than the one that had preceded World's End but looked far less natural, and as forests go, this one is actually surprisingly new. Planted as recently as the 1970s, the wood is mainly full of pine trees, in particular Sitka Spruce, with the odd larch thrown in to confuse the squirrels.

Both trees are non-native species, however. The larch was brought in from Europe around 400 years ago, while the Sitka Spruce arrived from America less than 200 years ago, in 1831, to be exact. Messing with the environment must have been something of a fun hobby for our well-to-do ancestors, as, if you remember, we had come across this at Leighton Hall where John Naylor had grafted two trees together, Frankenstein-style, and had ended up with the Leylandii.

Anyway, I always love it when I encounter larch, as its seeds are a particular favourite of Red Squirrels. Quite frankly, the Reds need all the help they can get, having been outcompeted by their American cousins, the Greys. In fact, Grey Squirrels steal resources and carry lots of filthy diseases that kill Reds, and, in many areas, the poor Reds are almost extinct.

And while it had long been thought that Grey Squirrels were spreading across the country as a single sort of wave, recent DNA analysis has suggested this is not the case. Squirrels caught in one or another part of the country have been identified as being genetically distinct from others, and it is even possible to find out where new populations have come from when they first spring up.

For instance, recent Greys caught in Aberdeen were shown to have come from the population in Hampshire and, in particular, the New Forest. As there is no way a squirrel could possibly have walked that far, there is only one direction in which to point the blame, and that is us humans, unfortunately. Greys, you see, have this unwitting knack for getting locked into things such as vans, lorries and even cars, and when we open the doors of such things at the other end of whatever journey has occurred, they just jump right out, often not even noticed by their respective taxi drivers, and live happily ever after in their lovely, new homes.

It's a shame that I never actually saw a Red Squirrel then. However, I did see half a dozen mountain bikers who flew around a bend and almost made me extinct. I later found out that this forest is very popular with the two-wheeled lot, so watch your step.

Leaving the forest behind, as well as the silent death that was the mountain bikers, a quick hop across a country lane led to a pleasant downhill section of squishy path towards Llandegla itself. One car briefly threatened to squash us and narrowly missed Rob, causing him to shout various things that were probably unprintable, which I thought was a bit ironic as Rob can be a bit of a fast driver himself. I can prove this, too, as his satnav says things like *in four hundred yards, stop and let me out.* In fairness, my driving is not much better. The other day, an angry woman yelled at me, saying she was going to make my life a living hell. I shouted back that I was grateful for the offer, but I was already married. And by the way, when I said the other day, I could be referring to any day between yesterday and fifteen years ago, something you will understand when you get to my age.

Emerging at a scarily busy main road, where juggernauts thundered by, wholly oblivious to smelly hikers, I wondered what would happen if one of them got me, and a popping water balloon sprang to mind. Hopefully, the drivers of these trucks would exercise some common sense and slow down at what was obviously a busy crossing point, but if I am brutally honest, I don't like the fact that my chances of survival are linked to the common sense of others.

Shaking that thought from my head, I dodged across the road and moved a few dozen yards along, looking for the resumption of the path at the other side, and almost missed it due to it being hidden and secreted in a hedge that, for whatever reason, the authorities had presumably decided to hide, and they had done an outstanding job of it, too.

For a minute, I doubted if I would even fit down the path, but somehow, I managed it, though I did have to hold my breath for a minute or two. In fairness, I probably only made it through because my friends had recently made the gap considerably bigger, and I made a mental note to thank Rob in particular when I caught him up.

Emerging at the other end onto a quiet village road, it was almost like I was born again, and I momentarily danced a little jig until I realised a little old lady was watching me, and I should say, she had a somewhat bemused look on her face. She had probably not seen something like me emerge from those trees since the 1930s, or possibly earlier, unless, of course, she had just seen Rob, James and Mark do exactly the same.

Anyway, this was Llandegla, and it was awesome, and when I say was, I emphasise the past tense. Nowadays, unfortunately, it is a quiet little backwater of a place, and all the houses were unpleasantly new. But my disappointment was not to last, for just half a mile and a few minutes later, I was in the centre of the village, and it was actually rather pretty, and as an added bonus, I found all of my friends, who were waiting for me just opposite the church.

I had popped in there on our little reconnaissance trip last year, which is precisely why I was not going in now. It had been Easter Sunday, and I had barged in right in the middle of the Easter service. Everything went quiet as everyone looked at me, which is when my stomach decided to demonstrate the mating call of a whale.

St Tecla's Church stands proudly where all the village's roads met, and beyond that, the most excellently named River Alyn splished and splashed beneath a fine stone bridge, though in my childish head, that river was really called Alan. Don't go digging near that river, by the way. In the 19th century, a wicked ghost spent quite some time haunting the rectory in the village. After considerable shenanigans, the wayward spirit was eventually captured by a Mr Griffiths, and he buried it in a box which he placed beneath a large stone somewhere near to the bridge, because that would keep a ghost imprisoned, obviously.

St Tecla herself is worth a mention. There is a well, just south of the village, that bears her name, and in days gone by, crazy people with too much money would come here to be cured of disease. Apparently, they would wash themselves after sunset, then walk around the well three times, hopefully without falling over in the darkness. After that, they would leave an offering of fourpence and spend the night in the church, presumably because they could no longer afford a hotel, having left all their money in a muddy ditch.

The church later discouraged this, probably

because they were sick of finding strangers asleep in the pews every morning, though I'll bet they kept the money, of course.

Anyway, other than that, Llandegla hasn't given the world all that much, other than a man called Elihu Yale. The village was the ancestral home of the Yale family, and Elihu was probably the most famous and lived quite a life, and if you think you've never heard of him, I can promise that you have.

Although he wasn't actually born here, he spent much of his life at the family home, but he also travelled far and wide. With good connections via his father, he managed to wangle a top job with the up-and-coming British East India Company, where he amassed a fortune of his own, and let's just say he didn't do this by following the rules. Insider trading was quite common, and he was perhaps one of its most ardent fans, so when he was inevitably sacked from his job, he returned to England with a sum of money equivalent to billions of pounds today.

So, with more cash than you could shake a stick at, old Elihu Yale decided to reinvent himself as something of a philanthropist, and one of his grand schemes was to fund a college in America. That college, as you may have already guessed, is Yale University, named in honour of Elihu, and is one of the top universities in America, if not the world.

And while we could leave this little fairy

tale at that, it is only fitting to mention that Elihu Yale had links to the most grotesque trade imaginable, that of slaves. This started when he was in India, and it is alleged that he authorised the shipment of slaves to Europe and, in some cases, even compelled it, stating that it was a shame to waste cargo space.

In his later years, it is possible that Yale recognised how cruel he had been. When he died, he was buried in nearby Wrexham, and it is worth noting the inscription on his tomb, which reads like an apology for his deeds and a warning to all that follow to be just in life:

Born in America, in Europe bred,

In Africa travelled and in Asia wed,

Where long he lived and thrived; In London dead,

Much good, some ill, he did; so hope all's even,

And that his soul thro' mercy's gone to Heaven,

You that survive and read this tale, take care,

For this most certain exit to prepare,

Where blessed in peace, the actions of the just,

Smell sweet and blossom in the silent dust.

And finally, there are those who strongly object to the claim that it was largely Elihut Yale who was responsible for the founding of Yale University. Another man actually provided the majority of the funds, according to them at least, and that would be Jeremiah Dummer, although there was no way on earth that the trustees were ever going to call it *Dummer University*. I absolutely swear this is true, and anyway, you just couldn't have made up a better story even if you tried.

After Llandegla, the path left the road for a while, veering off behind the church and following the course of the babbling brook that you may remember was called Alan, or at least should be called that. The going was initially fairly flat due to following the course of the river, but after crossing a small road and hedging along a sheep-infested field, where there were literally thousands of them, I spied hills ahead, and I knew what was coming.

At first, the slope was reasonably gentle, and with firm ground underfoot, it was not really an issue. A quick clamber over a wooden style and through an overgrown hedgerow next spat me out onto a tiny backroad, fenced in on either side by prickly-looking plants with lots of sharp things on them, with a steeper uphill section to greet me. I stopped for a minute to get my breath, and I'm glad I did. A few seconds later, a large truck came thundering down the lane, and if I hadn't stayed where I had, I would either have been squished beneath its wheels or would have had to secrete myself painfully within those nettles. I wondered if that same truck had squashed my good friends, who were somewhere ahead of me.

I made my way slowly but surely upwards, and thankfully, no more lumbering trucks came my way, which was good. However, as I crested the top of the hill, in front of me, I saw yet more hills, which was bad. I had one thing going in my favour, however, which was a relatively straight road, so at least I would be able to see my death before it arrived, but as I plodded on, I gradually became aware of something else which could be bad, and that was the gradual but definite onset of rain.

At first, I missed the signs, which was a splash or two across my glasses, and by the time I had realised what was coming, and as I was reaching into my bag for some waterproofs, a full-on shower had arrived, apparently right above my head.

As the cold rain battered against my face, pushed in by a chill wind, I struggled to get into my protective gear, and by the time I had done so, I was probably about as wet as it was possible to get.

Luckily, as the road here took a definite left turn, I left it too, joining first a track and then a path which immediately led me alongside a small forest, providing some much-needed and greatly appreciated shelter from the worst of the elements and which was where I caught back up with Rob, James and Mark.

I stopped for a minute, which became five, then fifteen, and then some more, and finally, after half an hour of hiding beneath a dense patch of trees opposite some kind of transmitter, we plucked up the courage to move on, as staying still is not the best option when you are cold and wet, no matter what the weather.

With visibility down considerably, we were probably missing some of the finest views of this walk, as I was aware that somewhere off to the west were the mighty peaks of Snowdonia and, to the north, possible views of the Irish Sea and with it, the end of our walk.

Thankfully, the track here never took us to the highest of the peaks among this small range of hills, which stood at the southern end of the Clwydian Range, but instead sheltered us in the leeward side of them and thus greatly protected us from the worst that mother nature had to offer today, which mainly involved water, apparently, and lots of it.

Occasional breaks in the cloud offered the chance to see valleys dropping below us, and if I could take one positive from this stretch of the walk, it was that the route didn't include lots of pointless ups and downs to the bottoms of those valleys.

With my head down and my hood up, I really didn't see much for the next few miles, and being of a superstitious sort, I didn't remove my waterproofs, even when the rain finally appeared to have stopped.

Eventually, when a brilliant sun suddenly and without warning popped out from behind a thick layer of rapidly receding cloud, and when the temperature shot up by around a hundred degrees, I finally removed my outer layers. The others did the same, and we began the long process of drying out, simultaneously enjoying the spectacular views that had suddenly and spontaneously appeared from behind a thick veil of foggy mist.

The view really was as good as I had hoped, offering a beautiful panorama across the Vale of Clwyd, with one extra little offering thrown in for good measure. Somewhere out there was Prestatyn, and that meant the end of this walk, something that my feet were really looking forward to, though in order to get to that point, there was only one thing for it, and that was to keep on moving.

After what seemed like an eternity, the path led us to a road, which, by the looks of it, was a rather big one, and as we descended the hills towards it, I saw what looked like a café of some sort, with a rather big car park, and realised this was the famous, for this path at least, Clwyd Gate.

My mind wandered to what snacks they might have on the menu, and things like eggs and bacon sprang to mind, though at this point, I would probably have eaten a scabby horse, to recount a popular saying from my childhood, such were the hunger pangs deep within my belly. I'm not sure I would have actually eaten a scabby horse had someone magically whipped one up and served it on a platter before me, but I have heard it said that when you are truly hungry, your standards tend to drop.

On second thoughts, I pondered, I probably would eat it. It has been said by many that when it comes to food, I will eat pretty much anything, which means I probably don't have standards as such, in which case, that scabby horse is suddenly beginning to sound rather tasty.

None of this mattered anyway. When we arrived at the café, we discovered it wasn't a café at all. In fact, it didn't look like anything much today, and the cars in the car park presumably belonged to walkers who had fled this place many hours ago and were yet to return.

We sat on a low brick wall for a few minutes and pondered our situation, and I ransacked the bottom of my rucksack. While I didn't find a scabby horse, I did find a scabby Snickers bar, which, although it looked like it had been there since I walked the Coast to Coast many years ago, tasted pretty alright and was only slightly rancid.

We looked at our map, and it soon dawned on us that there was nowhere nearby to either camp or eat. After the briefest of discussions, we decided to head to the nearest town, which was

Ruthin, just a couple of miles as the crow flies, or in our case, as the taxi drives.

Technically, it wasn't actually a taxi, of course. Young James went onto his phone and simply summoned up a car, as if by magic, through one app or another, which, when you think about it, was probably rather dangerous. Thirty years ago, you see, we were constantly advised not to get in a car with strangers. Twenty years ago, the advice was don't meet people off the internet. And here we were, getting into an Uber.

On the way there, I went on one of those apps that promised to get you last-minute hotel rooms at bargain prices, and I struck absolute gold. There is, quite luckily, a Wetherspoons hotel in Ruthin, and I managed to bag the last room. There was, however, one tiny problem. While there was only one room, there were four of us, so we were going to have to be cheeky. I asked the taxi driver to drop us just next to the hotel so we wouldn't be seen, outside an old timber-framed house that had some kind of giant stone outside, which probably had a story to tell, I thought to myself, but more of that later.

A cunning plan was devised. I would go into the hotel and check in with Rob, and after dumping our gear in the room and scouting the place out a bit, we would figure out the best way to smuggle James and Mark in. It sounded simple, as indeed it was, mainly because we, too, were simple.

The manager was amiable and didn't comment on either our dishevelled looks or pungent state, although I'm sure I saw his nose twitch at least once or twice. He also totally forgot to mention the fact that our feet were entirely covered in either cow or sheep shit, not that we could have identified which one ourselves, and as for the small family of squirrels living in my hair, he remained absolutely silent.

The room was cosy, to say the least, and was the last one on the top floor of what was clearly an ancient building. Secret corridors led this way and that, and we almost got lost as we made our way through what was essentially a maze.

We managed it, though, and then I made my way down to the back door to let James and Mark in, but only after we had come up with a suitable diversion.

Rob would set fire to the front of the building, I suggested, which would occupy the staff for just long enough to bundle our sneaky friends in, but in retrospect, this plan had a couple of flaws. The first was obvious, as burning the place down would take us back to square one with nowhere to sleep, and the second was the prospect of doing twenty years in prison for arson.

As it was, we simply ensured no one was around when we let them in. The plan went exactly to plan, so to speak, apart from the fact that we got lost within the bowels of the building once again and bumped into the very same nose-twitching manager who had checked us in, though he did kindly point us in the right direction to our room, which was now even cosier.

Having four grown men in a room designed for two is challenging, to say the least, but as I looked around, I surmised that we had slept in worse conditions, and on a positive note, there weren't any rusty farming implements hanging above our heads threatening midnight decapitations.

We took turns to shower, and after we had all had a go, the bathroom resembled something you would expect to find in a country whose name ends in Stan, but at least we were clean. On second thoughts, perhaps clean was not quite the right word, and it was probably more accurate to say something like we were no longer rancid.

We didn't bother to go out for three reasons. We didn't want to give the game away about the numbers in our room, we were all knackered, and finally, Ruthin is said to be full of ghosts. Apparently, it is perhaps the only town in the country to have a haunted cash machine, which, you have to admit, is certainly an unusual claim to fame. Unfortunately, when I say haunted, I should probably point out that it's not one of those cash machines that dispenses limitless free cash. Instead, many people have simply reported hearing a ghostly wail while using it, though this might just be someone having it off down the alley behind the bank, such is Ruthin's reputation.

The town has quite some history worth gossiping about, you see. In the early 1900s, it was one of the favourite holiday spots of perhaps one of our most wayward monarchs, Edward VII, who, incidentally, was the great-great-grandfather of our current king, Charles III. I had come across Edward before, on the Yorkshire Coast Path, though not literally, of course. However, I suspect many people probably had back in the day, as he was, quite frankly, a bit of a pervert. His nicknames included *Dirty Bertie* and *Edward the Caresser*, and he even had a custom-built sex chair made for his romantic entanglements.

He came here, so to speak, to get down and dirty with Lady Cornwallis-West of Ruthin Castle, who was better known as Patsy. However, she was only sixteen at the time, while he was a dirty thirty. Surprisingly, or perhaps not surprisingly, Patsy's own mother had once seduced Bertie's dad, Prince Albert, who was the husband of Queen Victoria, so at least they kept it in the family.

Throughout his long life, most of which he spent impatiently waiting for his mother, Queen Victoria, to pop her clogs so he could become king, Bertie had lots of mistresses, and I mean that in the most literal sense. Interestingly, one of those he had was a woman called Alice Keppel, who was the great-grandmother of someone named Camilla Rosemary Shand.

She is perhaps better known as Queen Camilla, wife of King Charles III, and legend has it that when she met him for the first time, she is supposed to have said *My great-grandmother was the mistress of your great-great-grandfather. I feel we have something in common.* You couldn't make it up.

Anyway, we stayed in, and Mark ordered us a takeaway on one of those apps that promised to deliver junk food and empty calories straight to your door.

I went down to grab it when his phone pinged to say it had arrived, only to bump into that manager again, who gets everywhere apparently and whose last comment was *that's a lot of food for two people*, which was probably just his way of telling me we had been well and truly rumbled.

Still, with full bellies and having had a bit of a wash, we all had a great night's sleep. The floor was very comfy and was not painful at all, and it only moderately broke my back. I only woke up twenty-five times, and the three blokes who were farting and snoring all night didn't bother me in the least.

And okay, once again, it was probably four blokes farting and snoring, but you never wake yourself up, do you?

And as for that stone I saw earlier, there is

indeed a story behind it. Known as Maen Huail, it is where King Arthur allegedly executed a man called Huail, who was the brother of the famous historian Gildas the Wise. They had been fighting over a woman, and while Huail had managed to injure the king by striking his knee with a sword, Arthur forgave him on the condition that Huail should never mention these events again.

Not long later, however, Arthur overheard someone talking about the injury to his knee, and that someone turned out to be none other than blabbermouth Huail. Because of this indiscretion, Arthur immediately condemned him to death and executed Huail the Gobby on that very stone by chopping his head clean off.

Unfortunately for King Arthur, Gildas the Wise was rather fond of his brother, and predictably, he was not very happy with this turn of events. As a final act of revenge, he is said to have cast into the sea all works, records and writings detailing King Arthur and his reign, thereby eradicating him from the historical record. This, it is said, is why so little evidence exists about our most famous king in history, which makes perfect sense when you think about it.

I had been dozing off while thinking about all this until someone who shall remain nameless, James, asked me if I was sleeping. It always puzzles me why, when people see you lying

down, they still ask, *"Are you sleeping?"*
    No, I'm training to die.

THE FINAL PUSH

Ruthin to Prestatyn

I didn't sleep much last night, but I did get a few hours of worrying done. I also put my back out from sleeping on the floor and tweaked my neck when I sneezed this morning, so I'm probably just one fart away from total paralysis. In fact, this morning started out like a galloping golden retriever on a freshly waxed hardwood floor. I nearly fell down the stairs, the manager caught all four of us sneaking out, and then Mark realised he had left his sticks behind in the room, which you may remember, had been slightly over-occupied last night. The older I get, the more I understand why roosters start their day with a scream.

An incredibly early taxi sped us back up the hill to Clwyd Gate, as there was no way we were going to add mileage to our final day, which was already going to be challenging. The issue wasn't just the mileage either, but the terrain too, as today would see us crossing the Clwydian Range of mountains towards Bodfari before tackling the last stretch into Prestatyn. The mountains meant a relentless series of ups and downs, not what we really wanted after almost two weeks of walking, and all of this, when combined together, was why we set off at the ridiculous hour of four o'clock in the morning. Even the taxi driver was still half asleep.

We fell out of the cab in the car park at Clwyd gate and silently put our rucksacks on, as none of us was in the mood to talk. The only positive was the weather, as a cloudless blue sky stood above us in all directions. It's the start of a brand new day, and we're off like a herd of sloths, I thought to myself as we slowly shuffled onwards and upwards.

The path followed the road for a few hundred feet before leaving it behind, once again heading uphill, this time towards the lofty heights of a summit I had forgotten the name of but was called Gyrn. On the way up, a small wood entertained us briefly as we witnessed the tail end of this year's bluebells, which carpeted the floor liberally.

Our first proper climb of the day came soon enough as we began to make our way up Foel Fenlli, on top of which once stood an iron-aged hillfort. Although best seen from the air, it is certainly possible to make out the ramparts if you know what you are looking for, and as a double bonus, the views from the summit are outstanding, and we could clearly see Moel Famau, which was our next target.

I stopped here to take a look behind me, and I'm glad I did, as it was even better than the view to the front. I could still make out Llandegla Forest to the south, and while the view along the ridge was incredible, I was nonetheless glad it was behind me.

We were soon heading downhill and towards a car park, where I was surprised to see a couple of cars. It was still early, and I did not expect to see anyone else out walking at such an early hour, yet ahead of us and halfway up Moel Famau were two red specks. They must be mad, I thought to myself, because I knew we certainly were.

After the car park, the hard work began as we started the ascent of Moel Famau, which is a bit of an odd rock. From a distance, it looks like it has a nipple, which is strange because mountains generally do not have nipples, and anyway, that nipple should have actually been a phallus if you are posh or a willy if you are not. In any case, Moel Famau has this feature because it has been subjected to surgery.

Way back in the early 1800s, a mad architect from nearby Chester decided to build something equally mad atop this mountain in tribute to perhaps our maddest-ever monarch, George III. This king of ours is now notorious for being something of a nutter, and the phrase *the madness of King George* is not only a book, a movie and a play but is a part of our everyday language. The reason for his madness is said by some to be hereditary, but others state his declining mental health followed several bouts of serious illness. Regardless, we have a lot to thank George for, and while some of it is good, some of it is equally bad.

For instance, it is he who bought Buckingham House, which we now all know as Buckingham Palace. Prior to his purchase, it was just a rich person's home and likely would have been demolished had it not passed into royal hands. George was also the one who ordered the State Coach, which is basically a famous golden horse-drawn carriage that is still in use nowadays and which has been used to carry kings and queens in luxuriant style ever since.

Unfortunately, it was also King George who lost the American colonies, although he probably blamed the corrupt Admiral George Rodney, who you may remember was in charge of the British fleet at Yorktown, but as stated before, what this king is best known for is going stark staring mad. For instance, when talking, he would often repeat himself, and he would talk constantly until foam ran out of his mouth, which is not a pleasant image at all to have in your head.

Despite all of that, he somehow managed to stay on the throne for a staggering 60 years, from 1760 to 1820. And so it was, in 1810 and to mark his golden jubilee, that Thomas Harrison, that mad architect from Chester, drew up his plans to celebrate the even madder king's reign. And how would they choose to do this? Well, for some unfathomable reason, they chose to do this by building a colossal neo-classical monument that looked a bit like a willy on the top of a Welsh mountain in the middle of nowhere. I told you they were crazy.

What resulted was something that was supposed to look like a cross between an Egyptian obelisk and a three-tiered wedding cake. Work started in 1810, but construction was slow due to a lack of funds, even more so after the king popped his clogs in 1820.

Unfortunately, before it could be completed, a massive storm blew down much of the tower in 1862. After partial demolition, and when they realised they couldn't get it up, so to speak, they abandoned the idea altogether, which explains why they ended up not with a willy, but with a nipple, albeit one which resembled some kind of Second World War bunker or maybe even a ruined castle. And while the tower turned out to be rubbish, the views from the top were immense, especially on a day like today. In the west was Snowdon, the highest mountain in Wales, and to the north was the Dee Estuary, while in the east, I could just about make out Beeston Castle in England, around twenty-five miles away. And finally, I could see Prestatyn to the north, which, of course, meant it was time to move on.

For the next few miles, the path followed the western edge of the Clwydian Hills, with fantastic views in all directions. Gentle ups and downs and twists and turns brought no significant problems, and as the day got older, a steady stream of dog walkers helped to pass the time.

One particularly entertaining encounter happened at a bench where a stressed-out dad was berating his two young toddlers for one reason or another and who were entirely ignoring him, while his dog ran around in circles. I can only guess that they were tired and were either refusing to go on or were incredibly slow. Anyway, as he told them off, one of them fell from the bench, and the only thing that saved her from cracking her head on a rock was the rather large pile of cow poo that she landed in and on with a satisfying splodge-like sound as the crust cracked and she went all in. I didn't hang about to see how he reacted to this mini disaster, but I'm sure he saw me laughing.

A steep path down a hill led to a car park, Moel Arthur car park, beyond which was another uphill climb to Moel Arthur itself. It took us considerably longer to get up the next hill than it took to get down the last one, not surprisingly, but we eventually made it, although the path technically and thankfully tends to go around most of these hills rather than over the tops of them. Apparently, there was a hill fort on the top of this one as well, but all I saw was gorse bushes and rabbit droppings everywhere, and I mean everywhere. Although there was nothing to see, I could understand why someone would build a fort up here, but it's not where I would have built mine. While it was easily defendable, you see, it was miles from the nearest pub.

Ahead of us, to the north, stood just a few more hills of the Clwydian Range, and after that, the flat plains of the Vale of Clwyd promised a long-overdue respite from the relentless climbs of the last few miles, as well as the end of our walk. We followed the path with our heads down, and I tried to ignore the miles as much as my throbbing feet. Eventually, I began to notice that the path was definitely starting to take on something of a downward trend, meaning we were finally descending from these hills, which, no matter how beautiful, I just wanted to leave behind. And the view ahead was still excellent, with a town off to the left, which I presumed to be Denbigh.

Skirting the village of Bodfari, signage for Offa's Dyke suggested it was not quite time to say goodbye to those hills, as I was directed steeply upwards between some comfy-looking cottages, and I imagined being in one, sat on a sofa, and resting my swollen feet.

A tree-lined track led us up the hill further still until we broke out into the open after crossing another minor road, where we could enjoy fine views across the flatlands to the west.

Muddy fields eventually turned into the firmer footing of a narrow road, which led us further still up whatever magnificent hill this was, hemmed in on either side by great hedges once again, which made me listen more carefully for the sound of any approaching vehicle that might want to flatten us.

None came, and after a mile or so, we happened upon a crossroads with a small bench. Someone was sitting on it, and as we approached, she gave a short wave, so I stopped and enjoyed the next few minutes chatting with Delia, who was very interested in our walk, although my so-called friends carried on.

She was local, she told me, and also enjoyed the odd walk but had not done much since her dog had passed away at the end of last summer. When I asked her if she would get another one, she thought for a minute and then said probably not, as she wouldn't want to leave it behind. I'm not sure how old Delia was, but she was perhaps north of seventy-five, I figured, and understood her point about the dog.

She had walked the dyke herself, she told me, many years ago, and she said for her, it had been a walk home, as she started in Chepstow heading north to her home in Prestatyn, which is where she then lived. This had been the 1970s, and she then volunteered much more detail about her walk and how she had done it during one of the hottest heatwaves on record. Her husband had hated it, she said, as he doesn't like hot weather, or rather, she corrected herself sadly, he didn't. He had died over a decade ago, which is how she had ended up with Dylan, whom I presumed had been the dog, something she soon confirmed when she said that he loved to lay in the sun and have a belly rub. Well, don't we all, I thought to myself silently.

I had joined her on that bench by now and told her of my dog, whom I had lost just a couple of winters before, and then immediately realised that it had been much longer than that, over a decade, in fact. And my new dog, as I called my Labrador cross Belle, was, in fact, not new at all. Even she was getting too old for these walks, which is why she was not with me now, I went on.

Eventually, the time came to move on as I figured I should probably try to catch up with the others. I had taken my shoes off to air my feet, and as I put them back on and laced them up, Delia told me it had been nice to meet me. Usually, when people say that to me, I advise them to give it time, but anyway, she bade her goodbyes, stood up, and hobbled off back towards Bodfari.

I watched her disappear slowly down the hill, and eventually, she went round the bend, but not in a mad way. It was almost as if she blended into this countryside, and perhaps she did. Maybe we all do, eventually, which is a bit philosophical when you think about it.

The hills beckoned, and I carried on skywards, passing one particularly fine house on the left that could more accurately be described as a mansion and would perhaps suit a footballer or a lottery winner, but I yearned for my own little home, so far away, and of course, my little dog Belle.

The road was at least straight for the next mile or so and thankfully remained traffic-free, but at a sharp bend, it was finally time to leave the tarmac behind, which was good, as it had given my feet a bit of a battering.

That tiny little acorn was the cue to leave, taking me through an overgrown prickly hedge that made me fear the worst. Thankfully, it failed to deliver, leading me instead to a pleasant though muddy path that ran alongside a small wood. It was unfortunate, then, that I still found myself heading uphill, and I began to wonder how long this could go on for.

The answer was not all that long, for after taking me over a small summit, the path dropped again, which was good, but it then deposited me back onto the tarmac, which was not so good, as my feet were still throbbing from the last bit.

At least it took me downhill, I thought to myself as I stumbled along beneath some crackly power lines. A short uphill section had me worried for a moment or two but soon flattened out into more or less nothing, and after crossing a main road via a staggered crossroads, I, too, staggered along, though I still felt absolutely shattered, despite it being only a short climb. Do you ever feel like your body's *check engine light* is on, and you're still driving it like, "*Nah, It'll be fine*?" Well, up that hill, that was me.

The tarmac didn't last too long, though. A sign with a picture of a horse on it soon directed me left and to the west, beneath some more buzzing power lines, into a seemingly darkened tunnel of trees.

The tunnel proved to be short-lived, and I soon found myself heading firmly downhill again, once more enjoying those spectacular views across the Vale of Clwyd. The next few miles were a blur, following a succession of countryside paths and signs that finally led me to a much-appreciated footbridge over a motorway, as I had been concerned about how I was going to cross it. Also, I wondered, where on earth were the others?

This was the North Wales Expressway, and while it might technically not have been an actual motorway, for all intents and purposes, it definitely was, particularly in relation to Offa's Dyke Path. After this, you see, the game is nearly up, and the road represents a much-welcome return to civilization.

The first hint of that civilization is the tiny

village of Rhuallt, which sits just north of the expressway. Unfortunately, it is only that, a mere hint, and other than some splendid houses, I failed to find a supermarket, a pub, or one of those salons where the fishes nibble on your feet, which makes me wonder if it actually counts as civilization.

North it was then, up yet another little lane, which was unfortunately named Cwm Road. While that might be fine in Welsh, the pronunciation, similar to *Come*, means it is rather unfortunate in English, especially for a fully-grown yet incredibly childish individual such as myself.

Thankfully, this taste of so-called civilization turned out to be brief, and in no time at all, I found myself once more heading off into the wilds. A steep hill, straddled on both sides by a lovely range of nettles and stinging plants, led me a mile or so up yet another hill, spitting me out on a forest road that was presumably built by some Romans with too much time on their hands. By that, I mean it was deadly straight and seemed to lead nowhere, although eventually, I left it anyway and once again found myself tramping across muddy fields full of moody cows, which caused me to wonder about something I had never thought about before. The guy who discovered milk. What was he doing?

I think I got lost after that. I had been heading towards a place called Henfryn Hall, and I should have approached it from the south, but for some reason, even though I read my map and thought I knew exactly where I was, I approached it from the west. Still, I managed to get there, so I just shrugged my shoulders and carried on, uphill, of course. It's always uphill, apparently.

A further succession of fields, signs, styles and paths, all similar to the last few miles, led me in an almost trance-like state to the small village of Bryniau, where, after a couple of twisting and turning miles of woodland and scrubland walk, I was awoken in the most amazing sense. I left the trees behind, rounded a bend, and there before me, in all its glory, was the beautiful, broad and expansive vista of the North Wales Coast and the Irish Sea. The end, which had been so long coming, really now was in sight. I had almost finished my walk. It was nearly time to go home.

The path, just a sliver of bare earth, followed the contours of the hill and offered exceptional views to the north and the west. Prestatyn was visible far below me, and even better, it was almost within touching distance.

And a minute later, I bumped into Pete, whoever he was, though he definitely seemed to know me. Rob, James and Mark were waiting for me in his garden shed, he said, which was just off into the bushes to my left, and he told me to follow him, which solved that mystery.

I did, as well, and I wondered if he was going to murder me in the woods, which would be a shame, as I had almost finished the walk. So near, yet so far.

Luckily, he didn't murder me, but he did lead me to my friends, who were sitting around a small campfire and having a rest. I dropped my bag and joined them, and Pete told me about the place, as apparently, he owned the whole hill. He had bought it with the idea of building a house upon it and managing it as a nature reserve, which was very noble, although he said he had run out of money. Still, as far as a work in progress goes, it was pretty damned good, and even better, it was technically a suburb of Prestatyn.

Prestatyn has always been something of a backwater. Although it has been occupied since Roman times, the population never really grew until the arrival of the railways in the 1800s. Nowadays, as well as being the cultural centre of the universe because of it being at the end of Offa's Dyke Path, it is a bustling little seaside town, and although I have been here once or twice before, it was not a place that I could really say I knew.

Sprawling before us on a sunny day as it was now, however, it was a very welcome sight. I should be honest, though, and say that this was simply because it meant we had almost finished our walk and had nothing to do with sandy beaches and seaside air.

It does, however, hold some exciting secrets.

Neil Aspinall is one of those secrets, born here in 1941, and while he is not very famous, he has often been described as the fifth Beatle, and if you don't know who the Beatles are, then I am afraid there is nothing I can do for you. Being born in this tiny seaside resort was merely an accident of history, however, as his mother had been evacuated from nearby Liverpool due to German bombing raids on the city.

Later on in the war, the family returned to the bright lights and the big city, and it was there that he found himself attending Quarry Bank High School in the same English and Art lessons as a young man going by the name of Paul McCartney. Not long after that, George Harrison became yet another friend, and what was becoming known as the Mad Lad Gang then recruited another member, John Lennon.

Upon leaving school, Aspinall became a trainee accountant but stayed in touch with his old friends with cool names, who had by then formed a band. And believe it or not, back in those early days, The Beatles would travel to gigs by bus, although at first they weren't called The Beatles, of course, but were The Quarrymen, named after their school. However, as their popularity slowly increased, they sometimes found themselves doing two or three shows in one night and soon decided that they needed their own transport.

A quick call to their old friend Aspinall solved

this problem, who got hold of a battered old van and drove the wannabee stars to their early shows in his free time. By now, Pete Best had joined the line-up, meaning the band now had four members, and furthermore, when Aspinall was introduced to Pete's mother, Mona, things got awkward, to say the least. Aspinall liked Mona, you see, and Mona liked Aspinall, and let's just say that nine months later, a baby magically appeared.

Anyway, Aspinall went on to do great things for the band and was soon promoted far beyond mere driving, although he did continue to ferry them around. This wasn't perhaps the best outcome, however, as a certain event occurred later on, one which involved my home town of Hull, in Yorkshire, which I always try to mention whenever my travels allow.

The Beatles had been performing in my home city, you see, specifically at the Majestic Ballroom on Valentine's Day of 1963. They had been driving back to Liverpool in the early hours, and Aspinall had let George Harrison take a turn at the wheel. This was in the days before motorways, so their journey took them from town to town as they made their way home across the whole of England, and British roads in the early 1960s were notoriously pot-holed and slow to navigate, which, incidentally, just goes to show how some things never change.

Unfortunately, when they hit the first of those

towns, Goole in Yorkshire, which incidentally, at fifty miles from the sea, is Britain's most inland port, they quite literally hit it. As this was back in the days when winters were cold and brakes were crap, the van skidded on ice, slid down a slope and crashed through seven concrete posts, finally coming to a rest on the fence of a Burton's menswear clothing factory.

Unfortunately, a donut-munching policeman had been parked up nearby and saw the whole thing, and he was not best pleased. To cut a long story short, Harrison ended up at Goole Magistrate's Court, where he was found guilty of *driving without due care and attention* and fined the princely sum of ten pounds, which was a lot of money back then, even for a Beatle.

There is another famous person worth mentioning, too, who also saw their start in life right here in Prestatyn, although I use the word famous somewhat loosely here if I am being totally honest.

John Leslie Prescott was born in the town in 1938, and if you don't know who he is, you're not the only one. To cut a long story short and to miss all the boring bits, of which there are many, Prescott became a seaman, a union representative and finally, a politician. He is perhaps best remembered for being the Deputy Prime Minister of the United Kingdom during Tony Blair's government in the early 2000s, but he was also a Member of Parliament for, you've guessed it, Hull.

And while he did some noble and notable politicky-type things, such as banning asbestos and signing up for the Kyoto Protocol on climate change back when Greta Thunberg wasn't even a dollop of spunk, what he should really be remembered for is punching the living daylights out of a random nutter who thought it would be a good idea to throw eggs at him.

What this lunatic failed to appreciate was that back in his early days, Prescott was something of a boxer. He particularly honed his skills on a long cruise to New Zealand in 1957, when his typical day varied between, on the one hand, serving drinks to newly-disgraced ex-Prime Minister Sir Anthony Eden, who had just pissed off America and the rest of the world with a botched invasion of Egypt, to fighting with his ship mates for money on the other.

Anyway, they say that there is no such thing as bad publicity, and in the end, Prescott was cleared of all wrongdoing, and quite rightly so. If someone threw an egg at me, I think I'd do the same.

Anyway, that somewhat infamous event took place in Rhyll, which, incidentally, is just a few miles up the coast from Prestatyn.

We thanked Pete for his hospitality and continued on our merry way, following the path along the contours of a hill with the town laid bare before us. Quite rudely, however, while we expected to be going only downhill from now on, there was one last climb, which, quite frankly, was neither expected nor welcome.

When the downhill finally came, it was more than welcome and was also unexpectedly swift. I think we all nearly slipped on that last stretch of slippery path, possibly because we were rushing, and at the bottom, we hit the tarmac for the last time as we suddenly found ourselves in an actual town, one with paths and signs and crossings and whatnot. We were nearly there, and it was here that we bumped into Vince, who was just starting his walk of Offa's Dyke and was heading south, and who had stopped to have a quick look at a giant sculpture of a Roman helmet, as had we. I could not tell you how old he was, though he certainly looked older than me, but then I'm at that delusional age where I think everyone my age looks way older than I do.

Vince was quite a character. I detected an accent that emanated from somewhere in the north of England, most probably Newcastle, the actual Newcastle this time, but it wasn't the accent that was the most interesting thing that came out of his mouth. It was the words he chose to use. Do you remember before the internet when it was thought that the cause of collective stupidity was the lack of access to information? Well, it wasn't that.

Vince, you see, was not a fan of the Welsh, apparently. He complained vigorously that the best thing that had ever come out of Wales was Tom Jones' voice and various bits of Cathryn Zeta-Jones, although it's probably best not to go into details right now. And he also mentioned the fact, and I use that word very loosely here, that the Welsh, in general, although I am going to specify that he probably meant Welsh men, are rather fond of sheep, and I don't mean lamb dinners.

I did wonder, given his animosity towards the Welsh, why Vince had decided to holiday in Wales, and when I mentioned this to him, he said that he wasn't. His walk along Offa's Dyke, he claimed, would keep firmly and exclusively to the English side. Good luck with that, I told him, in a manner that was laden with a lot more sarcasm than I had actually intended. I had, of course, intended it to be very sarcastic anyway, though he obviously thought I was trying to be funny. Just for the record, I'm not actually funny at all. I'm just mean, and people think I'm joking. For instance, people keep mistaking my wows for compliments.

Incidentally, saying *"Have a nice day"* to someone sounds friendly, but saying *"Enjoy the next twenty-four hours"* sounds threatening, but it worked. He grunted and moved on, and I hoped never to see him again in my life. I can be a grumpy old git sometimes, and although I didn't particularly take to Vince, he sure was right about Tom Jones' voice and, let's face it, Zeta-

Jones too.

As for the sculpture, which featured an impressive Roman helmet apparently half buried in the ground and hidden behind a rather innocuous-looking electrical substation, it was put here to celebrate the area's strong links with some of our earliest colonizers. There had been a settlement here around two thousand years ago, you see, which had probably been a port used for transporting lead and silver from nearby mines, although, in all honesty, that is mainly conjecture.

In fact, it may well have been the Romans who gave Wales its name. The name of the country is actually derived from the old Anglo-Saxon word *Wahlaz*, meaning foreigners, particularly foreigners who were under the influence of the Roman Empire.

Technically speaking, though, bearing in mind that the other nations nearby are England, Scotland and Ireland, Wales should rightfully be called Welshland. Obviously, to show all due respect, we would have to translate the name into Welsh, and we would start with the word Cymru, pronounced Cumri, which is the Welsh word for Wales. Naturally, being English myself, that name would then have to be Anglicised so that my dim-witted countrymen could actually understand it, which means that the proper name for Wales should, in fact, be Cumland.

Moving on, having offended everyone who

needs to be offended here, when the Romans disappeared, so did the settlement, and modern-day Prestatyn only sprang up much later. In 1934, architect and amateur archaeologist Francis Gilbert Smith unearthed a Roman bathhouse on what is now the edge of town, which gave the growing seaside holiday resort a unique identity which it happily embraced.

To promote this identity even more, the local council decided to commission a sculpture in the early 2000s, which is how a giant helmet came to be half-buried on the edge of a housing estate today. Originally, the helmet, and thus this spot, had marked the northern terminus of the Offa's Dyke Path, though the route was extended to the seafront a few years ago, which unfortunately meant we still had a couple of miles to go. But before we go, it was actually built by an unusually named outfit called *Cod Steaks*, which, I am thrilled to report, is the exact same company that built all the fantastic props for the Wallace and Gromit films, of which I am a great fan and which I watch religiously every Christmas.

I was just getting ready to move on when a bespectacled man started a wholly unwanted conversation with us all. However, James, Rob and Mark made an immediate and strategic exit, which left me talking to him alone. I wasn't having any of it, however, not at this late stage of the walk. One guaranteed way to end an unwanted conversation is to take off one of your socks and hand it to the other person. I can't help doing this kind of thing, either. I've reached that age where my brain has gone from, *"You probably shouldn't do that"* to *"What the hell, let's see what happens".*

Anyway, he would not shut up, but luckily, I'm a pacificist, which is why I was about to pass a fist across his face.

The walk towards the seafront was done in a straight line, and I imagined us marching defiantly into town, much like the Roman Legionaries, having broken Offa's Dyke Path. In reality, we were variously hobbling and limping along with our battered and blistered feet, as it was actually the path that had broken us.

One of the houses we walked past had a trampoline in the garden, upon which some young miscreant was performing surprisingly impressive belly bounces. I looked at Rob and then at myself, and reckoned that either of us could pull off an equally impressive manoeuvre quite easily. We wouldn't even need the trampoline.

Houses gave way to shops, and our last obstacle was a railway line, which had to be crossed via a bridge and which involved lots of horrible steps, after which we caught a glimpse of the sea and, eventually, the sign that announced the official end of the path and was a stone just like the one on Sedbury Cliff back at the beginning so many miles ago.

I don't think anyone knew quite what to say as we just stood there for a moment, but as James began to take his rucksack off, we all followed suit, at which point Rob asked if anyone fancied walking back to Chepstow.

We buried him by the bench.

BOOKS IN THIS SERIES

History Walks

54 Degrees North: A Walk Across England

A Walk On The Wild Side: The Yorkshire Wolds

Coast To Coast: Finding Wainwright's England

Rambling On: Lost On The Cleveland Way

Hadrian's Wall Wath: A Walk

Through History

Northbound On The West Highland Way

All Hills High And Low: Walking The Herriot Way

One Step At A Time: The Wilberforce Way

Coastal Capers: Walking The Yorkshire Coast Path

Southbound On The Viking Way

Printed in Great Britain
by Amazon